Call and Response

Call and Response

The Abingdon Guidebook for Liturgy and Preaching, Year A, 2025–2026

R. DeAndre Johnson, General Editor

Nashville

CALL AND RESPONSE:
THE ABINGDON GUIDEBOOK FOR LITURGY AND PREACHING, YEAR A

Copyright © 2025 by Abingdon Press

All rights reserved.

No part of this work may be reproduced or transmitted in any form or by any means, electronic or mechanical, including photocopying and recording, or by any information storage or retrieval system, except as may be expressly permitted by the 1976 Copyright Act, the 1998 Digital Millennium Copyright Act, or in writing from the publisher. Requests for permission should be addressed to Permissions, Abingdon Press, 810 12th Avenue South, Nashville, TN 37203-4704, or emailed to permissions@abingdonpress.com.

ISBN: 9781791035563

Library of Congress Control Number has been requested.

Scripture quotations unless noted otherwise are from the Common English Bible. Copyright © 2011 by the Common English Bible. All rights reserved. Used by permission. www.CommonEnglishBible.com.

Scripture quotations marked NRSVue are taken from the New Revised Standard Version Updated Edition. Copyright © 2021 National Council of Churches of Christ in the United States of America. Used by permission. All rights reserved worldwide.

The cover of the book *Call & Response: The Abingdon Guidebook for Worship and Preaching, Year A (2025–2026)* features a circular stained glass window design in blue and white on the top half of the cover.

MANUFACTURED IN THE UNITED STATES OF AMERICA

Contents

xi Introduction

PART ONE
CALLED TO WORSHIP: THE BASIC PATTERN

3 Gathering
   3 Opening Sentences
   4 Calls to Worship
   7 Opening Prayers
   7 Confession and Pardon
   9 Passing of the Peace

11 Proclaiming
   12 Prayers for Illumination
   13 Affirmations of Faith

15 Thanksgiving
   15 Prayers of the People
      15 Pastoral Prayers
      19 Bidding and Responsive Prayers
      21 Prayers for Special Occasions
      23 Prayers in Times of Crisis
   25 The Offering
      25 Invitations
      26 Prayers for Giving and Receiving
      27 Doxologies
   27 Baptism
      27 Introductions
      28 Thanksgiving Over the Water
   31 Holy Communion
      31 Invitation
      31 Great Thanksgiving
      35 Prayer After Receiving

Contents

37 Sending
    37 Invitation to Discipleship
    38 Blessings/Benedictions
    39 Dismissals

PART TWO
THE RESPONSE THROUGH WORSHIP: LITURGICAL YEAR A

43 Advent
    43 Year A Lectionary Texts
    43 A Framework, Themes, and Ideas for Advent
        44 At Last: A Worship Series for Advent
    49 Words for Worship, Advent
        49 Gathering
        52 Proclaiming
        55 Thanksgiving
        57 Sending

59 Christmas and Christmastide
    59 Year A Lectionary Texts
    59 A Framework, Themes, and Ideas for Christmas and Christmastide
        60 Now: A Worship Series for Chrsitmas and Christmastide
    68 Words for Worship, Christmas and Christmastide
        68 Gathering
        74 Proclaiming
        76 Thanksgiving
        78 Sending

81 Epiphany
    81 Year A Lectionary Texts
    81 A Framework, Themes, and Ideas for Epiphany
        82 Reset: A Worship Series for Epiphany
    87 Words for Worship, Epiphany
        87 Gathering
        91 Proclaiming
        92 Thanksgiving
        98 Sending

Contents

99 Lent
- *99* Year A Lectionary Texts
- *99* A Framework, Themes, and Ideas for Lent
  - *100* Where Are You: A Worship Series for Lent
- *107* Words for Worship, Lent
  - *107* Gathering
  - *110* Proclaiming
  - *112* Thanksgiving
  - *115* Sending

117 Holy Week and Easter Sunday
- *117* Year A Lectionary Texts
- *118* A Framework, Themes, and Ideas for Holy Week and Easter Sunday
  - *118* Disrupted: A Worship Series for Holy Week and Easter Sunday
- *123* Words for Worship, Holy Week and Easter Sunday
  - *123* Gathering
  - *128* Proclaiming
  - *135* Thanksgiving
  - *141* Sending

143 Eastertide
- *143* Year A Lectionary Texts
- *143* A Framework, Themes, and Ideas for Eastertide
  - *144* Redemption Songs: A Worship Series for Eastertide
- *151* Words for Worship, Holy Week and Eastertide
  - *151* Gathering
  - *152* Proclaiming
  - *153* Thanksgiving
  - *157* Sending

159 Pentecost and Trinity Sunday
- *159* Year A Lectionary Texts
- *159* A Framework, Themes, and Ideas for Pentecost and Trinity Sunday
  - *160* So Come: A Worship Series for Pentecost and Trinity Sunday
- *163* Words for Worship, Pentecost and Trinity Sunday
  - *163* Gathering
  - *165* Proclaiming

    165 Thanksgiving
    169 Sending

 171 After Pentecost
   171 Year A Lectionary Texts
   171 A Framework, Themes, and Ideas for After Pentecost
    172 I Will: A Worship Series for After Pentecost
   178 Words for Worship, After Pentecost
    178 Gathering
    181 Proclaiming
    182 Thanksgiving
    186 Sending

   188 Year A Lectionary Texts
    188 Like This, Like That: A Worship Series for After Pentecost
   194 Words for Worship, After Pentecost
    194 Gathering
    199 Proclaiming
    210 Thanksgiving
    203 Sending

   203 Year A Lectionary Texts
    203 Don't Let Go: A Worship Series for After Pentecost
   208 Words for Worship, After Pentecost
    208 Gathering
    209 Proclaiming
    210 Thanksgiving
    213 Sending

   214 Year A Lectionary Texts
    214 Because Mercy: A Worship Series for After Pentecost
   219 Words for Worship, After Pentecost
    219 Gathering
    220 Proclaiming
    221 Thanksgiving
    222 Sending

   223 Year A Lectionary Texts
    223 Go with Us: A Worship Series for After Pentecost

Contents

230 Words for Worship, After Pentecost
    230 Gathering
    233 Proclaiming
    233 Thanksgiving
    234 Sending

235 Year A Lectionary Texts
    235 The Kingdom Is Yours: A Worship Series for After Pentecost
241 Words for Worship, After Pentecost
    241 Gathering
    245 Proclaiming
    245 Thanksgiving
    247 Sending

249 Special Times of Worship

255 Contributors

259 Sources

Introduction

It seems fitting that a worship resource for liturgy and preaching might be entitled *Call and Response*. After all, it is the fundamental cadence of Christian worship and discipleship. Throughout scripture the faithful are invited to hear and listen for God's call upon creation, summoning all into intentional community with sacred purpose. Likewise, the patterned response of the faithful to this call becomes the echo of grace, heralding the dawn of new creation and the sureness of a future with hope. Call and response is the cadence of our life in Christ, providing the essential pulse for worship that is engaging without being performative and transformative without being manipulative.

Call and Response: The Abingdon Guidebook for Worship and Preaching, Year A aims to help pastors and worship leaders prepare meaningfully rich worship services that are relevant to their communities. Our objective is to provide inspiration for liturgy and preaching that engages people and deepens their discipleship, to provide information to edify leaders at all experience levels, and to provide actual words for worship services throughout the year. While this resource reflects the depth of United Methodist theology and practice, we hope discerning leaders from across the denominational spectrum will find it useful in the most practical ways on a daily and weekly basis.

As the title suggests, this volume is organized into two main sections:

The Call
This section provides a foundational understanding of the basic pattern of worship—Gathering, Proclaiming, Thanksgiving, Sending—and all its constituent elements. Within this pattern readers will find general examples for each liturgical moment and contextual prompts for particularly challenging occasions such as traumatic events, natural disaster, life transitions, and current events. Contributions in this portion come from a variety of sources—some new, some ancient—reflecting both the

breadth of liturgical expression and the ecumenical spirit within the United Methodist tradition.

The Response

Based on the revised common lectionary readings for year A, this section is organized by seasons of the liturgical calendar. Responding to the varied and contextual ways in which many congregations and pastors utilize either the lectionary or worship series, this section seeks a hybrid approach that organizes the complementary lectionary readings for each season into a suggested worship series based on emerging themes. Each season is then outlined thematically and contains a brief overview and commentary with suggestions for worship. A diversity of worship artists, pastors, and theologians have provided newly written liturgies for each season, offering the church a fresh liturgical expression for such a time as this.

Call and Response seeks to reflect the practical divinity—theology applied to daily life—so ubiquitous to the Wesleyan Christian tradition. As such we hope the contents of these pages will serve as a guide and inspiration for what may be contextually expressed within the liturgy of the local church, enabling it to creatively and faithfully respond to the move of the Holy Spirit within the world today. Likewise, this resource may function as its own kind of call to worship—calling all worship leaders, pastors, and congregations to allow the Holy Spirit to empower the church's voice and enliven its worship.

R. DeAndre Johnson
General Editor

How to Use This Book

Use **Part One** for teaching the basic pattern of worship and for coaching people on your worship teams. Use it as the basis for an all-church study of worship, or a sermon series about worship. Use the frameworks in **Part Two** for planning sermons and worship throughout the year. Use the commentaries as general inspiration or as templates for your sermons. If you prefer not to preach or plan worship in serial form, simply use the commentaries to guide your weekly preparation and set the "series" structure aside. Some liturgical pieces are based on lectionary texts or are written for certain days, but you may use the liturgies whenever and however they work best for your congregation. For responsive readings, the **bold text is for the congregation** to speak in unison, and the **regular text is for the leader** to speak alone.

Part One

CALLED TO WORSHP

The Basic Pattern

Gathering

"The people come together in the Lord's name" (from "An Order of Worship Using the Basic Pattern," *The United Methodist Book of Worship*). **The fundamental purpose of the Gathering is to enable the coming together of God's people, from the parking lot to the pew. Consequently, each part of the Gathering should focus on both nurturing a sense of community among the faithful and turning attention towards God.**

When planning the Gathering, think critically about how to provide:

- Hospitality
- Accessibility
- Preparation for the rest of the service

In addition to music and liturgy, worship leaders should think critically about the hospitality and accessibility of the worship space as essential aspects of the Gathering. Similarly, worship leaders should use this time to prepare the congregation for fuller participation later in the service—i.e., a brief rehearsal of unfamiliar hymns or instructions for ritual actions. All these should be done with the intent of enabling the people to know themselves as God's gathered people and to grow in their awareness of God's presence among the gathered. On the following pages, you will find examples of liturgies and prayers for the Gathering.

Opening Sentences

I will bless the Lord at all times;
    his praise shall continually be in my mouth.
My soul makes its boast in the Lord;
    let the humble hear and be glad.

O magnify the LORD with me,
> and let us exalt his name together.
—Psalm 34:1-3 NRSVue

O the depth of the riches and wisdom and knowledge of God!
How unsearchable are his judgments and how inscrutable his ways!
"For who has known the mind of the Lord?
> Or who has been his counselor?"
"Or who has given a gift to him,
> to receive a gift in return?"
For from him and through him and to him are all things. To him be the glory forever. Amen.
—Romans 11:33-36 NRSVue

Blessed be the God and Father of our Lord Jesus Christ, who has blessed us in Christ with every spiritual blessing in the heavenly places, just as he chose us in Christ before the foundation of the world to be holy and blameless before him in love. He destined us for adoption as his children through Jesus Christ, according to the good pleasure of his will, to the praise of his glorious grace that he freely bestowed on us in the Beloved. In him we have redemption through his blood, the forgiveness of our trespasses, according to the riches of his grace that he lavished on us.
—Ephesians 1:3-8a NRSVue

To those who are called,
who are beloved in God the Father
and kept safe for Jesus Christ:
May mercy, peace, and love be yours in abundance.
—Jude 1-2 NRSVue

Grace to you and peace from him who is and who was and who is to come . . .
and from Jesus Christ, the faithful witness,
the firstborn of the dead,
and the ruler of the kings of the earth.
—Revelation 1:4-5 NRSVue

Calls to Worship

Call to Worship

Gather us in, Lord.
Gather all our fears and dreams,
Gather all our brokenness and potential,
and show us how you will use it all.
Gather us in, Lord, for we are better together.

Gather us in, Lord.
Let the young and the old join together,
Let the poor and the rich share together,
Let the faithful from every corner raise the song,
Till we can see what we may yet become.
Gather us in, Lord, for we are better together.
Gather us in, Lord.
Gather us again with waters that tell of our shared calling.
Gather us again with bread that tells of our community.
Gather us again with wine that tells of our salvation
And by your Spirit make us one in purpose, mind, and heart.
Gather us in, Lord, for we are better together.

Call to Worship

We come because we love to tell the old story.
We come to sing the old song of God's salvation and healing love.
Give us courage, Lord, to trust what we know and obey what we hope.
We come because we know about impossible births and Exodus freedom.
Give us courage, Lord, to trust what we know and obey what we hope.
We come because we know the strangeness of
the blind seeing, the lame walking,
the dead living and the poor rejoicing.
Give us courage, Lord, to trust what we know and obey what we hope.
We come because we know Jesus,
who showed us how the old story can become a new, dangerous, transforming song.
Give us courage, Lord, to trust what we know and obey what we hope.
—adapted from Walter Brueggemann, "Old Stories Become New Songs"

A Micah 6:8 Call to Worship
(Britney Winn Lee)

Mercy without justice and humility is transactional.
Humility without mercy and justice is despair.
Justice without humility and mercy is punishment.
You have shown us, O God, what you require.
To act justly, love mercy, and walk humbly with you. Amen.

Call to Worship
(John Thornburg)

Jesus, our brother, went to the temple to meet with the teachers.
    He went to the seashore to gather disciples.

He went to the mountaintop to speak to curious crowds.
He went to the garden to pray for the world.
He went to Emmaus to show himself to the frightened and bewildered.
And now he comes to travel with us,
and with our sisters and brothers throughout the world.
And we will watch for him.

A Call to Worship for Complex Times
(Britney Winn Lee)

The world has spun since we were last together.
Its residents have built up and torn down.
Things have stayed the same and shifted forever among us this week.
We are a storied people—dynamic, hurting, curious, and in process.
We contain multitudes together.

Let us remember the complexities that exist between us and beyond us as we gather, knowing that we bring much to this space.
Let us also remember that love has been at work, not thwarted nor slowed, in the time that has passed.
Indeed, love is at work now.

We open ourselves to its presence and power,
that all of who we are and all that we bring will be met by all that it promises.
We open ourselves to you, loving God, this day.
Come, let us worship together.

Be Assured: A Call to Worship
(Britney Winn Lee)

Be assured that God is among us;
Open wide the sanctuary doors, there's enough love for all!
Be assured that God is not contained;
We are invited to create, to experiment, to evolve!
Be assured that God is on the move;
Let us join God in the redemptive adventure of the world
Where everything is being made new,
Even us, even now.

A Call to Worship for Liberation
(Britney Winn Lee)

With your voice alone, O God, you call to our bodies and spirits.
"Come into your healing," says the Lord.

Though we are chronically human, you have not left us in despair.
It is for freedom that we are set free.
In our rule-making, we can miss the heart of God. Help us to lead with love.
This Sabbath day is for liberation.
Let us worship together Christ Jesus who loosens the chains of oppression.
In our society and in our souls.
Come now, Holy Spirit.

Opening Prayers

Invocation
(John Thornburg)

Where there is joy in the world today,
where people rejoice in the rising of the sun and the dawn of a new day,
Come, Holy Spirit, Confirm Their Joy and Ours.
Where there is pain in the world today,
where people cry out in hunger and desperation,
Come, Holy Spirit, Bring Comfort to All in Pain.
Where there is strife in the world today,
where factions have forgotten what the fight is about,
but only remember that they hate each other,
Come, Holy Spirit, Cure the Warring Madness of Your People.
Where there is hope in the world today,
where people cling to the promise of new life that they have in you,
Come, Holy Spirit, Strengthen Them and Us in Hope.

Confession and Pardon

Prayer of Confession
(R. DeAndre Johnson and Jorge Lockward)

God of grace and community,
whose ties are stronger than culture or tribe,
we praise and bless your name
for you have knit us together into a tapestry of grace and forgiveness.

Even so, Lord,
though your Spirit is continually calling us
into deeper communion with you and each other,
we confess that, at times, we are resistant to your call
and reluctant to live as your true community.

For the ways in which we have subverted or denied
the gifts of your Spirit within each other,
Lord, have mercy. Christ, have mercy. Lord, have mercy.
For the ways our welcome hits the wall when it becomes inconvenient,
Lord, have mercy. Christ, have mercy. Lord, have mercy.
For the times when we are distrustful of new smells and new sounds
in our homes, churches, and communities
Lord, have mercy. Christ, have mercy. Lord, have mercy.
For the difficulty we have in moving from welcome to belonging and true sharing,
Lord, have mercy. Christ, have mercy. Lord, have mercy.
For all the ways in which we subvert the deep truth of our faith
by accepting the easier settlements of our society,
Lord, have mercy. Christ, have mercy. Lord, have mercy.

(brief silence)

You are the God of all forgiveness.
We do not ask for an easy way out,
but for courage, honesty, and faithfulness.
By your gracious forgiveness transpose us into agents of your will,
that our habits and inclinations may more closely follow
your humble, majestic lead,
that our lives may joyously conform to your vision and pattern of a new world.
This we pray in the name of your immigrant Son, Jesus our Lord.
Amen.

Hear the good news:
Nothing, absolutely nothing, can separate us from the love of God in Christ Jesus.
Anyone who is in Christ is a new creation.
The old life has gone; a new life has begun.
So, in the name of Jesus Christ, we are a forgiven people. Glory to God!
Alleluia! Amen.
—adapted from Walter Brueggemann, "On Controlling Our Borders"

Prayer of Confession
(John Thornburg)

God of power and might, we are so often afraid.
> You call us to greatness, and we protest that we are weak.
> You show us your ways, and we complain that they are too hard.
> You promise to protect us, and we do not trust your word.

Forgive our weakness, and our lack of faith.
Strengthen us for your work, and your ministry in the world. Amen.

Passing of the Peace

Invitation to Passing of the Peace

Since we have been reconciled,
let us share the peace that has been given us in grace.
May the peace of God be with you.
And also with you.
—Valerie Bridgman Davis, *Africana Worship Book, Year A*

Invitation to Passing of the Peace

As forgiven and reconciled people,
let us greet one another with signs of peace and reconciliation.
The peace of Christ be with you.
And also with you.

Proclaiming

Proclamation of the Word is the heartbeat of the church's worship and the world's salvation. Fred Craddock describes such proclamation as the "breaking of silence." He notes that the Word comes to us, is spoken to us, out of the backdrop of God's silence, breaking through into our world as God's revelation to God's people. "God breaking the silence with the Word—what an appropriate description not only of revelation but a sermon, a word tossed against the clear glass of silence behind which people sit waiting and asking, "Is there any word from the Lord?" (Craddock, *Praching*).

The sounding of the Word through proclamation enables those listening to encounter the risen Christ in very real and empirically tangible ways. So, when it comes to Proclamation, worship leaders should not shy away from purposefully and creatively using multiple scripture readings through the service—whether musically, visually, or dramatically. In doing so, considerations should be made for multiple learning styles as well as accessibility for pre-readers. Scriptural, historical, and ecumenical creeds or affirmations of faith can provide differing avenues for both preparing for and immediately responding to the Word.

On the following pages, you will find examples of liturgies and prayers for the Proclamation.

When planning the Proclamation, consider ways to:

- Use multiple scripture readings

- Share them with purpose and creativity

- Make them accessible for different learning styles

- Make them accessible for children and people who do not read

To prepare for and respond to the Word, consider ways to use:

- Scriptural creeds

- Historical creeds

- Ecumenical creeds

- Affirmations of faith

Prayers for Illumination

Prayer for Illumination
(John Thornburg)

Gracious and eternal God,

as we await the reading of your Word, make us still in this moment that we can hear that you are the source of every breath we draw and that you are breathing in and out with us;

take the worries that are resident throughout our hearts and minds and still them just now, just as your Son, our Savior, stilled the wind and waves so that his disciples could know who he was;

confirm any and all joy that is resident within us today, and amplify it, so that we may feel what it is like to rest in you;

when we fall into disobedience, take us to the Garden of Gethsemane, so we can hear our Lord say, "Not my will, but yours be done";

when we languish in apathy, take us to the Sheep Gate pool, so we can hear Jesus ask, "Do you want to be healed?";

when we elevate wealth or status or nation above you, take us to the hillside, so we can hear Jesus say, "No one can serve two masters";

when we doubt our calling and every impulse tells us to retreat, take us back to the hillside, so we can hear Jesus say, "You are the light of the world";

make us your body as we work, pray and study, as we cry together and laugh together, as we wrestle with your word and as we stand before you to be fools for you;

stand us each to our full height, so that we may see everything we are meant to see, and so that those who listen to us may see you shining through us.

In the name of our Risen Savior, Jesus Christ, we pray. Amen.

In the Name Of

O most holy and gracious God,
It is your name we reverence
    in mellifluous praise and dutiful obeisance,
it is your name we invoke
    for righteous justice and just mercy;

It is your name we confront
    in awed investigation and interrogation—
but do we really know who you are?
Do we really know Your Name
    or do we only know who we wish you to be?
Speak to us your sacred name
and tell us again who you are
so that our lives and our living
may be re-tuned to praise you more perfectly. Amen.
—R. DeAndre Johnson, *Yes and Amen*

Affirmations of Faith

An Affirmation About Who We Love and What We Trust
(John Thornburg)

I love God, the one who made heaven and earth.
I love Jesus, because when we look at him, we see God face to face.
I love him because he came from God, because he was humble, and told the truth, because he was willing to suffer and sacrifice and even die.
I'm joyful that he didn't stay dead.
I trust that the one who judges me most finally is the one
who loves me the most deeply.
I revel in the Holy Spirit, the Great Disruptor of what's normal, the Fresh Wind
that opens every shuttered window.
I am glad that there is a place for people to gather, worship and scatter, and I trust
that the Holy Spirit will comfort those who gather, inspire those who worship,
and embolden those who scatter.
I'm grateful that so many have gone before me,
and I hope to walk faithfully in their footsteps.
I'm relieved that even when we stray the most,
God calls us back and says, "I forgive you."
I trust that there is a day coming when all people everywhere
will fully embody the image of God in which they were made.
I trust God; Lover, Beloved and Loving, and look forward to my future in God.

An Affirmation of Faith (Psalm 46)

O Lord, we know you are our refuge and strength.
You are a very present help in times of trouble. And we know trouble Lord . . .
. . . but we believe:
We believe God is our refuge and strength.
We believe God is a very present help in times of trouble.

We believe and we will not fear. We believe and we will not fear!
We believe God, though the earth should change.
We believe God, though the mountains tremble.
We believe there is a river that makes glad the people of God.
We believe there is a river. We believe there is a river!

When our world seems dried up, we believe there is a river.
We believe God is in the midst of the city, in the midst of the people.
We believe God will help when the morning dawns.
We believe God, though nations are in uproar.
We believe God though kingdoms teeter and totter.
We believe God utters a voice and the earth melts.
We believe Almighty God is with us.
We believe and will not fear. We believe there is a river.
God is our refuge and strength.
God is our refuge and strength. God is our refuge and strength!

Thanksgiving

Thanksgiving is the church's response to God's movement towards us as explicated in Proclamation. Such response may include prayers and petitions of various kinds, offerings, ritual actions, baptism, and communion. All these acts of Thanksgiving reflect the continual recognition of the depth of mercy received then accepting and returning that same mercy with gratitude and generosity. **In Thanksgiving, all the joys, concerns, gifts, and praise of the people are collected and offered to God.** Worship leaders should carefully plan each act of Thanksgiving to allow full participation of all gathered, so that all might be empowered to offer their own sacrifice of praise. On the following pages, you will find examples of liturgies and prayers for the Thanksgiving.

When planning the Thanksgiving, consider including:

- Prayers
- Petitions
- Offerings
- Ritual actions
- Baptism
- Holy Communion

Prayers of the People

Plan carefully to ensure:

- All are invited to actively participate
- Participants are empowered to offer their own praise

Pastoral Prayers

A Prayer of the People

Awake, O Sleeper, rise from death,
And Christ will give you life!

Bring newness and change to your church, O God,
> that we might serve you with courage and grace.

Awake, O Church, rise from death,
And Christ will give you life!

Bring newness and change to your world, O God,
> that we all might know the goodness of your love.

Awake, O World, rise from death,
And Christ will give you life!

Bring newness and change to our nation, O God,
> that each person might share and honor the other.

Awake, O People, rise from death,
And Christ will give you life!

Bring newness and change for the suffering, O God,
> that they might know your saving help.

Awake, O Sorrowful, rise from death,
And Christ will give you life!

Bring newness and change to even the departed, O God,
> that they might forever grow in your likeness.

Awake, O Saints, rise from death,
And Christ will give you life!

Bring newness and change to our hearts, O God,
> that we might grow larger in faith and hope.

Awake, O Soul, rise from the death,
And Christ will give you life!

Awake, O Sleeper, rise from death,
> for Christ has burst forth from the tomb, making all things new.

Rise and live, says the Lord. God has made you for life and all joy!
Amen, Alleluia! Alleluia, Amen!
—Susan A. Bock, *Liturgy for the Whole Church*

A Prayer of the People

Covenant with me
To spread community
To worlds beyond this place.

Sing afresh again
God's image in each one
Reflect that face ourselves.

Acknowledge human blur
Destruction, hurt, and sin
Confession brings forgiveness.

Sing anew God's praise
Accept our ministry
Begin the healing task.

Unite with those who love
Enough to move toward change
Empowered by the Spirit.

Go on our way in joy
Create a celebration
God's likeness lives in us!
—Mary Freedlund, *Women's Prayer Services*

A Prayer for the Church

Holy Spirit, come and repossess your church. We grew tired in waiting for you
    and have strayed too far from the places
        we first met you.
We found more efficient ways to do business
    and have gone too long without listening
        for your direction.
We placed confidence in our own experience
    and have become too oblivious
        to your work around us.
Forgive us, Lord.
In your mercy and by your power,
    rush right into our hallowed spaces
        and disrupt all our scheming,
            all our dreaming,
            all our politicization,
            all our polarization,
            all our theologies,
            all our charities—
for none of it matters without you.
Without you, none of it matters.
Come, Holy Spirit. We desperately need you.
Amen.
—R. DeAndre Johnson, *Yes and Amen*

Praise for Today

Today is your day, Lord.
Not mine,
  not theirs,
    not ours,
but yours.
Help me to see each ray of sunlight,
  each drop of rain,
  each gust of wind,
as a constellation of grace,
  signs of your working in me,
    through me, and around me.
Keep my eyes open
  to see you in all the hidden places
    and hidden faces I encounter today.
Keep my mind ever marveling
  at the wondrous depth of your love
    and kindness to us.
Keep my heart malleable
  to your infinite, all-encompassing grace.
Keep my hands and feet courageous and bold,
  willing to risk the dare
  that whatever you have for me today
    is far greater than my fear.
This is your day, O Lord,
  and I am humbled again
by your merciful invitation to join you in it.
Thank you for this day. Amen.
—R. DeAndre Johnson, *Yes and Amen*

A Prayer for Exodus

O God of endless mercy,
you greet us in each moment,
  offering a revival of hope for renewed living
  in your kingdom—
but we are creatures interrupted by fear,
  enticed into believing both that
    life is controlled by fear
and that fear is the means to control life.
We need exodus, Lord!

By the power of your Spirit
release us into the freedom of expectancy
> so that we might learn again how to see
>> the miraculous potential of each moment and to trust again that
> your mercy outruns every moment.
And for love's sake,
> lead us to the place of
> humble, compassionate courage,
where honesty, integrity and kindness
> can overrule a culture of mistrust, suspicion
> and pretentious strength,
so that we may have a right mind
> to more fully know the true power of love.
In the name of the One who continues to say:
"Take courage! It is I. Do not be afraid."
Amen.
—R. DeAndre Johnson, *Yes and Amen*

Bidding and Responsive Prayers

A Prayer of Lament and Fear

The prayer begins with the following sung refrain. It should be repeated as many times as it takes to become meditative before proceeding with the rest of the prayer.

> Sung Refrain:
> Don't be afraid. My love is stronger, my love is stronger than your fear.
> Don't be afraid. My love is stronger, and I have promised,
> promised to be always near.
> —Wild Goose Resource Group, Iona Community, "Don't Be Afraid"

O God, your people have always had their fears.
So we come to you in humility and with honesty, naming our own.
Lord, we fear the future. What is coming next?
Our young people ask,
> "Will there be a place for me when I'm done with school?"
Our parents ask,
> "Will there be safe places for our children?"
Our seniors ask,
> "Will I die in peace and with dignity?" *[Refrain]*

**Lord, we fear the pain that comes
with illness and broken bones and aging.**

Some of us wonder how we're going to make it
> through more treatment and medication.
Some of us wonder how we can possibly face chronic illness.
Some of us wonder if prayers for healing even reach your throne.
Physical pain frightens us. *[Refrain]*

Lord, as a church, we wonder about our ministries and programs.
> **What if they don't "work"?**
What if outreach and faith nurture don't happen?
> **What if we fail?**
We fear the dependence we have to have on your Spirit
> to be the one to breathe life into Christians and non-Christians.

Lord, we are afraid of people who are different from us:
> those more powerful than us, those poorer than us,
> those of a different color or creed, those smarter than us,
> those with different personalities.
How do we talk to these people, O God? How do we make peace with them?
[Refrain]

Lord, we have acquaintances,
> **friends and family members whom we deeply love**
>> **but who do not know you.**
We are afraid for their salvation. *[Refrain]*

We admit, O God, that we're fearful of stillness and quiet.
It seems as if the last thing we want to do
> is slow down and be attentive to you.
Help us not to shy away from quiet times,
> from the simplicity of prayer, Scripture, and your presence.
It seems, O God, that, in the busyness of countless invitations
> we are afraid to say no. *[Refrain]*

And for all those fears for which we cannot name,
> we come to you, O God.
Those we cannot name because they're either unknown or unspeakable,
> receive them in our silence. *[Refrain]*

We are fearful so often, O Lord,
> because in our encounters with sin and evil
>> we find ourselves weak and poor.
We thank you so much then, Jesus,
> **for your actions and for your words—**
> **for love and the promise of nearness,**
which are our strength and our riches. Amen.
—John D. Witvliet, *Reformed Worship*

Thanksgiving

Prayers for Special Occasions

At the Retirement/Leaving of a Friend: I Thank God for You/Us

I thank God for you —
    for the light of grace that shines within you,
    for the warmth of love that radiates from you,
    for the depth of wisdom you bring,
    and for the strength of faith you inspire.
May you always know
    the constancy of God's presence with you
    and trust the power of God's gifts within you.
I thank God for you.

I thank God for us—
    for the joy of friendship,
    for the privilege of sacred work,
    for the beauty of excellence,
    for the ease of collaboration,
    for the comfort of forgiveness,
    and for the sincerity of respect.
May we always know and trust
    the Spirit to perfect our work to God's glory
    and strengthen our communion
        even as we work in separate places.
I thank God for us.

"Glory to God, who is able to do far beyond all that we could ask or imagine by his power at work within us; glory to him in the church and in Christ Jesus for all generations, forever and always. Amen."

Prayer at the Start of a New ____

Eternal God, thank you for the gift of time—
    for the letting go and the sting of loss,
    for the starting over and the embrace of newness,
    for the crying out and the hunger to make it right,
    for the sorrowing and the hope for better days,
    for the dying and the assurance of death's end,
    for the living and the lives of those who yet live,
    for the trying new things
        and the surprise of creative genius,
    for the failing and the comfort of forgiveness,
    for the waiting . . . and the waiting . . .
        and the waiting . . . and the holiness of waiting,

Thank you for the gift of time and
> the gift of grace for every time . . .
and the reminder that I cannot control or run away from either.

A Prayer for Decision Making

Lord, it's hard to know what to do sometimes.
There are too many decisions,
> too many opinions,
> too many risks,
> too many mistakes,
> too many lives to love and loves to live.
I don't know what do or how to be, Lord,
> but I know you. I trust you.

Give me wisdom to choose your good will for each moment.
Give me grace to live your good will in each moment.
Give me faith to believe again that no matter what I choose, your good will is still possible for each moment.

A Prayer for a Couple About to Marry

O God of Abraham, God of Isaac, God of Jacob, bless these Your servants.
Sow the seed of eternal life in their hearts,
so that whatever they learn in Your Holy Word they will profit from it,
and bring their learning to fulfillment by their deeds.

Look, O Lord, mercifully on them from heaven. Bless this couple.
As You sent Your blessing on Abraham and Sarah to their great comfort,
so send Your blessing on these Your servants.

Help them to obey Your will and always live in safety under Your protection.
May this pair live in Your love to the end of their days.
Through Jesus Christ our Lord, we pray. Amen.
—John Welsey, *Wesley's Daily Prayers*

A Prayer for Married Couples

O Eternal God, Creator and Preserver of all people, Giver of spiritual grace, and Author of everlasting life, thank you for sending Your blessing to us Your servants.
You have blessed our marriage in Your Name.
As Isaac and Rebecca lived faithfully together, so You have given us grace to honor our vows.

Keep us always in perfect love and peace together, living according to Your laws.
We pray through Jesus Christ our Lord. Amen.
—John Welsey, *Wesley's Daily Prayers*

Prayers in Times of Crisis

A Prayer Amid Chaos
(Britney Winn Lee)

Let us inhale. Now exhale. Inhale again. Exhale. One last inhale. Now exhale.
The earth was formless and empty, and darkness was over the deep. But God's Spirit was hovering.
God's Spirit hovers here, now.
Storms do not stop forming in the ocean, but there is community. Death and sickness break our hearts, but there are new mercies. Disorder seems unpreventable, but there is breath.
Breathe into us once again the breath of life, O God, that we may know the grace that is for us.
Let us not hold out for arrival to arrive at the peace that you make possible.
Which surpasses all understanding.
Amen.

In Times of Disaster: A Prayer of Praise and Intercession

In the midst of darkness, you call forth light.
In the radiance of your light, you invite us to walk into the mystery of your darkness.

You are our light in this darkness, O God.
Be our guide, that we may not be afraid to walk where no light shines.
You fill your creation with hope for peace,
but you also remind us of nature's destructive power.
Shelter us in the midst of storms,
May we show forth the light of your glory
by offering ourselves in love to all who are hurting,
When all we have is taken away,
still you hold us as your very own.
Blessed are you, Lord God of the universe,
now and forever. Amen.
—Discipleship Ministries

A Litany of Social Penance

O God, our Creator, who made us, your children, to be one family; so that what concerns any, must concern all; we confess the evils we have done and the good we have left undone. We have spent our strength too often upon the tower of Babel of our own pride. We have forgotten that the city's foundations, builder and maker is you, O God. We have been content that we ourselves should prosper, although many be poor; that a few should feast while multitudes starve both in body and in soul. And you, O God, have taught us that whatsoever we sow, that we shall also reap; help us to repent before your judgment comes.

For clouded eyes that see no further than our own advantage,
we confess our sin, O God.
For dulled imaginations that take no notice of the suffering of others,
we confess our sin, O God.
For willingness to profit by injustice which we have not striven to prevent,
we confess our sin, O God.
For selfishness that is quick to gain and slow to give,
we confess our sin, O God.
For carelessness that asks, "Am I my brother's keeper?"
we confess our sin, O God.

Ever merciful God, take away from us the wickedness of our conscious and unconscious wrongs. Forgive us for our unfaithfulness to the vision of your kingdom, and grant to us a better purpose for the days to come. From easy acquiescence to old iniquities,
save us, O God.
From indifference to the human cost of anything we covet,
save us, O God.
From the greed that wastes the lives of men and women through unemployment, poverty, and deprivation,
save us, O God.
From the cruelty that exploits the needy and defenseless,
save us, O God.
From the blasphemy against the Spirit that sells the bodies and souls of children to the golden idol of success,
save us, O God.
From false leadership in business and in government, and above all, from feebleness in the people that allows false leaders to rise to power,
save us, O God.

Unless the Lord builds the house,
their labor is but vain who build it.
But the One who sits upon the throne declares,
behold, I make all things new.

Even so, O God, let your Spirit be at work in us for your own redemptive purposes to build a new and better society on this earth for the blessing of your people, so that we may look toward your kingdom with hope, through Jesus Christ our Lord.
Amen.
—Walter Russell Bowie, in *The Wideness of God's Mercy: Litanies to Enlarge Our Prayer*

A Prayer During War Elsewhere
(Britney Winn Lee)

Even when we are so far removed in miles from the wall-rattling clangs and casualties of conflict, we are not so far removed from the human experiences of violence, loss, and unrestrainable societal threats to not be breath-halted by the words "we are at war."
It is our empathy that ties us over oceans. May that same empathy activate within us that which can tie us over divides, knowing all wars begin in the heart-cracks of othering.
Call us to the quiet places of evaluation—who am I at my core that would feed the beast of battle? What story am I ingesting? Who is it making me hate and fear? What voices am I allowing to build my lens? Do they sound like love? Do I trust grace enough to bet on it? Enough to put my weight against it? Enough to put my family's? Does abundance fall off of my lips freely and add to the inhale of my neighbors?
Or am I spreading scarcity like a virus?
Where we can be the hospitality after the catastrophe, the alternative narrative after the drawn lines, the resurrection after the grave, and the advocates of another way, let us. Make us brave and self-aware and honest and present enough to do so.
Give to those who need tonight that which they cannot earn or wield. Let them know they are not alone.
Let us know we are not alone.
Amen.

The Offering

Invitations

Invitation 1

The earth is the Lord's and all that is in it,
the world, and those who live in it.
—Psalm 24:1 NRSVue

Invitation 2

The point is this: the one who sows sparingly will also reap sparingly, and the one who sows bountifully will also reap bountifully. Each of you must give as you have made up your mind, not regretfully or under compulsion, for God loves a cheerful giver. And God is able to provide you with every blessing in abundance, so that by always having enough of everything, you may share abundantly in every good work.
—2 Corinthians 9:6-8 NRSVue

Invitation 3

Your ministry, and that of this congregation, makes a difference in the lives of people throughout the world. Like the church in Thessalonica, "your faith, love and steadfast hope in Christ" will be remembered. Worship God now with your tithes and offerings, so that others can experience God's love, hope, and liberation.
—Lillian C. Smith, *Africana Worship Book, Year A*

Invitation 4

God is a great God above all gods. God is greater than our problems and God's hand reaches to the depths and the heights, the sea and dry land. Come, let us worship the rock of our salvation with our giving; come into God's presence with our song, our thanksgiving, and the gifts of our lives and our substance. God is our God and we are the people of God's pasture, and the sheep of God's hand. Give. Give. Give.
—Valerie Bridgeman Davis, *Africana Worship Book, Year A*

Prayers for Giving and Receiving

Offertory Prayer

Lord, isn't your creation wasteful?
Fruits never equal the seedlings' abundance. Springs scatter water.
The sun gives out enormous light.
May your bounty teach me greatness of heart.
May your magnificence stop me from being mean.
Seeing you a prodigal and open-handed giver,
let me give unstintingly like a king's son, like God's own.
—Hélder Pessoa Câmara, OFS, *The Hodder Book of Christian Prayers*

Givers and Stewards: An Offering Prayer
(Britney Winn Lee)

O Lord, make us generous givers and trustworthy stewards.
Move us to give to keep lights on, but only if they are illuminating space for us to bring both our faith and our doubts.
Move us to give to keep the doors open, but only if they are open to the migrant, the poor, the ex-prisoner, and the other.
Move us to give to sustain programming, but only if that programming knows that it's only good news if it's good news for all people.
Move us to give the loaves and fishes we have, but also grant us the faith to see them multiplied for the common good of our neighbors and for your kingdom to come here on earth as it is in heaven.
In Jesus's name.

Doxologies

O the depth of the riches and wisdom and knowledge of God!
How unsearchable are his judgments and how inscrutable his ways!
"For who has known the mind of the Lord? Or who has been his counselor?"
"Or who has given a gift to him, to receive a gift in return?"
For from him and through him and to him are all things. To him be the glory forever.
Amen.
—Romans 11:33-36 NRSVue

To the King of the ages, immortal, invisible, the only God,
be honor and glory forever and ever. Amen.
—1 Timothy 1:17 NRSVue

Baptism

Introductions

Do you not know that all of us who were baptized into Christ Jesus
were baptized into his death?
Therefore we were buried with him by baptism into death,
so that, just as Christ was raised from the dead
by the glory of the Father,
so we also might walk in newness of life.
—Romans 6:3-4 NRSVue

As many of you as were baptized into Christ have clothed yourselves with Christ.
There is no longer Jew or Greek;
there is no longer slave or free;
there is no longer male and female,
for all of you are one in Christ Jesus.
—Galatians 3:27-28 NRSVue

You are a chosen race, a royal priesthood,
a holy nation, God's own people,
in order that you may proclaim
the excellence of him who called you
out of darkness into his marvelous light.
Once you were not a people,
but now you are God's people;
once you had not received mercy,
but now you have received mercy.
—1 Peter 2:9-10 NRSVue

Brothers and sisters in Christ:
Through the Sacrament of Baptism
we are initiated into Christ's holy Church.
We are incorporated into God's mighty acts of salvation
and given new birth through water and the Spirit.
All this is God's gift, offered to us without price.
Through the reaffirmation of our faith
we renew the covenant declared at our baptism,
acknowledge what God is doing for us,
and affirm our commitment to Christ's holy Church.
—"The Services of the Baptismal Covenant of The United Methodist Church as Revised to Align with the 2008 *Book of Discipline* and *Book of Resolutions*"

Just as Jesus began his ministry with baptism, so too in baptism we begin again.
Here we receive God's claim upon our lives, marking us as God's own for the world.
Here we are washed and raised into a new life of forgiveness and reconciliation.
Here we are anointed and empowered by the Spirit for the work of ministry.
This is God's doing—a work of grace—and it is marvelous in our eyes.

Thanksgiving Over the Water

I invite you to close your eyes, because some things can only be seen with the eyes closed. Now, listen to the water. Just listen. And dream.

> *Water is poured slowly and loudly into the font. Throughout the rest of the story create sound with the water as you are led to do so.*

And go now, to the beginning of time when there was nothing. Nothing. Nothing but deep, cold water, with a blanket of darkness stretching across it. The Spirit of God spent all its days hovering over that water, searching for something to love, someplace to plant God's feet and to be at rest.

Then came the day when God began to create the world. God spoke, and suddenly there was water above, held up in place by a great vault, and water below separated by dry land. If you listen hard, you will hear that water crashing upon the virgin beaches, and rolling softly away, in a gentle rhythm, crashing, rolling, again and again. The waters filled up with living things, and the earth and skies, too. And God made a people to love. And it was all beautiful, and noisy, and good.

Pause for silence and breathing.

Then one day, the rain came, soft and quiet at first, but then the windows of heaven were opened and the waters poured over the earth in a Great Flood. It rained and rained, three days, seven days, twelve, twenty, and on and on, thirty days, forty days. Then God sent a strong wind to blow back the rain, and hung a rainbow on the mist that was left in the air. You might be able to feel the water in the soggy ground under your feet as you emerge with Noah from the ark. And you can't help but notice the rainbow!

Pause for silence and breathing.

Now you are walking right through the Red Sea, whose waters are standing high to both sides, pressed back by God's own two hands, and the ground under your feet isn't even damp, and just as you step safely ashore, you can hear the thunderous crash of the sea, back into its place, covering your enemies. And you can't help but hear Miriam and our mothers and fathers, singing and dancing, wild with joy.

Pause for silence and breathing.

And now you are standing by Moses as he strikes the rock and water gushes out of it; and you are so dry and thirsty, you can't help but try to catch it in your hands and splash it all over and around you.

Pause for silence and breathing.

And now you are sitting at Jacob's well in Samaria, at high noon, with Jesus, and he is telling you all that is on his mind, while both of you drink the well's cold, clear, delicious water. You can't help but taste it.

Pause for silence and breathing.

Now you're with Peter, fishing in the water. Walking on it now, reaching for Jesus, thinking this must be a dream. And now you're with Philip and the Ethiopian eunuch, up to your waist in a tiny desert pond, pouring water over the eunuch's head and claiming him for Christ. And you can't help but say, "Amen, amen."

> *Pause for silence and breathing.*

And now, when you are ready, open your eyes.

In this water is the story of our life with God;
> From this water, we are lifted to dry ground, with Noah.
> Through it, we are rescued like the Israelites.
> In it, we are carried home over Jordan, into the church.

In and through this water, we are drowned and saved, washed and sustained.

In this water, the story of God's saving grace becomes our story too. From exile in Babylon, Ezekiel looked toward Jerusalem and dreamed of a cleansing, healing tide of water flowing out of the restored Temple in such abundance that it could be swam in. Can you imagine these waters flowing out from here to the farthest reaches of the earth to heal and soothe the whole world?

Sisters and brothers in Christ: through the sacrament of baptism God's Spirit has been poured out upon water, water poured over and immersing us, water that flows freely for all who will receive it, water from the streams of God's saving power and justice, water that brings hope to all who thirst for righteousness, water that refreshes life, nurtures growth, and offers new birth. Today we come to the waters, to renew our commitments in each other's presence to God who has called us, Christ who has sent us and the Spirit who has given us power to speak life.

Let the people of God say,
Thanks be to God!

Pour out your Holy Spirit, to bless this gift of water and *those* who *receive* it, to wash away *their* sin and clothe *them* in righteousness throughout *their* lives, that, dying and being raised with Christ, *they* may share in his final victory. Amen.

> *Here water may be used symbolically in ways that cannot be interpreted as baptism, as the pastor says:*

Remember your baptism and be faithful.
Amen.
—Susan A. Bock, *Liturgy for the Whole Church*

Thanksgiving

Holy Communion

Invitations

Invitation 1

Come to the table of grace. Come to the table of grace.
This is God's table; it's not yours or mine.
Come to the table of grace.
—Barbara Hamm, *Worship and Song*

Invitation 2

Jesus has invited everybody to dine at the table. Everything here is free!
Free from the bondage of sin to a life of peace. Everything here is free!
—Tim Warner, *The Africana Worship Book, Year A*

Great Thanksgiving

An Alternate Great Thanksgiving
(Jackson Henry)

In gathering at this table today, we remember that God is with us, and we are not alone.
Thanks be to God.

God, you created all things and gave us the gift of life. Time and time again, you have brought us through trials and tribulations and set us free through the Holy Spirit, all with a love that never ends.

And so, we lift up our hearts to you, and we offer you our songs and acts of praise. You are holy, and the earth, the cosmos, and all things in it sing to you with joy.

Into this world you made, you sent your Son Jesus Christ to be with us. He lived and died for the world, and he rose again that we might have life. The difficult road he walked led to a new covenant you offered to us—a covenant by water and the Spirit.

On the night in which he gave himself up for us, Jesus took a loaf of bread, and after blessing it he broke it, gave it to his disciples, and said, "Take, eat; this is my body that is given for you. Do this in remembrance of me." Then he took a cup, and after giving thanks he gave it to his disciples, saying, "Drink from it, all of you;

for this is my blood of the new covenant, which is poured out for you and for many for the forgiveness of sins. Do this, as often as you drink it, in remembrance of me."

Friends, there is Good News: Jesus Christ has died, yet lives! And Jesus will come again!

Come, Holy Spirit! *Hands above head in circular motions.*
Come, Holy Spirit!

Bless our bread and cup! *Hands in position of blessing, palms down.*
Bless our bread and cup!

Make us one body! *Hands turned over, at orans.*
Make us one body!
Hands remain at orans throughout conclusion of prayer.

Make us one, God—one with you, one with each other, and one in ministry to the world. May this table extend into the world until Jesus comes again and we join together at your heavenly table.
We pray all this in your name—Father, Son, and Holy Spirit. **Amen.**

An Abbreviated Communion Liturgy

We praise you, God our Creator whose love has no limits and whose splendor radiates both through the vast expanse of space and in the laughter of friends. Even when we ignore the signs of your life among us, you are always calling and inviting us to be where you are, to love whom you love, and to go where you go.
Thanks be to God.

We praise you, God our Savior, giving us Jesus to share our life and journey with us, to show us how to live as you desire. Through him, you destroyed the barriers that keep us from knowing you, and you continue to destroy the barriers that would keep us from loving each other.
Thanks be to God.

(taking the bread)
We praise you, God, remembering the night Jesus took bread,
blessed and broke it, and gave it to his disciples, saying,
"Take, eat. This is my body given for you. Do this in remembrance of me."

(taking the cup)
We praise you, God, remembering when Jesus took the cup,
gave thanks to you, gave it to his disciples and said,
"Drink this, all of you. This is my blood of the new covenant for you.
Do this in remembrance of me."

(lifting hands to bless the people. The people do the same.)
Come, Holy Spirit, come.
Come, Holy Spirit, come.

(. . . extending hands to bless the elements. The people do the same.)
Come, Holy Spirit, come.
Come, Holy Spirit, come.

(. . . extending hands to bless creation. The people do the same.)
Come, Holy Spirit, come.
Come, Holy Spirit, come.

Even so, come now Almighty God—Father, Son, and Spirit,
that we may be one with you and each other
and feast with you now as in the age to come,
praying as you taught us:

Our Father, who art in heaven, hallowed be thy name. Thy kingdom come, thy will be done on earth as it is in heaven. Give us this day our daily bread. And forgive us our trespasses, as we forgive those who trespass against us. And lead us not into temptation, but deliver us from evil. For thine is the kingdom, and the power, and the glory, forever. Amen.
—adapted from *The United Methodist Book of Worship* and *The United Methodist Hymnal*

Common Table Communion Liturgy
(Britney Winn Lee)

Here, at the common table, the holy presence within ordinary wood and nails is illuminated. This is mystery.
May it remind us that the ways of God are always unfolding from people to people.
Here, among the bread baked and juice pressed, our engagement in the story is confirmed. This is co-creation.
May it remind us that we are invited to participate in our own salvation.
Here, in our confession, our rebellion against your love at the expense of our neighbors is admitted. This is the beginning of healing.
May it remind us that while we were still sinners, Christ died for us.
Here, within the pouring and breaking of the elements, the self-giving love of Jesus is echoed. This is grace.
May it remind us that we have been given a new command, and as God has loved us, so must we love one another.
Here, in the sharing of the meal, the peace that accompanies belonging is present. This is the reconciliation through the Spirit.

May it remind us that we can be one with Christ, one with each other, and one in ministry to all the world.
Until Christ comes in final victory
And we feast at his heavenly banquet.
All honor and glory is yours, Almighty Father, now and forever, Amen.

God's Grace Is for You: A Communion Liturgy
(Britney Winn Lee)

God's grace is for you and in you.
God's grace is for and in every single person in this world.

We open ourselves to experience the Spirit, here and now.
Will you speak to us again, O God?

Christ's life reminds us that death is never the end. This Christ is here with us now.
Thank you, Jesus!

Loving Creator, Artist of every good and perfect piece of existence,
You have made us in your image.
You have made our friends, enemies, and neighbors in your image.

As your ancient name, YHWH, mimics our very breath,
Speaking your name is the first and last thing we do. We have always been yours.

Though we might forget how much you love us and be led by ego or fear,
Though we cope with pain and loss in ways that harm ourselves and others,
You run towards us every time. Every day, we are being saved.

And so, with your people on earth and all the company of heaven,
We proclaim that nothing compares to your love. And together, we say:
Holy, holy, holy Lord, God of power and might,
heaven and earth are full of your glory.
Hosanna in the highest.
Blessed is the one who comes in the name of the Lord.
Hosanna in the highest.

Holy are you, God, and blessed is your son Jesus
Who told us exactly where we would be able to find him:
Among the poor, the oppressed, the sick, and the suffering,
Giving food to the hungry and sharing tables with everyone
we think shouldn't be there.

His backward life, sacrificial death, and liberated life-again
Gave birth to the community of faith
Now invited into the same backwardness, sacrifice, and liberation.
Through the Spirit and at the water, you infuse this invitation with a promise:
"I am with you always."

On the night that Jesus absorbed violence to show us a better way,
he took bread, expressed his gratitude for *you*, broke the bread,
gave it to his friends, and said:
"Take, eat; this is my body which is given for you.
When you gather at the table, remember this love."
After supper, he took a cup of wine,
Expressed his gratitude for you again, gave it to his friends, and said:
"Drink from this, all of you;
Any covenantal symbol that makes you feel shame is gone;
The new covenant is here: God puts on skin and goes into the depths
of life and death
That you may know you have always been worthy of God's love.
Every time you share in this way,
Remember me."
This sacrament is an outward sign of an inward grace and an echo of this mystery:
Christ has died; Christ is risen; Christ will come again.

Prayer After Receiving

We thank you, God, for inviting us to this table
where we have known the presence of Christ
and have received all Christ's gifts.
Strengthen our faith,
increase our love for one another,
and let us show forth your praise in our lives;
through Jesus Christ our Savior. Amen.

Sending

Sending is the final movement of the church's worship. Just as Jesus commissions and sends his disciples out into the world, so too the church is sent out in the peace of Christ through the power of the Holy Spirit. Whether musical or liturgical, acts of sending should facilitate the blessing and the going out of the people. Just as in the Gathering, worship leaders should think critically about the hospitality and accessibility of the worship space as essential aspects of the Sending. Clear instructions on when and how people should go forth will avoid a haphazard conclusion that may feel disjointed from other aspects of worship. On the following pages, you will find examples of liturgies and prayers for the Sending.

When planning the Sending, focus on the blessing and sending out of the people. Think critically about ways to provide:

- Hospitality for all
- Accessibility for all
- Clear instructions
- Intentionality
- Cohesiveness with the rest of the service

Invitation to Discipleship

A Prayer of Commitment
(Eleanor Colvin)

In the Spirit of the Wesleyan Covenant Prayer

May your desires
    Be mine
May your thoughts
    Be mine

May your prayers
>   For me
>   Form on my lips.

May my hope
>   Be anchored in yours
May my will
>   Be tethered to yours
May your intentions
>   Toward me
>   Rise up in me.
Always.
Amen.

A Closing Prayer

God of every beginning,
Walk with us in our halting steps.
Prod us forward when we would stop.
Hold us up when we fall.
Love us when we pout because we do not want to change.
Change us into the image of Christ.
Grow us up and out.
May we spread into your grace,
blossom into your joy,
run into your mercy,
this day and always.
Amen.
—Valerie Bridgeman Davis, *The Africana Worship Book, Year C*

Blessings/Benedictions

Community Care: A Benediction
(Britney Winn Lee)

May you go further than insisting that someone deserves rest by investing in a culture of sabbath. Further than insisting that someone know they're enough by investing in a culture of non-judgement.
May you remember that while the former can be a little more than a reminder that another world is possible, the latter suggests we might just be able to get there together.
May you remember that community-care is a mercy when self-care is a chore.
We can do this. Go make the world better.

Surprise Us: A Benediction
(Britney Winn Lee)

God of hope, we speak the name of your son Jesus as we ask you to inspire us to dream outside of every box that we've ever assumed could limit you. Inspire us to do much with very little, to be curious and playful, to have faith like that of the children. When we feel drained, give us a spark. When we are burdened with business, grant us a dream. When we become stuck, send a friend, a word, a song, an idea to spur us on into the Good News that is the transformation of the world into which you have called us to participate.
Surprise us, God. Amen.

Dismissals

Dismissal 1
May God himself,
the God who makes everything holy and whole,
make you holy and whole,
put you together—spirit, soul, and body—
and keep you fit for the coming of our Master, Jesus Christ.
The one who called you is completely dependable.
If he said it, he'll do it!
—1 Thessalonians 5:23-24 The Message

Dismissal 2
Now to him who is able to keep you from falling and to make you stand without blemish in the presence of his glory with rejoicing, to the only God our Savior, through Jesus Christ our Lord, be glory, majesty, power, and authority, before all time and now and forever. Amen.
—Jude 1:24-25 NRSVue

Dismissal 3
You have been called and invited to experience God's abundant feast.
The invitation to experience God's kingdom, now, is yours.
Accept the invitation and live.
Go forth in love. Go forth in peace.
And may God's peace and love go with you. Amen.
—Lillian C. Smith, *Africana Worship Book*

Part Two

THE RESPONSE THROUGH WORSHIP

Liturgical Year A

ADVENT

Year A Lectionary Texts

At Last: Hope	Isaiah 2:1-5	Psalm 122	Romans 13:11-14	Matthew 24:36-44
At Last: Peace	Isaiah 11:1-10	Psalm 72:1-7, 18-19	Romans 15:4-13	Matthew 3:1-12
At Last: Joy	Isaiah 35:1-10	Luke 1:46b-55	James 5:7-10	Matthew 11:2-11
At Last: Love	Isaiah 7:10-16	Psalm 80:1-7, 17-19	Romans 1:1-7	Matthew 1:18-25

A Framework, Themes, and Ideas for Advent

This section provides ideas and information to inspire planning for worship and sermons. It is based on a suggested series—a framework for worship and preaching during this liturgical season. The series idea arises from the lectionary texts and aligns with the liturgical season. You may choose to lean into the series framework fully or not at all; these ideas and words for worship will be effective whether labeled by the series name or not.

This section includes commentary plus suggestions for themes and imagery for each week. In the next section, you'll find worship words for each part of the service—Gathering, Proclaiming, Thanksgiving, and Sending.

At Last: A Worship Series for Advent

> We live in the tension of now and not yet, but when Christ comes: Hope is renewed, peace is possible, joy is sparked, and love is embraced.

At last, my love has come along,
     my lonely days are over and life is like a song.
—Gordon, Mack, and Harry Warren, "At Last"

These lyrics from Etta James' signature song express the dual reality that encapsulates much of life—longing and hope. Here longing is the recognition that the present reality is not right, and hope is the certainty that things will be made right. Though we would like to think that much of life teeters between these two, the reality for far too many is that longing tends to be the dominant theme, creating a sense of loneliness as if we have been abandoned in a desolate wilderness. But like fresh water in a dry desert, hope can quite literally awaken the senses to new possibilities emerging even in the most desolate circumstances. *"At last"* becomes the soul's deepest sigh of relief that things are shifting and the recognition that the distance between longing and hope—the now and not yet—is fading into joy.

    The readings for Advent, Year A invite us to sigh "at last" again as we long and wait eagerly for Christ's second coming. In this *now and not yet* season, we are invited to name our present realities that keep us mired in sin and oppression, violence and injustice, and to remember how Christ's first coming confirmed the promise that God does not leave us alone. The overwhelming witness of the scripture is that we live in the tension of now and not yet, but when Christ comes: Hope is renewed, peace is possible, joy is sparked, and love is embraced.

    The thoughtful preacher or worship planner may want to consider ways to invite the congregation to name its longing—individually or corporately—considering the hope that Christ brings. This could be done as part of a prayer of confession, prayer of lament or as part of the lighting of the Advent candles (see accompanying liturgy). It may be important for the worship planner to craft carefully chosen words to help the congregation name a community concern.

Consider ways to name our longing as a congregation:

- prayer of confession
- prayer of lament
- advent candle lighting

Help people name their own longings individually:

- spoken aloud
- remembered in a moment of silence
- written out on paper or devices

Likewise, it may help to curate an opportunity or individuals to name their own longings—whether aloud, in a moment of silence or writing on paper. Whether sermonically or through the balance of the worship service, preachers and worship planners should aim to help answer the questions: How has God already begun to bring life in unexpected places? How do we hold on to hope in the middle of not yet moments—when transformation seems far away?

Though this commentary will focus primarily on the texts from Isaiah, many of the same themes can be easily traced through the other readings for each Sunday. Some of these will be highlighted throughout as an aide for preaching and worship planning.

Week One

Isaiah 2:1-5 | Hope Is Renewed

> **Key Images**: Mountain of the Lord, nations streaming to Zion, walking in God's paths, swords into plowshares, walking in the light
>
> **Themes**: Hope, justice, righteousness, peace, cessation of war/violence

> "They shall beat their swords into plowshares, and their spears into pruning hooks; nation shall not lift up sword against nation, neither shall they learn war anymore." (Isaiah 2:4)

Isaiah's vision of the "mountain of the LORD" stands as a beacon of hope, where those near and far receive instruction as hope agents. In the ancient Near East, mountains often symbolized divine presence. Here and elsewhere in scripture, Zion (Jerusalem) represents the center of God's reign to which every soul is drawn and from which hope is sent forth. Psalm 122 echoes this longing for Jerusalem as a place that embodies the peace of God's reign.

A key phrase here is "walk in his paths" (וְיֵלְכוּ בְּאֹרְחֹתָיו, v'yelekhu b'orḥotav). The verb "walk" (הלך, halak) in Hebrew often implies a continuous way of life, not just a one-time decision. In a world filled with war, division, and despair, this passage gives us a vision of eschatological peace where nations come to Zion to learn God's ways.

The contrast between warfare ("swords" and "spears") and agricultural flourishing ("plowshares" and "pruning hooks") is striking. The act of "beating" (כתת, kathath) implies forceful transformation, showing how God's kingdom radically reshapes the world. It speaks to the transformation of human conflict into divine peace, a hope that is not yet realized but is coming.

The *now* reality is that nations still war, injustice remains, and people long for security. But the *not yet* is breaking in—Christ's coming ushers in a kingdom where weapons are reshaped into tools of growth, where hostility is replaced with peace, and we become agents of hope. At last—hope is renewed, because God's promises are sure.

Romans 13:11-14 picks up the theme of wakefulness: *"The night is far gone; the day is near."* The present struggle will give way to the future reality of Christ's return. Similarly, Matthew 24:36-44 warns of Christ's sudden coming, reinforcing the tension of waiting.

> Advent is a season of hope because we anticipate this future, even as we catch glimpses of it in the present. How are we, as the Church, called to be a people who live into this hope?
>
> Where do we see God already at work turning swords into plowshares?

Week Two

Isaiah 11:1-10 | Peace Is Possible

> **Key Images**: Shoot from the stump of Jesse, the Spirit, child, predators and prey in harmony, the nursing child, my holy mountain
>
> **Themes**: New life, power of the Spirit, justice, righteousness, peace, cessation of war/violence, harmony, reversal

> "The wolf shall live with the lamb, the leopard shall lie down with the kid . . . and a little child shall lead them. They will not hurt or destroy on all my holy mountain, for the earth will be full of the knowledge of the LORD as the waters cover the sea." (Isaiah 11:6, 10)

Here is an audacious proclamation of peace, heralded by fragility. The imagery is radical—predators and prey coexisting, a child leading them all. This isn't just a call for people to get along; it's a vision of a deep, cosmic harmony where even the natural order itself is transformed.

In the opening verse, the word ḥoter (shoot) symbolizes a fragile but living remnant. A reference to the Spirit-anointed ruler who will bring about peace, its seemingly sudden appearance proclaims that even in destruction, life emerges. This seemingly fragile ruler will not be defined by might or war, but by the "Spirit of the LORD" (רוּחַ יְהוָה, ruach YHWH). The divine ruach (spirit/breath) empowers him with wisdom, knowledge, and righteousness, all for the sake of peace with justice. This theme is echoed both in Psalm 72, which describes the messianic king bringing justice to the oppressed, and in Romans 15:4-13 which interprets Isaiah's prophecy as fulfilled in Jesus, who brings Gentiles into God's peace.

In verse 10, the prophet draws our attention back to the "mountain of the LORD" (see commentary for Isaiah 2), which becomes the place where violence ends for every creature. This results in the earth being filled with the "knowledge of the LORD"

(דֵּעָה אֶת־יְהוָה, de'ah et-YHWH). It should be noted that knowledge (דֵּעָה) is more than intellectual understanding; it implies deep relational intimacy. The implication is that God's reign will transform and redefine every relationship. This is essentially John the Baptist's message to the Pharisees in Matthew 3:8-9.

The *now* is that we live in a world fractured by division—politically, socially, personally. But the *not yet* of Christ's reign is breaking in. Jesus, the shoot from the stump of Jesse, establishes a kingdom where peace isn't just a wish but a divine reality. At last—peace is possible, because Christ is the Prince of Peace.

> How can we be peacemakers in a divided world?
>
> What does it look like for us to live as if this peace is already here?

Week Three

Isaiah 35:1-10 | Joy Is Sparked

> **Key Images**: wilderness and dry land, blossoming crocus, streams in the desert, highway, leaping, joy
>
> **Themes**: joy, reversal, healing, restoration, renewal

> "The wilderness and the dry land shall be glad, the desert
> shall rejoice and blossom." (Isaiah 35:1)

This passage bursts with joy! The barren desert blooms, the weak are strengthened, and sorrow turns to singing. It's a passage of profound transformation—joy comes not because circumstances have changed *yet*, but because of the certainty of God's promise.

In a dramatic reversal, the "wilderness" (מִדְבָּר, midbar), a place of testing and dependence on God (e.g., Israel's 40 years in the wilderness, Exodus 16), will "be glad" (יִשְׂמַח, yismach). The uninhabited place of hardship will be transformed into joy and abundance. Likewise, it will "blossom" (פָּרַח, parach), meaning to sprout, bloom, or flourish. This word is used in Psalm 92:12 ("The righteous shall flourish like a palm tree") and Numbers 17:8 (Aaron's rod "budded and blossomed") and has the connotation of thriving. God's renewal is not just about survival but thriving—life abundantly where there was once only scarcity and death.

The arrival of joy begins to reshape the contours of life. "Weak hands" and "feeble knees" (רָפוּ, rafu and כָּשַׁל, kashal) are strengthened and restored, and "the redeemed" (פְּדוּיֵי, paduim), from the verb padah (פָּדָה), meaning to ransom, buy back, or rescue (see Exodus 13:13), come home. Salvation is not merely an escape; it is a return to God's presence.

Jesus explicitly references Isaiah 35 in Matthew 11:2-6 when John the Baptist asks if He is the Messiah. Jesus responds by listing miraculous healings—the blind see, the lame walk, the deaf hear—all direct indications that God's reign has begun.

The now may feel like a dry and weary land—people are burdened by grief, despair, or uncertainty. But the not yet of God's kingdom brings joy even in the waiting. The coming of Christ is the spark that sets joy ablaze, even before the fullness of redemption is realized. At last—joy is sparked, because the world is being made new.

> How can we find joy even in the wilderness seasons of our lives?
>
> What does it mean to live in joyful anticipation?
>
> Can we tell stories of those who have experienced restoration after loss—perhaps a person who found faith again after walking away, a church rebounding from decline, or a family healing after years of brokenness?

Week Four

Isaiah 7:10-16 | Love Is Embraced

> **Key Images**: sign, young woman, child, Immanuel, curds (milk) and honey, kings
>
> **Themes**: asking and receiving, trust, faithfulness, presence of God, fear, fulfillment

> "Look, the young woman is with child and shall bear a son,
>   and shall name him Immanuel." (Isaiah 7:14)

The context for this passage is the Syro-Ephraimite War (735–732 BCE), when King Ahaz of Judah was under threat from Aram (Syria) and Israel (Ephraim). Ahaz was considering an alliance with Assyria, but Isaiah urged him to trust in God instead of foreign powers. The command to "ask" (שְׁאַל, sha'al) is given in the imperative form showing that God is willing and eager to be known. This is not a divine trap; Ahaz is not being tested. Rather, God is giving him an opportunity to strengthen his faith by seeing God's faithfulness first hand.

It should be noted that Ahaz uses scripture to refute what God has spoken to him. He quotes Deuteronomy 6:16 (*"Do not put the LORD your God to the test"*) which refers to demanding a sign in doubt (as Israel did at Massah, Exodus 17:2), whereas here, God commands Ahaz to ask. Perhaps Ahaz's refusal is a lack of faith or is motivated by fear. Or perhaps he demonstrates a similar false piety as the Pharisees in Jesus's day (see Matthew 12:38-39) whose "holier-than-thou" posture blinded them to the signs of God's presence among them.

Even so, God still gives a sign—a child called *Immanuel*, "God with us." This sign is the certainty that new life is possible even during great distress and fear. It is what Howard Thurman refers to as *a boundless vitality*. And this vitality is secured, not through strategic alliances or negotiated compromises, but through the certainty of God's presence alone.

The other readings from Psalm 80, Romans 1, and Matthew 1 will all pick up on the theme of God's promise of presence and its fulfillment in and through Jesus. If the perennial existential question is "*Is the Lord among us or not?*" (see Exodus 17:7), then God's emphatic answer is always "Yes!"

The *now* is that we still struggle to trust in God's presence, especially in uncertainty. But the *not yet* is that Christ *is* coming—God's love takes on flesh, enters our world, and dwells among us. In Jesus, love is not just an idea but a person we can embrace. At last—love is embraced, because *Immanuel* has come.

> How do we live as people who believe in *Immanuel*—God with us?
>
> How can we embody God's love to those who feel abandoned or afraid?

Words for Worship, Advent

Gathering

Call to Worship (Isaiah 2:1-5)
(Eleanor Colvin)

Some say "'hope' is the thing with feathers;"
But we have come to the Lord's house seeking something more sure, more certain.
Hope is not a soft word, nor is it a lofty, unattainable ideal.
It is as real as a light, shining in a dark room.
Come, let us walk by the Lord's light.

Prayer of Confession (for Advent 1)
(Diana Sanchez-Bushong)

> Sing: ***O Come, O come Emmanuel and ransom captive Israel. That mourns in lonely exile here, until the Son of God appear.***
>
> *(Continue underscoring the following prayer but save the refrain for the final response after the Assurance and Pardon.)*

Hopeful God, Creator of light and darkness, day and night,
as we begin this journey of Advent,
we confess that we often choose our own paths instead of yours.
We choose the way of conflict instead of peace.
We seek to build our lives on our own terms,
rather than following the foundation you have laid for us.
Forgive us, God. Teach us to seek you,
even when your way is the harder road.
Help us to walk humbly in your light,
that we may reflect your love and hope to the world around us.

[Moment of Silent Confession]
Hear the good news: Jesus Christ came into the world
to offer hope in the midst of our darkness.
In the name of Emmanuel, God with us, you are forgiven.

**Rejoice! Rejoice! Emmanuel
shall come to thee, O Israel.**
(Refrain from "O Come, O Come, Emmanuel") You may wish to also sing the stanza "O Come Desire of Nations bind all peoples in one heart and mind. To us the path of knowledge show and cause us in her way to go. Rejoice! Rejoice! Emmanuel shall come to thee, O Israel."

Call to Worship (Advent 1)
(Diana Sanchez-Bushong)

The season of Advent is here—a time of waiting, a time of hope.
We come to worship the God of light and life, the Creator of day and night.
God calls us to leave behind the paths of darkness and walk in the light of love and peace.
With humble hearts, we turn toward God's way, seeking the hope that Emmanuel brings.
Come, let us walk together in the light of the Lord.
Let us worship the God of hope, who comes to us with love and salvation.

A Bilingual Call to Worship (Advent 2, Isaiah 11:1-10)
(Diana Sanchez-Bushong)

A shoot shall grow from the stump of Jesse, and a branch will sprout from his roots.
Un retoño brotará del tronco de Isaí, y un vástago surgirá de sus raíces.
The Spirit of the Lord will rest upon him—wisdom and understanding, counsel and strength.
El Espíritu del Señor estará sobre él—sabiduría e inteligencia, consejo y fortaleza.

He will bring righteousness and faithfulness, judging with equity and bringing peace to the land.
Él traerá justicia y fidelidad, juzgará con rectitud y traerá paz a la tierra.
The wolf will live with the lamb, and a little child will lead them.
El lobo vivirá con el cordero, y un niño pequeño los guiará.

Come, let us worship the One who brings hope and peace to all nations.
Vengan, adoremos a Aquel que trae esperanza y paz a todas las naciones.
All/Todos:

We will rejoice in the knowledge of the Lord, for God's glory will cover the earth as the waters cover the sea.
Nos regocijaremos en el conocimiento del Señor, porque la gloria de Dios cubrirá la tierra como las aguas cubren el mar.

Call to Worship (Advent 3)
(Diana Sanchez-Bushong)

People of God, rejoice with gladness and song, for the Lord is near!
We come with joyful hearts, for God comes to save us.
Beloved, let us lift our voices, for the splendor of God's glory is all around.
We worship the God who is, who was, and who is to come!

Prayer of Confession
(Diana Sanchez-Bushong)

God of splendor,
We come to worship today longing to feel the joy of Your presence, yet grief and sorrow often weigh us down. We yearn for signs of hope, but fear and uncertainty cloud our vision and too often we rely on our own strength and lose sight of Your steadfast love.
Forgive us, O God, for doubting your presence.
Steady us when we falter and strengthen us when we are weak.
Help us to live fully in your light, trusting in your promises of joy and renewal.

Silent Meditation

Hear the good news: God comes to dwell among us, to bring joy that overcomes sorrow and hope that casts out fear.
In Christ, grief and groaning will flee away, and we are made whole.
In the name of Emmanuel, God with us, we are forgiven.
Thanks be to God! Amen.

Prayer of Confession (Advent 4)
(Diana Sanchez-Bushong)

God of Abiding Love,
You have given us the sign of Emmanuel—Your promise to be with us. Yet, we confess that we often fail to live as people shaped by Your love. We doubt Your presence and seek additional signs of reassurance, even though You have already shown us the depth of Your faithfulness.
Forgive us, Lord, when we, like Ahaz, resist Your call and fail to trust in Your promises.
Forgive us when fear, pride, or selfishness overshadow the love You have planted within us.
Forgive us for forgetting to embody the grace and compassion You have so freely shown to us.
In Your mercy, turn our hearts back to You. Help us to live as faithful bearers of Your love in a world longing for hope.
Silent Reflection
Hear the good news: God comes to be with us, renewing, restoring, and preparing us to receive the fullness of His love this Advent season.
In the name of Jesus, the One who came to dwell among us, we are forgiven.
Glory to God. Amen.

Proclaiming

Advent Wreath Candle Lighting Liturgy: The Work of Christmas
by Howard Thurman
(Diana Sanchez-Bushong)

Week 1: Hope—Seeking the Lost

Today we light the first candle, the candle of hope. This light reminds us of Christ's mission to seek and save those who are lost. In this season of Advent, we look forward with hope to the One who restores, heals, and makes all things new.

God of hope, as we light this candle, fill our hearts with expectation. May we trust in your promises and share your hope with a world in need.

Come, Lord Jesus, our Hope. Shine your light in our hearts.
(Light the first candle.)

> **Sing: "In him there is no darkness at all. The night and the day are both alike. The Lamb is the light of the city of God. Shine in my heart, Lord Jesus."**
> *refrain of "I Want to Walk as a Child of the Light"*

Week 2: Peace—Healing the Broken

As we light the second candle, the candle of peace, we remember Christ's call to bring healing and wholeness to a broken world. Jesus, the Prince of Peace, comes to reconcile us to God and to one another, showing us how to live in harmony.

God of peace, as this candle shines, may your peace take root in our hearts. Help us to work for healing in our relationships, our communities, and our world.

Come, Lord Jesus, our Peace. Shine your light in our hearts.
(Light the second candle.)

> **Sing: "In him there is no darkness at all. The night and the day are both alike. The Lamb is the light of the city of God. Shine in my heart, Lord Jesus."**
> *refrain of "I Want to Walk as a Child of the Light"*

Week 3: Joy—Restoring Communities

Today we light the third candle, the candle of joy. As we light this candle we are reminded of Christ's mission to rebuild, reconcile and restore. Joy is found in the enduring presence of Christ with us as we carry out the work of renewal in our lives and in our communities.

God of joy, as this light grows brighter, may your joy overflow in our lives. Lead us to be co-workers in your mission of restoration, bringing joy where there is despair.

Come, Lord Jesus, our Joy. Shine your light in our hearts.
(Light the third candle.)

> **Sing: "In him there is no darkness at all. The night and the day are both alike. The Lamb is the light of the city of God. Shine in my heart, Lord Jesus."**
> *refrain of "I Want to Walk as a Child of the Light"*

Week 4: Love—Building Peace Together

As we light the fourth candle, the candle of love, we remember that Emmanuel comes to bring unity and peace to all people. Christ's love transforms and calls us to live as reflections of compassion and grace in a world longing for connection.

God of Love, may this candle's light remind us of the depth of Your care for us. Teach us to love as you love and to bring peace wherever we go.

Come, Lord Jesus, our Love. Shine your light in our hearts.
(Light the fourth candle.)

> **Sing: "In him there is no darkness at all. The night and the day are both alike. The Lamb is the light of the city of God. Shine in my heart, Lord Jesus."**
> *refrain of "I Want to Walk as a Child of the Light"*

Conclusion (Christmas Eve or Christmas Day): The Christ Candle

Tonight, we light the Christ candle, representing the fulfillment of all that we have waited for: hope, peace, joy, and love. Christ, the Light of the World, has come to dwell among us and to show us the way to live as God's people.

Christ, the Light of the World, fill our hearts with your light. Empower us to carry forward your work of hope, peace, joy, and love in our homes, our communities, and our world.

Come, Lord Jesus, our Emmanuel. Shine your light in our hearts.
(Light the Christ candle.)

Read the full poem—The Work of Christmas by Howard Thurman

When the song of the angels is stilled,
When the star in the sky is gone,
When the kings and princes are home,
When the shepherds are back with their flock,
The work of Christmas begins:
To find the lost,
To heal the broken,
To feed the hungry,
To release the prisoner,
To rebuild the nations,
To bring peace among others,
To make music in the heart.

Choral anthem: https://beckenhorstpress.com/the-work-of-christmas-satb/
(Dan Forrest setting of The Work of Christmas)

Prayer for Illumination (Isaiah 2:1-6)
Ideally read after the scripture and before the sermon
Mighty God—

In the days of the prophet, you spoke of a time when streams of people would flock to the doors of your house. We are here, now, O God. Blow wide open the doors of our hearts and make your home in them. Teach us your ways, Lord, that we may walk in your paths; for instruction comes from you alone. Amen.

Thanksgiving

An Advent Great Thanksgiving

The congregation is invited to sing "Already Here" (from Zion Still Sings*) in a spirit of hopeful anticipation. The Hallelujahs may be repeated at the discretion of the worship leader as a gathering meditation before proceeding into the liturgy.*

We watch and we wait,
Lord, we anticipate the moment you choose to appear.
We worship and praise until there's no debate,
And we recognize you're already here:
Hallelujah, Hallelujah, Hallelujah.

[Music continues to underscore as celebrant continues]
All our hallelujahs can never match your greatness, O God of heaven and earth.
You spoke creation into being, formed us in your image
and breathe life into our frame.
When we hid from you, you never stopped searching for us.
When we turned away from you, you never abandoned us.
When our love reached its limit, you never stopped loving us.
You keep coming to us proving your love through signs and wonders,
through prophets and dreamers, and through the spectacularly ordinary.
For all this we join our voices with all of heaven and creation in praising you, saying:

Holy, Holy, Holy Lord, God of Power and Might!
Heaven and earth are full of your glory!
Hosanna in the highest!
Blessed is He who comes in the name of the Lord!
Hosanna in the highest!
[sung as before] **Hallelujah, Hallelujah, Hallelujah.**

[Music continues to underscore as celebrant continues]
Holy and blessed are you, O God, because you sent us Jesus—
a friend and a brother, a healer and a teacher,
a servant and a savior—
to be our "Immanuel," the sign that you will never leave nor forsake us.

With us and for us, through the power of the Spirit,
    Jesus ate and celebrated,
    he wept and lamented;
    he suffered and died and was raised to life,
        all to demonstrate the wideness of your mercy and the depth of your love.

[Music underscoring stops here before the celebrant continues]
On the night in which he gave himself up for us,
Jesus gathered around the table with his closest disciples,
including the one who would betray him with a kiss.
While they were eating together,
[Celebrant takes bread, mirroring the actions]
Jesus took bread, and after blessing it, he broke it and gave it to them saying:
"Take, eat. This is my body."
    After the supper was over,
[Celebrant takes the cup, mirroring the actions]

he took a cup, and after giving thanks he gave it to them, saying:
"Drink from it, all of you; for this is my blood of the new covenant,
which is poured out for you and for many for the forgiveness of sins.

[Music underscoring resumes till the end as celebrant continues.]
    And so, because through Christ you have given yourself to us,
we now give ourselves to you as holy, living sacrifices—
proclaiming this mystery of faith:
Christ has died. Christ is risen. Christ will come again.
    [sung as before] **Hallelujah, Hallelujah, Hallelujah.**

    Come, Holy Spirit!
    Come, Holy Spirit!

    Bless these gifts!
    Bless these gifts!

    Bless this church!
    Bless this church!

    Bless your people!
    Bless your people!

    As you come to us now, bless and consecrate us, O God,
till we become the sign of your Immanuel to all the world,
and our lives are only Hallelujahs, for you are already here!
    [sung as before] **Hallelujah, Hallelujah, Hallelujah.**

Sending

Benediction
(Diana Sanchez-Bushong)

Go forth as people of hope, walking in the light of God's love.
Choose the paths of peace and humility, reflecting Christ's light to the world.
May Emmanuel, God with us, guide you on your journey,
and may the blessing of the Creator, the Redeemer, and the Sustainer
be with you now and always.
Amen.

CHRISTMAS AND CHRISTMASTIDE

Year A Lectionary Texts

Now: Wonder	Isaiah 9:2-7	Psalm 96	Titus 2:11-14	Luke 2:1-20
Now: Glory	Isaiah 52:7-10	Psalm 98	Hebrews 1:1-4, (5-12)	John 1:1-14
Now: Mercy	Isaiah 63:7-9	Psalm 148	Hebrews 2:10-18	Matthew 2:13-23
Now: Newness	Ecclesiastes 3:1-13	Psalm 8	Revelation 21:1-6a	Matthew 25:31-46
Now: Grace	Jeremiah 31:7-14	Psalm 147:12-20	Ephesians 1:3-14	John 1:(1-9), 10-18
Now: Vision	Isaiah 60:1-6	Psalm 72:1-7, 10-14	Ephesians 3:1-12	Matthew 2:1-12
Now: Belonging	Isaiah 42:1-9	Psalm 29	Acts 10:34-43	Matthew 3:13-17

A Framework, Themes, and Ideas for Christmas and Christmastide

This section provides ideas and information to inspire planning for worship and sermons. It is based on a suggested series—a framework for worship and preaching during this liturgical season. The series idea arises from the lectionary texts and aligns with the liturgical season. You may choose to lean into the series framework fully or not at all; these ideas and words for worship will be effective whether labeled by the series name or not.

This section includes commentary plus suggestions for themes and imagery for each week. In the next section, you'll find worship words for each part of the service—Gathering, Proclaiming, Thanksgiving, and Sending.

Now: A Worship Series for Christmas and Christmastide

> Through Jesus, God with us is a constant, present reality—
> an eternal now that both gives and calls us into wonder,
> glory, mercy, newness, grace, vision, and belonging.

Now the silence
Now the peace
Now the empty hands uplifted
Now the kneeling
Now the plea
Now the Father's arms in welcome
Now the hearing
Now the power
Now the vessel brimmed for pouring
Now the body
Now the blood
Now the joyful celebration
Now the wedding
Now the songs
Now the heart forgiven leaping
Now the Spirit's visitation
Now the Son's epiphany
Now the Father's blessing
Now Now Now
—Jaroslav J. Vajda, "Now the Silence," *The United Methodist Hymnal*

Vajda's communion hymn provides a remarkable rumination on the immediacy of Christ's presence in the sacrament. The word "now" is repeated twenty-one times in short succession, and combined with the lack of punctuation, it conveys a startlingly insistent tone and suggests forward movement that intentionally remains unfinished. In fact, the hymn tune that accompanies the text ends on the dominant chord, creating a kind of musical cliffhanger that suggests that there is more to come. Whether in preparation for or during the sacrament, singing this hymn is a daring declaration of God's inbreaking into our lives and the promise of hope is *now*.

So too is the central message of the Christmas season—that **the incarnation is God's emphatic now.** Now is the wonder and the glory of God with us. Now is the need for mercy, the revelation of newness, and the unveiling of grace. Now is vision clarified and belonging claimed. The Incarnation is the heartbeat of our present. This is the real gift of Christmas.

Worship services will vary in this season based on the context of your community and its traditions. Though not every community will celebrate worship on each of the days offered here, worship leaders might consider how they might invite the congregation into intentional reflection and formation through the season—perhaps offering short devotionals for the twelve days of the season and/or short liturgies for individual reflection. These could be adapted from the resources offered here. Additionally, worship leaders are encouraged to lean into their community's existing traditions with the reflective question *How might this tradition embody _____ now?*

Consider inviting the congregation into intentional reflection and formation:

- offer short devotionals for each day of the season
- offer liturgies for individual reflection
- lean into your community's traditions with the reflective question *How might this tradition embody _____ now?*

Christmas Eve (Proper II)

Luke 2:1-20 | Now Wonder

> **Key Images:** shepherds in the field, manger, night, angels, swaddled child
>
> **Themes:** wonder, God in the ordinary, God's peace vs. Caesar's peace

> Now in that same region there were shepherds living in the fields, keeping watch over their flock by night. (Luke 2:8)

As Luke narrates, up to this point, the birth story of Jesus includes a lot of names to remember—Herod, Abijah, Zechariah, Elizabeth, Aaron, Elijah, John, Gabriel, David, Jacob, Abraham, Augustus, Quirinius, Mary, Joseph, Simeon, Anna. Names and identity seem to be an important feature of the gospel, with each name (and the respective characters they represent) conveying meaning and depth to the story. So, it begs the question: *Why don't we know the names of the shepherds?*

The fact that much of the story centers on their experience rather than the actual birth would make it seem appropriate for the gospel writer to have at least made up names for these common workers. Yet, in a world dominated by title and status—

where Caesar's peace comes through manipulation, regulation, and measurement of others—God sends a messenger at night to these essential workers whose names will never be remembered or recorded, heralding a peace (εἰρήνη eirēnē) that elicits so much joy that even the angels sing.

God summons forth peace and joy through the humility, wonder and gifts of the lowly. As Esau McCaulley writes,

> Christmas is the grand miracle that makes space for all the smaller miracles. It gives us enough hope to walk a little farther in the dark toward the glimmer of something that seems too distant to reach.

Perhaps the shepherds remain unnamed, not because of lack of importance or significance, but as a reminder that God's good news (εὐαγγέλιον, euangelion) cannot be decreed or imposed by force or sheer will; rather, it comes through the witness and faith of ordinary people marveling at the wonder and glory of God amid their ordinary lives.

> What keeps us from noticing the "glory of the Lord" in daily life?
>
> How can we cultivate awe amid the ordinary?

Christmas Eve (Proper III)

John 1:1-14 | Now Glory

> **Key Images:** brightly shining lights of various kinds, a pitched tent or encampment of tents
>
> **Themes:** incarnation, Jesus embodies and reveals God's presence

> And the Word became flesh and lived among us, and we have seen his glory, the glory as of a father's only son, full of grace and truth. (John 1:14)

In his meditation entitled "God Is Present," Howard Thurman writes:

> One thing I know concerning my anxieties: they are real to me. Sometimes they seem more real than the presence of God. When this happens, they dominate my mood and possess my thoughts.

Too often we live in the tyranny of the now, where our lives become so defined by what's happening to us in the present moment, that we lose sight of the light and grace embedded within and around us since the very beginning—that is, the presence of God.

Perhaps this is why *seeing* (θεάομαι *theaomai*, "to look at attentively, to behold with contemplation") is so important to John's gospel— . . . *and we have seen his glory, the glory as of a father's only son, full of grace and truth* (v.14). This "glory" (δόξα doxa) denotes splendor, radiance, and directly implicates God's manifest presence (*kavod* in Hebrew: כָּבוֹד), as in the cloud that filled the tabernacle (Exodus 40:34) and later the Temple (2 Chronicles 5:14).

For John the fullness of God's presence is seen or revealed precisely in a series of dichotomies—creator meets creation, light meets darkness, knowing meets unknowing, unbelief meets believing, Word meets flesh—where instead of mutual destruction all are held in tension with each other. Christ's incarnation is a testament of God's real presence in the stuff of real life. To see this is to see God's glory amid our now.

Thurman goes on to say, *The presence of God does not always deliver me from anxiety, but it always delivers me from anxieties.*

> How might the presence of God disrupt the tyranny of now?
>
> Have I seen God's glory—in broken places, in faces, in moments I almost missed?

First Sunday after Christmas Day

Matthew 2:13-23 | Now Mercy

Key Images: a family fleeing, someone dreaming, mothers crying

Themes: God's presence in grief and injustice

> Now after they had left, an angel of the Lord appeared to Joseph in a dream and said, "Get up, take the child and his mother, and flee to Egypt, and remain there until I tell you, for Herod is about to search for the child, to destroy him." (Matthew 2:13)

Matthew's gospel shatters our romanticized, soft version of Jesus's birth by introducing us to the murderous rage of Herod the Great. Non-biblical sources confirm that, though he was gifted as an incredible architect, over time Herod became increasingly paranoid that his place and sense of belonging was not secure. By the end of his reign, Herod had murdered his wife, her two sons, her brother, her grandfather, her mother, his firstborn son, and countless others who were rumored or not to have threatened his sense of belonging.

And like the king *who did not know Joseph* (Exodus 1), the reality of God and God's promise made real in our lives can feel threatening. It can feel as though we are losing or have lost control of the carefully crafted ways in which we have held things together and created security for ourselves. The surprising introduction of Jesus into the world can and should utterly disrupt our well-ordered lives, because Jesus confronts our selfish ambition with other-centered humility. Jesus confronts our hunger for power with unfeigned vulnerability. Jesus confronts our scheming with faith in the triumph of mercy.

As we put away our well-appointed nativity scenes and move further away from the sentimentality of Christmas, we are confronted with the *realness* of Jesus's birth—the *realness* of our lives and the world today. It is messy and chaotic. It is scary at times. It is sometimes clouded with uncertainty and mired in death and violence. With strong allusions to the tragedies within the Exodus story, the defeat by Assyria, and the exile into Babylon, Matthew makes clear that God's mercy will triumph over every violent and oppressive power.

And so, God with us meets the real us. God's mercy is never absent—it flees with the family, cries with the wounded, and promises restoration.

> Where is mercy meeting or confronting your community today?

New Year's Day

Revelation 21:1-6a | Now Newness

> **Key Images**: a shining city or new home, a spring of water
>
> **Themes**: reign of God as present reality

> And the one who was seated on the throne said, "See, I am making all things new." (Revelation 21:5)

While in the Spirit, John is given this revelation of *things that must soon take place* (1:1) and begins to describe a vision of a hostile world and the spiritual forces at work within it. And throughout this vision John sees that Christ is the final victor, and those who bear his name will overcome through him.

So, John writes of a new heaven and new earth being revealed through Christ's victory over all the forces of evil and darkness in the world. "New" (καινός *kainos*) does not mean "recent" or "new in time" but "new in character" or "fresh." This newness culminates and is encapsulated in the proclamation of God's ongoing, present-oriented work: "See, I am making all things new."

John could only see this newness after being confronted with the horrors of the present. Even John's immediate reality as a political exile on a remote island belies the truth that the world isn't all it should or could be. To receive the newness God offers, we must be willing to see the world as it is and know that something must change. This seeing is a gift of the Spirit.

What is the Spirit empowering your community to see about its present amid God's newness?

Second Sunday after Christmas Day

John 1:(1-9), 10-18 | Now Grace

> **Key Images**: pitched tent or tabernacle, images of generosity and abundance, acts of kindness
>
> **Themes**: discipleship as relationship with Christ, grace, newness

From his fullness we have all received, grace upon grace. (John 1:16)

From the beginning of the gospel, John emphasizes the importance of relationship. This is Jesus's purpose and mission since before creation—to dwell or "tabernacle" with us. *Grace and truth*—revealed kindness that is faithful and reliable—move into the neighborhood, and it is this intentionality of relationship that reveals God's character in the most personal, tangible way possible. In contrast to legislated codes or dogma, grace, and truth are not things Jesus offers—they are who He is.

Jesus is the conduit of grace, and in him nothing is lacking. To receive (παραλαμβάνω *paralambano*, "to take with" or "companion") Jesus is to receive God's active goodwill towards us—that is God's loving intention to do us good, to bless us, and to bless others through us. Like a ship that is well staffed and equipped, so is the *fullness* (πλήρωμα *plērōma*) we receive from Christ. *Grace upon grace*—successive waves of ongoing, superabundant generosity—becomes both the benefit and the side effect of relationship with Christ. With him, we become conduits of grace.

This is not merely an origin story about Jesus entering our world but also about how we are able to start again because of grace. In a season marked by post-holiday fatigue, early-year anxieties, or lingering grief, this text grounds us in abundance: not scarcity, not striving, but grace upon grace.

What would it mean to live this year from a place of fullness?

Epiphany of the Lord

Matthew 2:1-12 | Now Vision

> **Key Images**: star or stars, any number of wise ones, images of joy, seeing for the first time
>
> **Themes**: the sacred in the mundane, seeking Christ leads to joy

> When they saw that the star had stopped, they were
> overwhelmed with joy. (Matthew 2:10)

It is unknown exactly how many Magi there were or even who they were. Coming from somewhere east of Jerusalem, they were likely non-Jewish priests or political advisors who studied the movements of the heavenly bodies to determine meaning and clarity for human affairs. And though we cannot pinpoint their exact place of origin, it seems likely that the Magi were at least near some of the Jewish colonies that had been scattered throughout the Parthian empire.

That said, what is certain is that the Magi traveled to Jerusalem because they saw a star that meant something to them, and they decided to take it seriously. These ordinary guys doing their ordinary job observed something that was not all that unusual for their ordinary job and took seriously the possibility that this might be different. Instead of looking for ways to dismiss the moment as unimportant or unworthy of any particular attention, they decided that it just might lead to something different—that the promise might be real.

It is unknown whether they followed any of the other stars they may have observed before, but they followed this one with curiosity and wonder about its possible meaning and purpose for their lives. What star has risen in our world—and are we paying attention?

Their attentive pursuit leads them to joy. Verse 10 may be rendered more literally as "they rejoiced with great vehement joy." Their openness to the possibility that the promise might be real ultimately gives them vision for the kind of joy they could not have imagined could be theirs.

It is the kind of joy that gives vision to see the worth and potential a poor child of questionable parentage in a backwater town and emboldens them to say to this family through their actions "Your lives matter." It is the kind of joy that gives vision to go home "by another road," empowering them to subvert powers and systems to protect those who are vulnerable even at the cost of their own privilege.

| What it could be like to have that kind of joy, to receive that kind of joy?

Baptism of the Lord

Matthew 3:13-17 | Now Belonging

> **Key Images**: crossing a flowing river, images of baptism, doves
>
> **Themes**: new creation and transformation, identity and belonging

> Then Jesus came from Galilee to John at the Jordan,
> to be baptized by him. (Matthew 3:13)

Crossing the Jordan was a pivotal event for the ancient Israelites, because it signaled entrance into a new life (Joshua 3–4). Oppressive forces and wilderness wanderings are left behind and through the waters a life marked by promise emerges. It is no wonder then that John would be found near the Jordan, choosing its waters as the location for heralding entrance into new life.

More than arrival, the verb *came* (παραγίνεται *paraginomai*) implies a public appearing and presence with, often used in contexts of divine mission (cf. Matthew 2:1; 3:1). This is a revealing, not just a relocation. As Jesus presents himself to be baptized by him, he demonstrates an intentionality that both affirms and fulfills the way into newness that John has been preparing.

Jesus insists that his participation and belonging to this new way inaugurated by John is necessary to fulfill all righteousness. This righteousness or justice is about right relationship, and the way into newness is not defined by law-keeping but by right-acting according to God's saving purposes. And God confirms this by opening the heavens (ἀνεῴχθησαν aneōchthēsan, indicating a permanent tearing open similar to Matthew 27:51) and naming Jesus as my Son, the Beloved (ἀγαπητός, agapētos, used in Isaiah 42 for the Servant of the Lord). This naming affirms Jesus's identity before his ministry begins. It is relational and royal, indicating that belonging precedes doing.

And so, entrance or belonging to God's plan is revealed when John appears at the Jordan (v.1), fulfilled when Jesus comes to the Jordan (v.13), and confirmed at the Jordan when God opens the heavens, unveiling the way to renewal (v.16). Now emerges a vision where belonging is relational and spiritual, not institutional nor performative.

> What would it look like to live from belonging, not toward it?

Words for Worship, Christmas and Christmastide

Gathering

A Call to Worship for Christmas Eve
(Bromleigh McCleneghan)

Beloved, will you come? Fix your mind's eye on a far-away field. Can you see the deepness of the night?
We can see the stars spread across that endless sky.

See that unfamiliar star? The one that burns more brightly – the one whose light seems to reach down to the horizon over Bethlehem.
Shall we fix our eyes on the star? On the horizon? Shall we look to Bethlehem?

Not yet. For now, look again to the night sky. Do you see how it is now filled with holy messengers? They are singing!
Fear not, the angel says. Good news, the angel proclaims!

Now, tonight: in that far away village and in our hearts right here, a child is born. A child who is God among us, a child who is good news for all people.
Let us not be afraid. Let us sing and rejoice.

Come and rejoice for the Christ child is born!

Call to Worship (Isaiah 9:2, John 1:4-5)
(Kallie Green)

The people who walked in darkness have seen a great light.
On those who lived in deep darkness, light has dawned.
The light shines in the darkness,
And the darkness did not overcome it.
Christ has come and in him is life.
Life that is the light for all people!

Opening Prayer (Isaiah 9:2, John 1:1-5, Revelation 21:5)
(Kallie Green)

Emmanuel, God with us, we come today to hear your story, of ancient things that happened long ago, and of a light that shone so bright, it shines even here

and now. You were there in the beginning; through you, all things came into being. You are in the future, making all things new. And you are here and now, calling us into your love and light. Help us to be unafraid, as we hear today, the eternal invitation of Christ our Lord, who calls us to wonder, glory, mercy, newness, grace, vision, and belonging. Amen.

An Acclamation for Christmas Day
(Bromleigh McClanaghan)

We have seen his glory; the Gospel writer proclaims. His "high renown or honor won by notable achievements" or his "magnificence or great beauty"? What is the glory of the Word? It is the glory of God's own, the glory—the great beauty, the renown—of one whose life bears witness to God, whose whole life is grace and truth.

Glory to God in the highest. Christ is born. The Word is flesh and lives among us. Amen.

Prayer of Confession (Luke 2:10-14, John 3:19-20, Matthew 24:35-40)
(Kallie Green)

Almighty God,
We shrink before your majesty. Even while angels sing of your glory, we turn away. We have turned away from your light and your people, we have loved the darkness. Hiding from your light, we have not seen you in our neighbor, we have walked past those who are hungry, we have ignored the stranger, we have not clothed the vulnerable, and we have not gone to those imprisoned in darkness. Forgive us, we pray. Free us for joyful obedience, through Jesus Christ our Lord. Teach us to sing with your angels and to be bearers of good news and great joy. Amen.

Hear the good news! The light shines in the darkness and the darkness has not overcome it. In the name of Jesus Christ, who was, and is, and is to come, you are forgiven. Here and now, you are called to new life as you walk in the light of God's glory!

In the name of Jesus Christ, who was, and is, and is to come, you are forgiven. Here and now, you are called to new life as you walk in the light of God's glory!

Glory to God in the highest heaven and peace on earth! Amen.

Call to Worship for First Sunday after Christmas
(Bromleigh McClanaghan)

When tyrants rage, and the innocent are slain, our hearts should break.
We tend to skip this story.

There's no historical record of it. Matthew is referencing the story of Moses.
But even if it didn't happen then, it happens all the time.

When tyrants rage, and the innocent are slain, our hearts should break.
We may long for deliverance to come through a dream, for God's mercy to bring an end to violence.

God's mercy knows no end; not so for tyrants.
Let us worship, raising our broken hearts to our merciful God, praying and working for the day when no child need be afraid, for the day when mercy overcomes rage and love, the powers of death.

A Watchnight Prayer for Wisdom and Courage

Blessed be God, our Creator, who protects the children of God and never spurns their prayers. Let us humbly implore God:
Enlighten us, Lord.

We thank you, Lord for enlightening us through your Son. Fill us with his light throughout the year.
Enlighten us, Lord.

Let your wisdom lead us this year, Lord,
That we may walk in the newness of life.
Enlighten us, Lord.

May we bear hardships with courage for your name's sake and be generous in serving you.
Enlighten us, Lord.

Direct our thoughts, feelings, and actions this year.
Help us to follow your providential guidance.
Enlighten us, Lord.

Our Father, who art in Heaven,
Hallowed be thy Name. Thy Kingdom come,
Thy will be done, on earth as it is in Heaven.
Give us this day our daily bread,
and forgive us our debts, as we forgive our debtors,

And lead us not into temptation, but deliver us from evil.
For thine is the Kingdom, and the power, and the Glory
forever. Amen.
—African Amreican Lectionary, adapted from Maryland Province Society of Jesus, "A Year of Prayer Guide Book: Co-Laboring with the Living Lord, Ignatian Companions on Mission"

Prayer of Confession for New Year's Day
(Bromleigh McClanaghan)

Eternal God, this life you have given is a glorious mystery. But we confess that we don't actually like mystery all that much. Or change for that matter. We would like to know where we stand. We would like to know what to expect. We feel this is not too much to ask. And yet you answer as you have from age to age: "there is a time for everything, and I will be with you through it all. When you are brave and full of achievements, when you are vulnerable or grieving. I have always been with you, and I will be with you as you are transformed, made more perfect, in love." You call us, O God, to seek your face where we least expect it: in people who are suffering, in people we could help. You call us to see them, to see you, and to reach out in love. We do not do so as often as we should. Continue to work on us, O God, in this new year and always. Wipe every tear and transform us, that we may reflect your glory. Amen.

Opening Call to Worship and Prayer: Seeking Light

In this season of waiting, of longing,
of looking for you to come into our world
We are seeking light
[Light candles]
In our own lives
We are seeking light
In our neighborhoods
We are seeking light
In our families
We are seeking light
In our work
We are seeking light
In Grace
We are seeking light
In our nation
We are seeking light
In our world
We are seeking light

In . . . *[add your own longings]*
We are seeking light
Seek and you shall find
Knock and the door will be opened
Ask and it will be given to you
Jesus Christ, you are the light of the world
May we have eyes to see you
And ears to hear you
Come into our world today
Amen
—Grace Church in Ealing, London

An Epiphany Call to Worship
(Britney Winn Lee)

What is it that the world learns as the Magi approach the dwelling's door, if not that God will reveal God's self to unlikely people in intimate ways?

Christmas has kicked off a new story.
The outcast is invited, the foreigner is family.

Paradigms are shifting, lines are moving, narratives are being rewritten with the coming of the Christ child. It is not that those who are worthy are rewarded.

It is that those who follow will find.

Come, let us worship together our ever-surprising God.

A Call to Worship for Epiphany Sunday
(Bromleigh McClanaghan)

Arise, beloved, in body or spirit or both!
We rise, enlivened by the light that has come to dwell among us.
Open the eyes of your hearts, that you might see what is being revealed.
Our salvation has come; our God is with us.
Our salvation—not for one, or a few, but for all. God's reign is being born among us.
This revelation is good news for all but Herod.
The powerful of this world may fear God's reign, but we are always given a choice.
We will not heed them; we will go another way, creating new paths of love and justice with our God.

Christmas and Christmastide

Gathering Words for Epiphany/Baptism of the Lord

"Belonging is not too great an ask. Find your sacred company. And may they find and cherish you."
—Cole Arthur Riley, *Black Liturgies: Prayers, Poems, and Meditations for Staying Human*

Call to Worship for Baptism of the Lord

The Voice of God prods our hearing
The activity of God stretches our seeing.
Together they invite us down into the waters of life where the Spirit flows.
From there we may rise to go, to dare, to walk, and to serve beyond where we have been before.
—Martha Brunell, *The Abingdon Women's Preaching Annual, Series 2, Year A*

Litany: "Lord, I Want to Be a Christian"

>*(Sing)* **Lord, I want to be a Christian in my heart, in my heart.**
>**Lord, I want to be a Christian in my heart.**

You alone can change me, Lord.
Wash me in the waters of baptism that I may become a new person.
Wash away everything that stands between me and your holiness.

>*(Sing)* **In my heart, in my heart.**
>**Lord, I want to be a Christian in my heart.**

You alone can change me, Lord.
Wash away this temper that gets me into more trouble than I can handle.
Wash away the massive wants that place me in constant financial jeopardy.

>*(Sing)* **In my heart, in my heart.**
>**Lord, I want to be a Christian in my heart.**

You alone can change me, Lord.
Wash away my envy that separates me from the people I should love.
Wash away everything that stands between me and your holiness.

>*(Sing)* **Lord, I want to be a Christian in my heart, in my heart.**
>**Lord, I want to be a Christian in my heart.**

You alone can change me, Lord.
Wash me with your cleansing power that I may be a child of God.
You alone can change me, Lord.

>*(Sing)* **Lord, I want to be a Christian in my heart, in my heart.**
>**Lord, I want to be a Christian in my heart.**

—Kwasi I. Kena, *The Africana Worship Book, Year A*, with lyrics from "Lord, I Want to Be a Christian"

Proclaiming

Christmas Eve Worship Pattern Idea: "Not Quite Lessons and Carols"
(Kallie Green)

Christmas Eve can be tricky in a smaller church. There are often fewer leaders (whether volunteers, staff, music, childcare, etc.) and more visitors, both children and adults alike who are not as accustomed to listening to a sermon or sitting through a service. A helpful format in some years has been to break up Luke 2:1-20 into smaller pieces and instead of one long sermon, do a series of shorter reflections, with carols between the readings and reflections. This allows people more places to enter back into the story if they get distracted. It also helps to maximize the number of Christmas carols. It even opens up the possibility to share the load of writing or sharing reflections among different speakers. One of the reflections can be a time to invite the children to the front for a children's reflection. As a visual and to involve younger leaders, during each song you can invite a child to bring up the nativity piece of the previous reflection.

> First Lesson: Luke 2:1-5, Reflection: Joseph
> Second Lesson: Luke 2: 6-7, Reflection: Mary and Jesus
> Third Lesson: Luke 2: 8-14, Reflection: The Angels
> Fourth Lesson: Luke 2:15-20, Reflection: The Shepherds and the Animals

Prayer for Illumination
(Bromleigh McClanaghan)

Holy God of Mystery and Love: as this ancient and familiar story is shared this night, open our minds and hearts to receive it as if for the first time. Fill us with wonder, we pray, that a long-ago birth could change the world, now as then. Amen.

Christmas Eve—Light
(Britney Winn Lee)

We light each candle of Advent as an act of faithfulness in the holy company of mystery, remembering that as the darkness grows, so does the power of the flame's presence.

Tonight, as we welcome the lights of Christ's hope, peace, joy, and love, we celebrate the Spirit's illumination of God through the incarnation of Jesus.

Our faith has not been in vain. For to us a child is born, to us a son is given, and the government will be on his shoulders.

And he will be called Wonderful Counselor, Mighty God, Everlasting Father, Prince of Peace.

Come, let us worship God together.

I Believe: An Affirmation of Faith (John 1:1-5)

Jesus Christ, brother of Light,
I believe.
I believe
that in the beginning was the Promise
and the Promise was with God
and the Promise was God.
I believe
in the infinite, nurturing creativity of God,
in the incarnate, crucified humility of God,
in the intimate, inspiring liberality of God.
Jesus Christ, brother of Light,
I believe.
—Bruce Prewer

Prayer for Illumination for the 2nd Sunday after Christmas
(Bromleigh McClanaghan)

Holy God, Divine Parent of us all, as we receive the scripture readings this morning, help us to remember that the primary way you make families is through adoption. Not blood or marriage or ritual or nation. You adopt us and call us your own. You invite us to live as your children, to be loved as your children, and to be siblings to all. Open us to this gracious love—offered not because of what we have done or not done, but because you are Gracious Love—and help us to love as you do. May we heed the reminder from the Gospel writer, too, that even in God's own family, we do not always accept or recognize one another. Open our hearts to this Word, to your grace, and to one another, we pray. Amen.

Prayer for Illumination for Epiphany Sunday
(Bromleigh McClanaghan)

Holy God, today we recall the story of that day on the banks of the Jordan; the two cousins having a little argument about what is right and proper and righteous. We remember the older capitulating, and lowering Jesus under the water. We recall hearing of the dove swooping down and the voice from heaven. *This is my beloved, with whom I am well pleased.* Help us to remember, we pray, that Jesus's request to be baptized is actually the first thing he does of his own volition in Matthew's Gospel. Before this, he has been born, and whisked off to Egypt, and brought home again. *This is my beloved, with whom I am well pleased,* you say. Help us to know that your love for us is similarly unearned; we are beloved and pleasing to you because we are yours, because of who we are, not what we have done or accomplished, not even because of how we have served. Just because, you call him beloved. Just because, you are well pleased with us. What a wonder. To be seen and known and loved. To belong.

Let us give thanks for this gift, and commit to creating places of belonging for each and every one of God's beloved. In the name of the baptized Jesus, we pray; Amen.

Thanksgiving

Offertory Prayer
(Bromleigh McClanaghan)

God of all eternity, God of ancient lands, God of here and now:
The story of the long-ago night of your birth among us has quite the cast of characters, quite the setting. We hear of Emperor Augustus and the governor of Syria, Quirinius, of a young couple and a group of shepherds. We hear of towns and nations, of an empire and a countryside. We hear their names—of these people and places—and we recall the people and places who comprise the stories of this community, this church, this life. It is a wonder, that rich and poor, powerful and vulnerable, are brought together in the unfolding story of your love. As we share our offerings this night, may we continue to wonder that we—across any differences we might know or claim—are all a part of the same story. Bless our wonder and our offerings we pray, that they might bear witness to your abundant love and the sacred worth of every person.

Christmas Eve Great Thanksgiving for Children
(Jackson Henry)

God is with us.
Thanks be to God!
Lift up your hearts.
We lift them up to God!
Let us say "thank you" to God.
This is the story of our thanks:
God, you created the heavens and the earth, and we were born from your love.
You have always been faithful to us, from the beginning, even when we turned away from you.
We know this because you sent Jesus to be our Savior.
When he was born, the angels sang, and so we do, too:

> *SING:* **Holy, holy, holy Lord, God of pow'r and God of might,**
> **Heav'n and earth are full of your glory,**
> **Hosanna in the highest!**
> **Blessed is the One who comes**
> **In the name of the Lord,**
> **Hosanna in the highest! Hosanna in the highest!**

Christmas and Christmastide

Felix Mendelssohn, arr. William H. Cummings
adapt. by Jackson Henry

Jesus was born in a stable and lived among the poor, yet he loved everyone with a full heart.

Even so, he was rejected by the people he loved, and he eventually died for us and for the world. His love saves us even today.

In his last days, Jesus ate with his disciples, just like we do now around his table. He took bread; gave thanks to you, God; broke the bread; and shared it with his disciples. He said, "Take and eat; this is my body which is given for you. Whenever you do this, remember me."

After the meal, Jesus took a cup, gave thanks to you, and shared it with his disciples, saying, "Drink from this all of you; this is my blood of the new covenant, poured out for you and for many for the forgiveness of sins. Whenever you drink this, remember me."

To remember your loving acts in Jesus Christ, we thank you, God, and we give ourselves to you as you gave yourself to us. Even though Jesus died, we know he is alive, and he is still with us.

SING: Christ has died; Christ is risen; Christ will come again.

God, pour out your Holy Spirit on us and on this meal. Let it be for us a sign of Jesus's love, that we may be his body—his hands, his feet, his heart—in the world. Make us one until Jesus comes and welcomes us at his heavenly table, where there is a place for everyone. We pray this in your name, gracious God, now and always.

SING: Amen.

Sending

Benediction for Christmas Eve

May the everlasting love of God enfold you in blessing,
May the Spirit's light shine before you,
And may the embrace of the Holy Child
Keep you this night and always. **Amen.**
—Heidi Neumark, *The Abingdon Women's Preaching Annual, Series 2, Year A*

A Sending Forth for the Christmas Season

Come and see!
**The light of God has come into our world
to proclaim God's justice and love;
It has overcome the darkness and brought new life.**

Come and follow!
**Christ our companion has redeemed our world
He draws us into a loving family
From every tribe and family and culture.**

Go and tell!
**The Spirit has equipped us for service
To love our neighbors as we do ourselves
To bring God's salvation to the ends of the earth.**

Come and see, come and follow, go and tell!
In God's Love the nations of the earth will put their hope.
—adapted from Christine Sine, Godspace

A Watchnight Benediction

Go from this place; not into darkness, although it is night!

Go into the Light of God's eternal, inspiring Love.
Go to be those who bring peace, love, hope, and joy.
And God will always be with you. **Amen.**
—Nancy Townley, MinistryMatters.com

Benediction

Greet yourself as God's beloved. Greet one another as God's beloved. Greet all you encounter as God's beloved. In that greeting, we will be and we will become the Body of Christ. In that greeting, we will behold the image of God, ever among us and around.
—Martha Brunell, *The Abingdon Women's Preaching Annual, Series 2, Year A*

EPIPHANY

Year A Lectionary Texts

Resetting Identity	Isaiah 49:1-7	Psalm 40:1-11	1 Corinthians 1:1-9	John 1:29-42
Resetting Relationship	Isaiah 9:1-4	Psalm 27:1, 4-9	1 Corinthians 1:10-18	Matthew 4:12-23
Resetting Power	Micah 6:1-8	Psalm 15	1 Corinthians 1:18-31	Matthew 5:1-12
Resetting Discernment	Isaiah 58:1-9a (9b-12)	Psalm 112:1-10	1 Corinthians 2:1-12 (13-16)	Matthew 5:13-20
Resetting Perception	Exodus 24:12-18	Psalm 99	2 Peter 1:16-21	Matthew 17:1-9

A Framework, Themes, and Ideas for Epiphany

This section provides ideas and information to inspire planning for worship and sermons. It is based on a suggested series—a framework for worship and preaching during this liturgical season. The series idea arises from the lectionary texts and aligns with the liturgical season. You may choose to lean into the series framework fully or not at all; these ideas and words for worship will be effective whether labeled by the series name or not.

This section includes commentary plus suggestions for themes and imagery for each week. In the next section, you'll find worship words for each part of the service—Gathering, Proclaiming, Thanksgiving, and Sending.

Reset: A Worship Series for Epiphany

> God's claim upon us resets and reframes who we are,
> whose we are, and how we show up in the world.

May we all thus experience what it is to be, not almost only; but altogether Christians; being justified freely by his grace, through the redemption that is in Jesus; knowing we have peace with God through Jesus Christ; rejoicing in hope of the glory of God; and having the love of God shed abroad in our hearts, by the Holy Ghost given unto us!—John Wesley, "The Almost Christian"

Preaching to St. Mary's Church in Oxford—a place of deep affection and spiritual significance—Wesley calls out those who display only a form of godliness, an *almost* Christian. He insists that the *altogether* Christian life must involve more than mere belief in God or good actions. Rather, the movement from *almost* to *altogether* is a work of the heart made possible only through unmitigated trust in Jesus. In short, faith in Jesus resets everything.

In the light of Epiphany, we encounter the claim of Christ upon our lives. God's grace doesn't merely improve us; it *resets* us—rewriting our identity, reclaiming our belonging, and reframing our daily witness. This series is an invitation into the journey of grace—from appearance to authenticity, from habit to holiness, from passive religion to passionate discipleship. Focusing on the epistle readings through the season, this series reflects a movement toward this full-hearted faith, resetting our identity, unity, wisdom, understanding, growth, foundation, and vision.

Add richness and depth to this worship series by incorporating sacramental acts throughout:

- offer remembrance of baptism as a part of worship service
- offer remembrance of baptism as part of another ritual action
- offer holy communion weekly for this season, if that is not your typical pattern

Worship leaders should consider incorporating remembrance of baptism throughout the series. This may be done directly as a designated part of worship or indirectly as part of another ritual action (e.g. entering/exiting worship or during the passing of the peace). Leaders may also consider instituting weekly communion for this season. Centering these sacramental acts in worship will add richness and depth to the series.

Lastly, highlight the progression of the series by creating a progressive worship art installation or sanctuary shift where something is *reset* each Sunday:

- Backdrop colors: Begin with muted winter tones and gradually move toward richer, warmer hues (deep blues, purples, golds).

- Visual altar element: Use a layered tablecloth (light cloth under broken, cracked pottery or stones). Over the series, remove the broken items and reveal a glowing light (e.g., candle, flame, glass cross).
- Transfiguration Sunday: End with radiant gold or white, a lifted cloth or banner of light, representing being "altogether Christian."

This season is an opportunity to *reset*—not just our habits, but our hearts. As we dwell in the light of Christ's Epiphany, we hear anew the invitation not to settle for being almost, but to altogether live as people reset by grace.

Week One (Second Sunday after the Epiphany)

1 Corinthians 1:1-9 | Resetting Identity

> **Key Images**: baptismal waters, cracked pottery mended with gold (kintsugi)
>
> **Themes**: grace names and mends us, calling and sanctification

> To the church of God that is in Corinth, to those who are sanctified in Christ Jesus, called to be saints . . . (1 Corinthians 1:2)

The church at Corinth was rife with dysfunction. With theological, political, and class divisions, the church struggled to find its footing within a culture of competing values and questionable ethics (1 Corinthians 5:1). And so, Paul calls the church to remember who they are and to what they have been called.

The letter begins by affirming the Corinthians' identity as sanctified (ἡγιασμένοις hēgiasmenois, set apart for a sacred purpose; made holy through God's action) and called (κλητοῖς klētois, invited or summoned by God to a specific purpose or identity). The emphasis here is on God's action and claim upon all those who call upon the name of our Lord Jesus Christ (v.2)—a communal claim that flattens all other claims of "chosenness" that may lead to divisions. Believers are no longer defined by worldly standards, divisions, or achievements, but by their calling and sanctification.

Despite their imperfections, they are recipients of God's grace and participants in the fellowship of Christ. This fellowship (κοινωνία koinōnia) is a deep communal sharing and participation in the life of Christ, which empowers and strengthens their witness.

> How does recognizing ourselves as sanctified and called by God change our self-perception?

Week Two (Third Sunday after the Epiphany)

1 Corinthians 1:10-18 | Resetting Relationship

> **Key Images**: interwoven threads, clasped hands, mosaic of faces
>
> **Themes**: the unity-in-diversity of the Church

Has Christ been divided? (1 Corinthians 1:13)

Recognizing the threat inherent in ideological corners (σχίσματα *schismata*, "divisions, rifts"), Paul exhorts the Corinthians to *be in agreement* (literally "speak the same thing") and *be united in the same mind and the same purpose* (v.10). Significantly, the verb *katērtismenoi* implies a completed action with continuing results, that this "uniting" is done to them not by them. It conjures imagery of restored nets, or broken limbs set back in place—a body mended for effective function. It strongly suggests God's initiative in restoring relationships, mending the fractured community into proper alignment.

In Greco-Roman society, factionalism—especially in philosophical schools and patronage systems—was normal. Yet for Paul the cross is transformed from a symbol of shame into a powerful message that heals divisions beyond social tolerance toward spiritual cohesion. The cross is the central unifying factor that defines and harmonizes Christian community. The well-known coritos "Dame la Mano" captures this well:

No me importa la iglesia que vayas	It doesn't matter what church you go to
Si detrás del calvario tu estás	If you are behind Calvary,
Si tu corazón es como el mío	If your heart is as mine,
Dame la mano y mi hermano serás	Give me your hand and you will be my brother

> How might preferences be subverting our shared participation in Christ?

Week Three (Fourth Sunday after the Epiphany)

1 Corinthians 1:18-31 | Resetting Power

> **Key Images**: a cross overshadowing a crown, discarded things, light breaking through clouds
>
> **Themes**: power in vulnerability, God's wisdom, the impact of redemption

> But God chose what is foolish in the world to shame the wise; God chose what is weak in the world to shame the strong; God chose what is low and despised in the world, things that are not, to abolish things that are, so that no one might boast in the presence of God. (1 Corinthians 1:27-29)

After their respective presidencies, rivals John Adams and Thomas Jefferson began corresponding with each other, developing a long-distance friendship that lasted till their deaths. In one such letter, Adams writes:

> Power always sincerely, conscientiously, [very candidly], believes itself right. Power always thinks it has a great soul, and vast views, beyond the comprehension of the weak; and that it is doing God service, when it is violating all his laws.

Adams offers a chilling insight that sounds a lot like Corinth. In a society obsessed with status, rhetoric, lineage, and intellect, Paul delivers a stunning theological reversal. The Corinthians—spiritually boastful and socially divided—are reminded that God chooses the outcasts. God deliberately calls the foolish, the weak, and the lowly—not by accident, but to unmask the illusions of human power.

More than poetic flourish, it is a core theological conviction rooted in the cross: that divine strength is revealed in vulnerability, and true wisdom is revealed in what the world despises.

The cross resets our understanding of status. It declares that our worth comes not from merit, success, or pedigree, but from the free and loving choice of God. No one boasts—not because we are nothing, but because in Christ, we have received everything.

> How might the message of the cross challenge the power structures—visible and invisible—in your community?

Week Four (Fifth Sunday after the Epiphany)

1 Corinthians 2:1-12 (13-16) | Resetting Discernment

> **Key Images**: an ear listening, open book with light, flame over a head
>
> **Themes**: spiritual growth and insight

Now we have received not the spirit of the world but the Spirit that is from God, so that we may understand the gifts bestowed on us by God. (1 Corinthians 2:12)

Here Paul continues his corrective to the Corinthian obsession and dependence on outward performance. He reminds them that he is neither persuasive nor impressive but came to them in weakness (c.f. 1 Corinthians 1:27) and *a demonstration of the Spirit and of power* (v.4). His point is not self-deprecation, but a theological protest against performative religion which is antithetical to grace.

And so, Paul resets their understanding of discernment. True spiritual wisdom (σοφία *sophía*) does not come from clever reasoning or inherited tradition alone, but through the revelation (ἀποκάλυψις *apokalypsis*) of the Spirit of God. Human wisdom, no matter how brilliant, cannot unlock the mind of Christ.

This is a contrast between two operating systems: the spirit of the world, which values influence, dominance, and success; versus the Spirit of God, which unveils grace, reveals Christ crucified, and enables discernment (v.13-15). Discernment (ἀνακρίνειν *anakrinein*, meaning to discern/judge/examine) is a word used for careful investigation, but here it is qualified: only the one who is spiritual can "judge" rightly. This is not about condemnation, but perception. Spiritual discernment is not merely a decision-making process—it is a spiritual grace that enables spiritual gifts (χάρισμα *charisma*). It is the Spirit's active work to shape our imagination and will toward the things of God.

Resetting discernment does not discard reason; instead, it subjects it to the renewing presence of the Holy Spirit. This kind of discernment allows the believer to:

- See through false narratives of power and success,
- Understand suffering through the lens of the cross,
- Perceive others not as competitors but as beloved,
- Live by grace, not performance.

> How is the Spirit reshaping imagination in your community?
>
> What gifts of grace are emerging?

Week Five (Transfiguration Sunday)

2 Peter 1:16-21 | Resetting Perception

> **Key Images:** mountain peak view, lamp in the dark, a bright star, gradual lighting like at sunrise
>
> **Themes:** interpretation of scripture, guidance and discernment

> So we have the prophetic message more fully confirmed. You will do well to be attentive to this as to a lamp shining in a dark place, until the day dawns and the morning star rises in your hearts. (2 Peter 1:19)

Mountain top experiences do not last, but Jesus does. In addressing internal dissent and division within the Church, Peter recalls his own experience of the Transfiguration (see Matthew 17:1-7) where he, along with James and John, saw Jesus in *majesty* (μεγαλειότης *megaleiótēs*, meaning glory or splendor)—a glory that gave them insight into Jesus's relationship with the Law (represented by Moses) and the prophets (represented by Elijah). Yet, the point of the transfiguration is not about Moses and Elijah, nor is it really about the glory. No, the point is Jesus—that everything needed for understanding the purpose or will of God is found in Jesus. The voice from the cloud makes clear that the important thing to take away from this mountain top experience is not who showed up but the fact that Jesus came down from the mountain too.

So then, in the light of Jesus the prophetic message (προφητικὸς λόγος prophētikos logos, i.e., the entire witness of Scripture and divine revelation) is made "firm, stable, secure" (βέβαιος bébaios). Amid cultural conditions that at times seem confusing and unstable, Jesus provides the light (φοσφόρος phōsphoros, light-bearer) that enables and empowers interpretation. Through Jesus both what was spoken then and what is said today become clearly understood as God speech or not.

Peter's message is not only retrospective but prospective—you, too, can live by the light of Christ. The ultimate reset is not just seeing the glory of Christ on the mountain but experiencing the dawning of that glory within—a reorientation of inner perception about ourselves, about others, and about God. How then shall we live? Look to Jesus. For in this way, entry into the eternal kingdom of our Lord and Savior Jesus Christ will be richly provided for you (v. 11).

> What illusions—about myself, others, or God—need to be transfigured by the light of Christ?
>
> What would change if I trusted that this light already shines within me?

Words for Worship, Epiphany

Gathering

Call to Worship
(Michelle Mejia)

We gather today as your church
ready for a reset,
to be formed anew by God's abundant grace.
We gather today to worship
and remember your claim upon us,

that we are your saints,
enriched in Christ Jesus and not lacking in any gift.
We gather today to renew our calling
to be partners with God,
in loving the world and joining your work of healing within it.

Call to Worship (all/any weeks)
(Ginny Griggs)

God is our light and our salvation!
God renews the song in our mouths.
Let us worship the One who has claimed us.
Let us celebrate a Love that knows our name.

A Call to Authentic Witness
(Katie McKay Simpson)

In an era awash in half-truths and quiet compromises, we are summoned to stand bare and unflinching before the world.
We answer the call, aware that true transformation begins in the raw, unguarded depths of our being.

Let our lives, rough-hewn and real, be the living evidence of a grace that does not shy away from truth.
Together, we bear witness as salt and light—a reset that challenges every dark corner of our world.

Call to Worship (Exodus 24:12–18)
(Katie McKay Simpson)

Come, we invite you to climb with us into the quiet majesty of that inner mountain—
where the air thins, and every step becomes a prayer, every silence a hymn.

In that hallowed space between earth and sky,
we encounter the profound mystery of transformation—a reset that is both startling and tender.

Let us lift our eyes and our hearts into the bright unknown,
where the ordinary is transfigured by the touch of divine presence and grace.

A Call to Follow (Matthew 17:1–9)
(Katie McKay Simpson)

On that fateful mountaintop, the very face of Christ was unveiled in a glory that redefined destiny
resetting the hearts of His disciples with a love as fierce as it was unexpected.

In that searing moment of truth, we find the courage
to leave behind our dead weight and rise, transformed.

Let the transfigured light of our Savior ignite in us a passion to carry His brilliance into every darkened place of our lives.
We embrace this divine metamorphosis, our souls forever marked by grace and truth that redeems all.

Opening Prayer
(Michelle Mejia)

Spirit of God, in your infinite wisdom search us and know us. Reveal to us the way that you see us, O God. Help us know that before we belong to anyone or anything—we first belong to you. Remind us that you choose what we consider weak, foolish, less than, and despised for your saving work in the world, so that we might learn to trust in you and not our own abilities. As we embrace our own belovedness, may we share this good news with others. In Jesus's name, we pray. Amen.

Prayer of Confession & Assurance of Pardon
(Michelle Mejia)

**God of mercy and grace,
we confess that we have not trusted you with our whole selves.
We have not seen ourselves as your claimed and beloved people.
We have not seen others as your claimed and beloved people.
We have separated ourselves from our neighbors.
We have focused on our differences instead of our shared humanity.
We have boasted in our own importance and abilities.
Forgive us, we pray, for the ways we have failed to be your church in the world.
Knit us together once more with the same mind and purpose that is in Christ Jesus our Lord. Amen.**

Friends, hear the good news:
Christ Jesus became for us wisdom and righteousness, sanctification and redemption so that our faith would rest in the power of God. In the name of Jesus Christ, we are forgiven! Thanks be to God! Amen.

Prayer of Confession and Renewal
(Katie McKay Simpson)

As salt and light, we are called to transform our communities
with Your love and truth.

Yet in an age where the church's mission is often distorted by false prophets,
we confess that we too have sometimes allowed the shadows of these voices to
obscure our purpose.

Forgive us, O Lord, for the times we have lost sight of Your call
to be genuine, to care for the poor, the hungry, and the oppressed.
Remold us and remake us when we experience a failure of nerve in the face of hate.
Restore in us the integrity of authentic worship which calls us higher place of the heart
And grow in us the fierce courage to break the yoke of injustice.

Prayer of Confession (all/any weeks)
(Ginny Griggs)

Merciful God,
> **you have named us as your own and called us into a new way of being;**
> **yet we are prone to wander from your voice.**

Where we have abandoned your wisdom for the wisdom of the world,
> **forgive us.**

Restore us now, and ground us in your grace;
through Jesus Christ our Lord. Amen.

Prayer of Confession (Weeks 4 and/or 5)
(Ginny Griggs)

Merciful God, you have shown us your way to walk toward justice:
> **to seek repentance over performance,**
> **action over appearances,**
> **humility over acclaim.**

Where we have lost sight of you and become enamored with other paths,
forgive us. Recenter us in your way of salvation, and restore to us your joy;
through Jesus Christ our Lord. Amen.

Proclaiming

Prayer for Illumination (all/any weeks)
(Ginny Griggs)

May the Spirit, who searches the depths of all being, reveal the wisdom of God's Word to us today; through Jesus Christ our Lord. Amen.

Prayer for Illumination
(Michelle Mejia)

Reveal to us, O God,
by your Spirit that searches everything,
what no eye has seen,
nor ear has heard,
nor human heart conceived,
that you have prepared for those who love you,
so that we may understand the gifts that you have given to us
through Jesus Christ our Lord. Amen.

A Responsive Reading—Psalm 40:1–11
(Katie McKay Simpson)

In the bitter silence of our waiting,
we pour out our hearts to a God who knows our suffering.
"We wait patiently for the Lord."
In a world of demands made on particular timelines,
we grow anxious for not yet receiving your deliverance,
"We wait patiently for the Lord."

When our voices crack from the weight of despair, God's promise echoes: renewal comes at the edge of our brokenness.
"We wait patiently for the Lord."

Let each word be a declaration against the darkness,
a stubborn cry that even in anguish, hope remains.
"We wait patiently for the Lord."

So we now dwell in holy patience is a countercultural posture.
"We wait patiently for the Lord."

Responsive Reflection—Psalm 27:1, 4–9 (3rd Sunday of Epiphany)
(Katie McKay Simpson)

The Lord is my unwavering light amid the darkness—a beacon that scares the shadows away.
In Your presence, fear dies a quiet death.

Show us Your face, O Lord, that we might stand unashamed, hearts ablaze with a truth that defies despair.
In Your fierce love, we are reborn.

Even as tempests lash and night deepens, we hold fast to the sanctuary of Your promise.
Your light is our defiant song.

Thanksgiving

A Congregational Prayer for Lightbearers (2nd Sunday)
(Katie McKay Simpson)

Lord, through the course of the ages,
we remember that You chose Your servants to shine—
to bring hope to the nations and healing to the broken.
Though the journey is arduous and our spirits may falter,
remind us that Your strength is made perfect in our weakness.
When our energy wanes and the expectation feels overwhelming,
infuse us with the comfort of Your everlasting love.

May we who labor in the dark hours,
carrying the delicate flame of hope in a heavy, uncertain world—
know that our exhaustion is sacred.
In the long night before dawn, the weariness we know becomes the crucible
in which God's transformative promise is forged.

O Divine Artisan, renew our tired limbs and quivering hearts;
let the faint spark within us burst into a radiant reset
where every faltering step is graced with the assurance of Your love.
Let Your promise be our renewal:
that even in exhaustion,

Your light perseveres and our labors are not in vain.
Grant us rest in our weariness,
and courage in our moments of isolation.
Help us to lean into Your embrace,

finding solace in the assurance that You walk beside us—
guiding our every step in the dark.

May we, through our trials, become beacons of Your hope,
knowing that our exhaustion is transformed by Your grace,
and that every flicker of our light brings us closer to the dawn.
In the name of the One who calls us to shine, we pray.
Amen.

A Prayer for Those Who Are Exhausted
(Katie McKay Simpson)

Being a light
takes energy
and involves expectation.
This fatigue comes
when the weight of the world
is simply
too
hard
to bear in the isolating work of light-casting.

O God, who called us from the darkness into deeper purpose,
grant renewal in our weariness.
Trust in our timidity and terror.
When our strength is spent, may Yours begin—
a reset of heart and spirit. Amen.

Prayer of Renewal (3rd Sunday after Epiphany, Isaiah 9:1-4)
(Katie McKay Simpson)

O God, You once declared in ancient song,
"The people walking in darkness have seen a great light."
O Divine Light, in the shadowed hours of despair,
we gather our hearts like scattered embers—
each a spark of hope amid relentless night.
You declared in ancient song,
"The people walking in darkness have seen a great light."

So we rise,
joy our banner, a sacred act of resistance against the forces of oppression that grow.
Here, we claim our joy as both inheritance and defiance,
a harvest reaped from our ancestors

and the seeds of your everlasting love.
Our laughter rings like battle-cry,
a jubilant proclamation in the face of despair;
breaking the chains that bind us, filling us with the light of Your salvation.

O Source of all renewal,
infuse our souls with the strength of your radiant truth:
that joy, though delicate as a blossom,
carries the fierce power of sacred resistance.
May our hearts forever be alight with your grace,
each act of rejoicing a quiet rebellion against the tyranny of gloom.

We pray this in the spirit of Isaiah's ancient vision,
where sorrow is vanquished by the brilliance of your love,
fragile embers of hope become a beacon against the night
and every joyful step is a testament
to the unyielding hope born from your light.
Amen.

Prayer for Justice and Mercy
(Katie McKay Simpson)

Lord, empower us to bring justice to the oppressed
and mercy to the hurting, for the safety we seek belongs to us now
It is now our turn to carry the world.

We are each other's safety when the world seems dangerous,
Our lives become living miracles—
each action, every word a shield,
Our lives to serve as a safe harbor when all other sanctuaries are plundered.
Let us resist a unity that masquerades as false peace—
one that silences voices,
Suppresses inconvenient emotions,
and hides brokenness.

May we flood one another with belonging,
discover wisdom in the whispers of our ancestors,
and find our future amid the rubble—
the seeds of hope hidden in our songs.
For we know something better is coming.

A Pastoral Prayer (1 Corinthians 2:1–12)
(Katie McKay Simpson)

O Spirit of the Living God, fall afresh on us.

In the quiet spaces of our hearts and in the tender whispers of the world around us, we come before You, acknowledging that true wisdom is not found in human learning or in the fleeting accolades of this age, but is a sacred gift, a revelation of Your Spirit. As we grow, may we rely not on the wisdom of this world but on the profound mystery revealed only by Your Spirit. You have shown us that wisdom is not merely an accumulation of facts or intellectual prowess; it is the deep knowing of Your presence, the gentle guidance that transforms our brokenness into beauty.

By Your wisdom, we learn to step into the uncertain terrain of life with openness and wonder, recognizing that each moment of vulnerability holds the potential for a new beginning.

By Your wisdom, we see that even in the everyday, the mundane can become a portal to the sacred—a space where our hearts encounter Your grace in unexpected ways.

By Your wisdom, we are invited to embrace the paradoxes of life, understanding that in surrendering to the mystery of the cross, our pain is transformed into hope, our failures into stepping stones toward redemption.

O Divine Spirit, remind us that true wisdom comes from Your ever-present grace, revealing the hidden treasures of Your kingdom in the silence of our souls and the beauty of the natural world. Help us to discard the vain efforts of worldly knowledge and to trust in the living, breathing mystery of Your love. May Your Spirit guide us as we journey together, illuminating our paths with insights that transcend human understanding—is a gift freely given, a testament to the eternal love that unites us all. Amen.

A Great Thanksgiving (Matthew 5:1-12)
(Katie McKay Simpson)

The Lord be with you.
And also with you.
Lift up your hearts. *(The pastor may lift hands and keep them raised.)*
We lift them up to the Lord.
Let us give thanks to the Lord our God.
It is right to give our thanks and praise.

It is right, and a good and joyful thing,
always and everywhere to give thanks to you,
Father Almighty God, creator of heaven and earth.
You formed us in your image and breathed into us the breath of life.
When we turned away, and our love failed, your love remained steadfast.
You delivered us from captivity, made covenant to be our sovereign God,
and spoke to us through your prophets,
who embodied the journey of enduring faith with You—
when the path is steep, and the burdens seem too heavy—
we cling to these promises of our own blessedness.
And so, with your people on earth and all the company of heaven we praise your name and join their unending hymn:
(The pastor may lower hands.)
Holy, holy, holy Lord, God of power and might, heaven and earth are full of your glory. Hosanna in the highest. Blessed is he who comes in the name of the Lord. Hosanna in the highest.

(The pastor may raise hands.)
Holy are you, and blessed is your Son Jesus Christ.
Your Spirit anointed him to preach good news to the poor,
to proclaim release to the captives and recovering of sight to the blind,
to set at liberty those who are oppressed,
and to announce that the time had come when you would save your people.
He healed the sick, fed the hungry, and ate with sinners.
By the baptism of his suffering, death, and resurrection you gave birth to your Church,
delivered us from slavery to sin and death,
and made with us a new covenant by water and the Spirit.
It is in Christ's words we remember the paradox of the cross,
where suffering is transformed into redemption,
our trials become testimony,
and our weaknesses are made strong through your love.

From the witness of scripture, we remember:

*(The pastor may hold hands, palms down, over the bread,
or touch the bread, or lift the bread.)*
On the night in which he gave himself up for us, he took bread, gave thanks to you, broke the bread, gave it to his disciples, and said: "Take, eat; this is my body which is given for you. Do this in remembrance of me."

(The pastor may hold hands, palms down, over the cup, or touch the cup, or lift the cup.)

When the supper was over he took the cup, gave thanks to you, gave it to his
disciples, and said: "Drink from this, all of you; this is my blood of the new
covenant, poured out for you and for many for the forgiveness of sins.
Do this, as often as you drink it, in remembrance of me."
As we drink from this cup, let it remind us that within the paradox of the cross,
our deepest suffering is met with the promise of new life and redemption.

In this sacred act, God's children throughout time are invited
to embrace the paradox of the cross
where sacrifice becomes our source of hope,
and our brokenness is transformed by your redeeming love
which offers blessing to all creation.

(The pastor may raise hands.)
And so, in remembrance of these your mighty acts in Jesus Christ,
we offer ourselves in praise and thanksgiving as a holy and living sacrifice,
in union with Christ's offering for us, as we proclaim the mystery of faith.
Christ has died; Christ is risen; Christ will come again.

(The pastor may hold hands, palms down, over the bread and cup.)
Pour out your Holy Spirit on us gathered here,
and on these gifts of bread and wine.
Make them be for us the body and blood of Christ,
that we may be for the world the body of Christ, redeemed by his blood.

(The pastor may raise hands.)
By your Spirit make us one with Christ,
one with each other, and one in ministry to all the world,
until Christ comes in final victory, and we feast at his heavenly banquet.
Through your Son Jesus Christ, with the Holy Spirit in your holy Church,
all honor and glory is yours, almighty God, now and forever.
Amen.

Lord's Prayer

Giving of the Bread and Cup

Prayer After Receiving
In the quiet simplicity of the Beatitudes, we hear afresh the paradox of the cross—
> that blessedness comes not from power, but from meekness;
> not from might, but from mercy.

Today we give thanks for those who, though burdened by life's trials, choose to
seek justice, to offer compassion, and to stand as beacons of hope in troubled

times. Nourished by this sacred meal, may we join in their number again today. May our lives speak of the gentle strength that transforms sorrow into a promise of everlasting peace. Amen.

Prayer After Receiving (all/any weeks)
(Ginny Griggs)
Fed and filled at your table, O God
we remember who we are and to whom we belong. As we go from this place, knit us together in purpose, that we may join as partners in your work in the world. Amen.

Sending

A Call to Follow—Matthew 4:12-23 (3rd Sunday after Epiphany)
(Katie McKay Simpson)

As Jesus beckoned the fishermen from the depths of their worn-out lives, so He calls to us—those weighed down by guilt and failure—to leave behind the nets of our past.
We step forward, trembling but determined, into the burning light of His mercy.

In this new life, we embrace the paradox of following a Savior who meets us in our brokenness and transforms it into beauty.
We gather as those transformed by His love, ready to cast aside our nets and walk boldly into the future He has prepared for us.

Each step away from the familiar is an act of defiance against despair—a surrender to the wild, unyielding grace that transforms every misstep into a sacred beginning.
In His call, we find the courage to be remade.

Today, we stand at the threshold of a sacred journey—a journey that embraces hope, and declares that our past does not define our destiny. We commit ourselves to the call of Jesus, knowing that in His light, every ending is but a beginning.
With open hearts and willing spirits, we answer the call to follow, and in doing so, we become bearers of God's eternal light.

LENT

Year A Lectionary Texts

Where Are You? Distant	Joel 2:1-2, 12-17	Psalm 51:1-17	2 Corinthians 5:20b-6:10	Matthew 6:1-6, 16-21
Where Are You? Hiding	Genesis 2:15-17; 3:1-7	Psalm 32	Romans 5:12-19	Matthew 4:1-11
Where Are You? Searching	Genesis 12:1-4a	Psalm 121	Romans 4:1-5, 13-17	John 3:1-17
Where Are You? Thirsty	Exodus 17:1-7	Psalm 95	Romans 5:1-11	John 4:5-42
Where Are You? Forgotten	1 Samuel 16:1-13	Psalm 23	Ephesians 5:8-14	John 9:1-41
Where Are You? Grieving	Ezekiel 37:1-14	Psalm 130	Romans 8:6-11	John 11:1-45

A Framework, Themes, and Ideas for Lent

This section provides ideas and information to inspire planning for worship and sermons. It is based on a suggested series—a framework for worship and preaching during this liturgical season. The series idea arises from the lectionary texts and aligns with the liturgical season. You may choose to lean into the series framework fully or not at all; these ideas and words for worship will be effective whether labeled by the series name or not.

This section includes commentary plus suggestions for themes and imagery for each week. In the next section, you'll find worship words for each part of the service—Gathering, Proclaiming, Thanksgiving, and Sending.

Where Are You? A Worship Series for Lent

God is always looking for us, even as we search for God (or hide from God).

I don't know where I'm headed
But I know where I'm from . . .
    —J. J. Heller, "Coming Home"

Heller describes the sense of displacement she felt as a freshman college student—far from home, alienated from meaningful community and generally dispirited. Yet, amid her displacement, she never lost the idea of home as a "safe haven" where she would be known and wanted and buoyed back to life. Returning home enabled her to quite literally locate herself.

This Lenten series explores the spatial language of Scripture—not merely geography, but the inner terrain of the soul: exile and return, ascent and descent, hiding and seeking. The searching question *"Where are you?"* resounds throughout, not as condemnation, but as invitation. Whether returning or awakening to place, the invitation is to locate oneself within the ubiquity of God's presence. **Wherever we find ourselves—where we have been or where we are going—every place is pregnant with divine purpose and call.**

From the call to return in Joel to the breath of life in Ezekiel, the Lenten series *Where Are You?* traces the journey of return, recognition, renewal, and resurrection. It explores how God meets humanity in places of shame (Genesis), questioning (John 3), exclusion (John 4), obscurity (1 Samuel), and death (Ezekiel). The consistent thread is that God seeks us first, even when we are unsure where we are ourselves.

This series begins with Ash Wednesday and intentionally stops on the 5th Sunday of Lent, so that the events of Holy Week might be understood and celebrated as a separate, unified unit (see the *Disruption* series). Notwithstanding, because location is so significant to the events of Holy Week, it would not be difficult to include it as part of the *Where Are You?* se-

The scope of this series:

- The series begins with Ash Wednesday.
- The series ends with the 5th Sunday of Lent.
- The 6th Sunday of Lent and Holy Week are included in the *Disruption* series, page 117.
- Planners may instead choose to extend this *Where Are You?* series to include Holy Week.

ries. Worship leaders should use pastoral discretion in determining what is best for the worshipping community.

As part of a journey of place, those designing worship should consider gradually introducing visual elements tied to each text (e.g., a tree branch for Eden, a vessel of water, anointing oil, dry bones) as the weeks progress. Or use visual markers (e.g., paper or projected footsteps) leading into or through the sanctuary, representing the journey toward God and God's journey toward us. The leading question of the series could also be used as a liturgical frame for calls to worship, prayers of confession, or benedictions for the series.

When God asks, "Where are you?", it is not because God has lost us, but because God longs to restore us. *Where do we stand in relation to grace? Are you hiding? Searching? Thirsty? Overlooked? Dry and lifeless?* As we walk with Jesus to the cross, we are also walking back into the presence of the God who is always searching for us.

So, where are you?

Consider gradually introducing visual elements as the weeks progress.

- tree branch
- vessel of water
- anointing oil
- dry bones

Use visual markers to lead people into and through the sanctuary:

- paper footsteps
- projected footsteps

Use *Where Are You?* as the frame for liturgical elements.

Ash Wednesday

Joel 2:1-2, 12-17 | Where Are You?—Distant

> **Key images:** torn garments, ashes shaped into a spiral or pathway
>
> **Themes:** forgiveness, repentance, grace, mercy

> Return to the LORD your God, for he is gracious and merciful, slow to anger, abounding in steadfast love, and relenting from punishment. (Joel 2:13)

Through the noise of judgment and exile comes the divine call to *return*. This Hebrew word (שׁוּב *shuv*) is rich in covenantal and relational resonance. It implies not only physical return but a restoration of relationship, a reorientation of life toward God. The phrase "with all your heart" (בְּכָל־לְבַבְכֶם, *bekhol-levavkhem*) intensifies the appeal—it is not mere ritual, but total inner transformation.

Because it is too easy to view every disaster as punishment, it is important to emphasize that this is not a march of shame but a path of homecoming. *Even now* (v.12) signals a window of opportunity that remains open. This return is not about appeasing God—God is not to be manipulated. Rather, it is a reminder that God is fundamentally gracious and merciful, slow to anger and abounding in steadfast love and relents from punishing (v.13). This is home. Returning is a journey of remembering home as we draw closer to the place that may feel simultaneously new yet so familiar.

No matter how distant you may feel—whether spiritually numb, busy, bitter, or burned out—no one is too far from grace.

> So, where are you?
>
> What distances have grown between you and God, your community, or yourself?
>
> How might God be moving to close the gap?

Week One

Genesis 2:15-17; 3:1-7 | Where Are You?—Hiding

> **Key images:** a bare tree branch in a pot of earth; a cloth partially covering it to symbolize hiding
>
> **Themes:** shame and separation, God's seeking love

> Then the eyes of both were opened, and they knew
> that they were naked . . . (Genesis 3:7)

Perhaps one lesson to glean from this origin story is that we have capacity to choose. We choose how we want to relate to others and creation. We choose which voices to hold as authoritative. We choose how to respond to each other and to God. We have capacity to choose, and choosing is power. Maybe the *opening of their eyes* is less about a newfound knowledge and more about the awareness of choice and its accompanying power.

Though the lectionary reading ends at v.7, the impact of the transgression continues and intensifies into v.8:

> They heard the sound of the Lord God walking in the garden at the time of the evening breeze, and the man and his wife hid themselves from the presence of the Lord God among the trees of the garden.

Here again is a choice: the man and his wife choose to *hide*. First, they choose to hide their vulnerability (עֵירֹם *erom*, meaning "naked, nudity") from each other. This becomes the first physical barrier to the communion previously enjoyed between people. Vulnerability is how community flourishes.

> So, where are you?
>
> What barriers continue to keep us apart?

Second, they hide from God. Even though they hear and recognize God's presence near them, they choose to hide. Whether because of shame, guilt, or desire, they choose to push away from God's presence—perhaps because what God brings is either too hard to bear or too impossible to entertain.

Yet, it is worth noting that their choice is not a deterrent nor hindrance to God. God does not leave them alone nor let them stay in hiding. God comes anyway, searching and calling for them, because God chooses us even when we don't.

> So, where are you?
>
> Where are you withdrawing from truth, community, or God?

Week Two

John 3:1-17 | Where Are You?—Searching

> **Key images**: a bowl or images of water (symbolic of birth and baptism), suspended cloth to represent wind/breath
>
> **Themes**: justifying grace, faith/doubt, process of transformation

> Now there was a Pharisee named Nicodemus, a leader of the Jews. He came to Jesus by night . . . (John 3:1-2a)

That this encounter occurs at night is a deliberate choice in John's Gospel, where light and darkness are symbolic of understanding, revelation, and moral/spiritual posture. In John, night is often a time of confusion, fear, or uncertainty—but also of transition and potential. Night is the space between known and unknown.

Nicodemus may be hiding his visit out of fear (of the Pharisees). Or perhaps he is searching, wrestling with spiritual questions he can't yet ask in daylight. Maybe he represents all of us who are yet unsure—half-formed in faith, hesitant but hungry.

Whatever the case, night becomes the vehicle that allows Nicodemus to move from teacher to student to disciple. Whereas the other Pharisees posture themselves against Jesus throughout the gospel, Nicodemus humbles himself. By the end of the gospel, he gradually moves into the light of day, becoming a defender (John 7:45-52) and loving caretaker (John 19:38-42).

Though it is not instant, it is undoubtedly transformation. Sometimes, you must sit in the dark with Jesus long enough for transformation to take root and begin its work. Whether in the clarity of day or in the uncertainty of night, encountering Jesus always makes the difference.

> So, where are you?
>
> Are you willing to sit in your night . . . with Jesus . . . long enough to be transformed?

Week Three

John 4:5-42 | Where Are You?—Thirsty

> **Key images**: well, heat of the day, a clay jar with flowing fabric representing water
>
> **Themes**: encountering God in the ordinary, crossing boundaries, true worship

> The woman said to him, "Sir, give me this water, so that I may never be thirsty or have to keep coming here to draw water." (John 4:15)

Despite valiant attempts to explain, there is really no indication as to why this woman of Samaria comes to the well when she does. Perhaps it is a lack of adequate planning that has her coming in the hottest part of the day. Perhaps she eschews participating in the conventional roles of women at the time—like fetching water together in groups and the general association of wells with marriage (cf. Genesis 24, 29 and Exodus 2). Perhaps she just needed more water for her daily activities and there is nothing particularly odd here.

Except it is noon—the brightest part of the day, which in John's gospel symbolizes understanding, revelation, and spiritual clarity. This woman doesn't come to the well to hide but to live. She encounters Jesus amid her daily routine. Instructive here is both that Jesus shows up in her daily routine and she shows up with curiosity that transforms routine into a means of grace.

In his book *Encounters with Silence*, Karl Rahner writes to the "God of My Daily Routine:"

> I now see clearly that, if there is any path at all on which I can approach You, it must lead through the very middle of my ordinary daily life. If I should try to flee to You by any other way, I'd actually be leaving myself

behind, and that, aside from being quite impossible, would accomplish nothing at all.

Notably Jesus does not judge, criticize, or condemn her. Rather, Jesus simply reveals who he is, and she is implicated. Jesus breaks into her routine so that she might live and become more authentically her—free from expectations (then and now) and free to define her story on her own terms. Perhaps this is the living water she was thirsty for all along.

> So, where are you?
>
> Where in your daily routine might Jesus be waiting?
>
> How is Jesus inviting you to live more authentically and free?

Week Four

1 Samuel 16:1-13 | Where Are You?—Forgotten

> **Key images**: anointing oil, images of shepherding, a covered box or container symbolizing hiddenness (could be gradually uncovered during the sermon)
>
> **Themes**: God's hidden work, seeing with God's eyes, anointed for mission

> Samuel said to Jesse, "Are all your sons here?" And he said, "There remains yet the youngest, but he is keeping the sheep." (1 Samuel 16:11)

While the reader understands the purpose of Samuel's visit, it is not clear to the residents of Bethlehem—least of which, to Jesse and his sons. Samuel's visit causes a stir, prompting the elders of the city to meet him *trembling* (חָרַד *chârad,* "to shudder with terror, fear"). Samuel's high-profile creates a public spectacle, hence his earlier concern in verse 2. The prophet's exclusive invitation to Jesse and his sons should be seen in this light. This was a can't miss event.

So, It begs the question: how did Jesse *forget* David? Was it accidental or intentional? Perhaps David was considered an embarrassment or a pariah because he was *ruddy* like Esau (Genesis 25)? Or maybe his youth or employment disqualified him from the invitation and its implications? Or maybe his good looks and reputation—
. . . skillful in playing, a man of valor, a warrior, prudent in speech, and a man of good presence (v. 18)—has fueled tension and division within the family (like Joseph and his brothers, see Genesis 37)? Whatever the case, while the scripture is unclear about Jesse's motivation, the emphasis is on the divine motivation to *see*.

The word "see" (רָאָה *ra'ah*) is used repetitively in verse 7 to highlight the contrast between human perception and divine insight. David, like others at the margins of family, society, or vocation, is quite literally forgotten in the human process of discernment. Yet God sees differently. God consistently calls those who are otherwise ignored: the barren (Hannah), the enslaved (Hagar), the foreigner (Ruth), the young (David), the marginalized (Mary). Grace ignores human hierarchy. The forgotten are not forgotten by God.

> So, where are you?
>
> Who yet remains unseen in your life, in your community?
>
> How might grace be searching for you today?

Week Five

Ezekiel 37:1-14 | Where Are You?—Grieving

> **Key images:** twigs and bones (or white-painted sticks), a valley scene, a gentle wind chime
>
> **Themes:** the weight of grief, systemic death, Spirit-enabled life, vocation

The hand of the LORD came upon me, and he brought me out by the spirit of the LORD and set me down in the middle of a valley; it was full of bones. (Ezekiel 37:1)

From the perspective of the exilic community, for whom the destruction of Jerusalem and the Temple signified a total collapse of covenantal identity and eschatological expectation, these bones represent not only physical death but the theological death of hope: *Our bones are dried up, our hope is lost; we are cut off completely* (v. 11). This is a place of deep pain and anguish, where the stench of death lingers and the weight of grief will not relent.

Ezekiel is brought to this place of national grief by *the hand of the LORD* (v. 1). This phrase indicates both divine power and divine intimacy. It is not just force but guidance. God does not remain distant but walks Ezekiel into the grief. God wants Ezekiel to understand and acknowledge the totality of systemic death in this place and that God is not OK with any of it.

The dynamism of the Spirit (רוּחַ ruach) so dominates this passage that from the first verse it subverts the totality of death. The word appears ten times in this short passage and functions as the theological hinge for transformation. Though the bones are dried up (יָבֵשׁ yavesh, evoking a complete lack of vitality), the Spirit creates progressive restoration—first bone to bone, then sinews and flesh, and finally the breath of life.

And again, the Spirit guides Ezekiel through grief into full participation in this

Spirit-enabled resurrection. Perhaps the point is that death, grief, and resurrection are interconnected by the Spirit.

> So, where are you?
>
> How might the hand of Lord be guiding you and your community through grief?
>
> How might the Spirit be nudging you to prophesy to these bones that God is not OK with the systemic death within your community?

Words for Worship, Lent

Gathering

Call to Worship for Ash Wednesday
(Joseph Yoo)

Where are you, people of God? Are your hearts near to the One who created you?
We come searching for You, O Lord, longing to draw closer to Your presence.
Where are your treasures? Are they in the things of this world
    or the treasures of heaven?
We seek to store our treasures in You, where they will endure forever.
Where are you in this journey of faith? Are you ready to return to God
    with all your heart?
**With humble hearts and contrite spirits, we come to worship, to repent,
    and to be renewed.**
**Lord, here we are. Meet us in this sacred time and draw us
    into Your steadfast love.**

Opening Prayer for Ash Wednesday
(Joseph Yoo)

Let us pray:
Merciful and loving God,
As we gather on this sacred day, you ask us, "Where are you?" You call us to examine our hearts, our priorities, and our lives. Are we near to you, or have we wandered far?

Today, we confess that we have often strayed, storing up treasures that fade and seeking approval from the world instead of you. Yet, over and over, you invite us back, not with condemnation, but with grace and love.
Help us to return to you with all our hearts, to worship not with empty rituals but with sincerity and truth. Teach us to give, to pray, and to fast in ways that reflect your light in the world.
Mark us this day with the ashes of repentance and the hope of renewal. Guide us through this season of Lent to rediscover where we are—in Your love, in Your grace, and in the eternal life you offer through Jesus Christ.
In Jesus's name we pray, Amen.

Prayer of Confession: Ash Wednesday (Joel 2:12-17)
(Jackson Henry)

Merciful God,
> We come to you humbly and ask your forgiveness.
> We have made choices that offer a poor witness to your Name.
> Because of our sinful action or inaction,
>> People have likely looked upon us and asked, "Where is their God?"
> We repent of the sin we have knowingly chosen,
>> And we repent of the sin that we have inadvertently committed.
> We are tired of wandering, and we desire to return to you.
> Receive us, O God, and set us free to lovingly serve you
>> In ways that bring honor to you and our neighbors.
> We pray this in Jesus's most holy name. Amen.

Call to Worship: Where Are You, God?
(Laura Jaquith Bartlett)

Voice 1: God, where are you?
Voice 2: The God who created us is calling us to worship.
All Voices: God, we long to hear your voice.
Voice 1: Christ, where are you?
Voice 2: The Christ who leads us into discipleship is beckoning us forward.
All Voices: Christ, we long to follow your path.
Voice 1: Spirit, where are you?
Voice 2: The Holy Spirit who empowers us is blowing us into new life.
All Voices: Come, Spirit, come! Inspire our worship.

Prayer for Ash Wednesday
(Laura Jaquith Bartlett)

Gracious and merciful God,
we gather in your holy name on this holy day.

We pray that our hearts will return to you
during this season of Lent.
Where there is hunger in our neighborhoods,
may we work to feed your people.
Where there is homelessness in our communities,
may we offer shelter.
Where there is oppression in our world,
**may we choose to loosen
the bonds of injustice.**
Take our hearts and make them clean, O God.
Take our lives and make them your own. Amen.

Prayer of Confession
(Laura Jaquith Bartlett)

Return to me with all your hearts, says the Lord!
We are lost.
Help us find our way back to you, O God.
Christ has made all things new. Faith is all that is needed.
We are lost.
Help us strengthen our faith, O God.
Stop pretending humans know all the answers. Humble hearts is what God desires.
We are lost.
Help us strip away the layers of pride and pretense, O God.
New life in Christ is waiting for all those who believe.
We are lost.
Help us fully open our hearts to you, O God.

Jesus Christ stands ready to guide us back into the arms of love. Amazing grace flows abundantly, quenching our thirst and sweeping away our guilt and fear.
We lift our hearts in gratitude! Amen.

Prayer of Confession: Lent 1 (Genesis 2:15-17, 3:1-7)
(Jackson Henry)

God of mercy and grace,
>We confess that we have not followed your instruction.
>We have considered our own thoughts higher than yours,
>>We have thought of ourselves more than our neighbors,
>>We have neglected those crying for help,
>>And we have not considered how these actions have grieved your loving heart.
>We humbly ask you to not give up on us.
>Forgive us, and help us to live into the salvation we are so graciously offered,
>>For we desire to joyfully serve you.
>Amen.

Call to Worship: Lent 2 (John 3:1-17)
(Jackson Henry)

Come, people of God, and speak! Speak of the wondrous things God has done!
We will testify to God's goodness and grace!
Praise the holy Name of Jesus!
We lift up your name, O Jesus! May your glory shine in this place!
Come and believe in the hope and promise of our Savior—
The promise of new life, reconciliation, and resurrection!
May our hearts be opened and our voices ready for prayer and singing as we celebrate the gift of new birth in Jesus Christ!

Call to Worship: Lent 3 (John 4:5-42)
(Jackson Henry)

The living water is flowing! Come and drink.
The well is unending, and the water is eternally refreshing!
Drink from the water of life!
Who is it that tells us to drink? Who invites us?
The Lord Jesus Christ offers this water for us and the world.
May this water quench the thirst that runs deep within us.
Fill our cup, Lord, to overflowing! Hallelujah! Amen!

Collect: Lent 4 (1 Samuel 16:1-13)
(Jackson Henry)

Lord God,
Your gaze has pierced through the biases we have
    Toward the strong and powerful,
And you have often anointed those of low stature
    To be leaders among us.
Work within us to see as you see,
    Love as you love, and bless as you bless,
        That we might faithfully be a part of your unfolding story. Amen.

Proclaiming

Prayer for Illumination
(Laura Jaquith Bartlett)

God, we pray that our ears will be opened to hear your voice speaking through these words.
God, open our ears.

We pray that our eyes will be opened to see your vision illuminated by these words.
God, open our eyes.
We pray that our minds will be opened to understand your wisdom
contained in these words.
God, open our minds.
And we pray that our hearts will be opened to believe that in these words,
in our prayers, and in the hearts of all who are gathered together,
you are here with us today.
God, open our hearts. Amen.

Prayer for Illumination: Lent 2 (Psalm 121)
(Jackson Henry)

O Living Word, we lift up our eyes to the hills,
    wondering from where our help will come.
As we encounter the written word today,
    may we be attentive to the movement of your Holy Spirit.
Bring us to know of your loving purposes
    through the reading and hearing of the word.
Come and help us. We need you. Amen.

An Ash Wednesday Reflection
(Britney Winn Lee)

What unsustainable version of me (or my narratives, or my institutions) could use a little death today?

The little deaths that I avoid (in my avoidance of balls dropped, weakness exposed, limits left unresolved) speak directly to my relationship with big Death—
am I rested in resurrection?

Do I believe that somewhere down the road and down the calendar—maybe by hands not my own or in ways not my own or for reasons not my own—that seeds and shoots can come from soil made rich by soot?

Can I trust the long game of my own weakness?

That power is made perfect in actuality and not just poetry?
That life is gift, not granting.

Ashes to ashes, my faith makes room for my humanity today—
its limits, its mortality, its needs—maybe so, too, can I.

Thanksgiving

Prayer of Thanksgiving (John 4:5-42)
(Joseph Yoo)

Let us pray:
Gracious and ever-present God,

We come before you with grateful hearts, for you are the God who always meets us where we are. Like the Samaritan woman at the well, you see us in our thirst, our questions, and our struggles. You ask, "Where are you?"—not to shame us, but to invite us into your grace and truth.

We give thanks for the living water you offer, a wellspring of hope and eternal life that quench every longing in our hearts. In your presence, we are known fully and loved deeply. You cross every boundary to reach us, offering healing where we are broken and belonging where we feel excluded.

Thank you for the gift of Jesus, who shows us how to worship in spirit and in truth, not bound by place or tradition but rooted in the love and mercy of your kingdom. Thank you for the opportunity to leave behind the burdens of our past, like the woman leaving her jar, and to run forward with the good news of your salvation.

Where are we, Lord? We are here, at your feet, grateful for your unending grace. We are here, ready to drink deeply of the living water and to share it with others. Help us to go out as witnesses of your love, proclaiming that you are indeed the Savior of the world.
In the name of Jesus Christ, the source of all our hope and joy, we give you thanks. Amen.

Offertory Prayer: Lent 5 (Ezekiel 37:1-14)
(Jackson Henry)

God, you do amazing things! You breathe your Spirit upon a dry and thirsty land and bring the dead to life. It is only by your grace that we are able to live as new people, and we give you our thanks through this offering. Just as you make the impossible possible, take these gifts and multiply them, that they may lead to great works in your holy name. We pray this in the name of the resurrected Christ. Amen.

Prayers of Intercession
(Laura Jaquith Bartlett)

(needs two leaders; there are a number of unlit tea lights in a large bowl or basin filled with sand, visible to the congregation)

Leader 1: As we pray together for the world and all its peoples, I invite you to keep your eyes open and to look at the people around you, for we are indeed on this journey *together*. When we come to the traditional prayer petitions, I'll pause at each one so that you can silently lift up specific prayers in your heart while [*Leader 2*] lights a prayer candle. Let us pray.

God of the journey,
We pray with confidence that you will travel with us throughout these 40 days. You have marked us with the ashes of repentance, death, dust, and you have claimed us with the water of baptism, new life, hope. We praise you for being the giver of life and the victor over death.

God of the journey,
We acknowledge that all of life is sustained by you, so we pray:
    For creation and its care . . . *Leader 2 lights a tea light*
    For the nations of the world . . . *Leader 2 lights a tea light*
    For our nation and those in authority . . . *Leader 2 lights a tea light*
    For this community and its leaders . . . *Leader 2 lights a tea light*
    For the church universal, its mission, and those who minister . . . *Leader 2 lights a tea light*
    For the United Methodist Church in its struggle for justice . . . *Leader 2 lights a tea light*
    For our local parish and its ministry . . . *Leader 2 lights a tea light*
    For persons with particular needs . . . *Leader 2 lights a tea light*

We pray all this in the name of the triune God, the giver and sustainer of life. Amen.

Communion Liturgy for Lent
(Michelle L. Torigian)

God is with you!
And God is with us all.
Open wide your hearts.
We open them completely to the Spirit of God.
May God's love nurture your wandering spirits each day.
May God's light sustain your souls each night.

This is a season of wilderness.
The season we grasp to understand the Divine just a little more.
This is the time for us to reach inwards to find the self that God sees.
This is the chance for us to gaze outwards, caring for the Christ in our midst.
The Lenten roads are long
Yet full of gifts.
The Lenten paths often seem chilly
Yet warm with the winds of the Spirit.
The Spirit of God is the light that leads us in the hushed nights.
The Christ is our companion on the journey in the intense sunlight of day.
We remember his time in the wilderness-
The struggles. The hunger. The peace.
And as we seek the Divine in our midst,
On this journey, we crave the bread of life.
On our desert roads, we thirst for the fruit of the vine, the cup of blessings.

Through Jesus the Christ's story, we remember the night before his arrest,
The night of serenity, solemnity, and love.
Jesus took in his hands bread from the table.
He broke it and blessed it.
Eat in remembrance of me, he said.
And after supper,
As the night grew long,
Jesus took a cup, and filled it with the fruit of the vine.
As he blessed it, he spoke aloud to them
Take and drink and always remember me.

May the Spirit who traveled with Christ in the wilderness
And fills us with the hope of God
Surround these elements.
May the Spirit speak to us in this season of wilderness
Becoming our strength on this journey
And filling our lives with love. Amen.

Divine Light of Our Journey—
In a spirit of gratitude we give thanks for this time at your Holy Meal.
This time at the Table filled us with strength,
Knowing that as we continue on this Lenten journey,
We will find your peace surrounding us.
Amen.

Sending

Benediction (John 11:1-45 for the 5th Sunday of Lent)
(Joseph Yoo)

Go forth into the world, remembering the One who calls you by name and meets you where you are. Like Lazarus, even in the places of despair or darkness, Jesus comes to you, calling you to rise.
May you walk with the assurance that Christ is the resurrection and the life, bringing hope where there is sorrow, light where there is shadow, and life where there is death.
Go now with hearts unbound, ready to live as witnesses of God's power and love, knowing that wherever you are, God is there, offering grace and calling you forward In the name of the Father, the Son, and the Holy Spirit, go in peace to love and serve. Amen.

Dismissal with Blessing
(Laura Jaquith Bartlett)

Deacon: May God, who has forgiven us, now make us strong for these days ahead. May Jesus lead us, and we be found faithful to follow.
May the Spirit drive us into the wilderness, burning away the chaff of our lives, and purifying our hearts for all to see and be blessed.

Elder: And may the love of God, the grace of Jesus Christ, and the fellowship of the Holy Spirit be with us on our Lenten journey and remain with us always! Amen.

Holy Week and Easter Sunday

Year A Lectionary Texts

Palm/Passion	Isaiah 50:4-9a	Psalm 118:1-2, 19-29	**Matthew 21:1-11**	Matthew 26:14-27:66
Holy Monday	Isaiah 42:1-9	Psalm 36:5-11	Hebrews 9:11-15	**John 12:1-11**
Holy Tuesday	Isaiah 49:1-7	Psalm 71:1-14	1 Corinthians 1:18-31	**John 12:20-36**
Holy Wednesday	Isaiah 50:4-9a	Psalm 70	Hebrews 12:1-3	**John 13:21-32**
Maundy Thursday	Exodus 12:1-4, (5-10), 11-14	Psalm 116:1-2, 12-19	1 Corinthians 11:23-26	**John 13:1-17, 31b-35**
Good Friday	Isaiah 52:13-53:12	Psalm 22	Hebrews 10:16-25	**John 18:1-19:42**
Holy Saturday	Job 14:1-14	Psalm 31:1-4, 15-16	1 Peter 4:1-8	**Matthew 27:57-66**
Easter	Acts 10:34-43	Psalm 118:1-2, 14-24	Colossians 3:1-4	**Matthew 28:1-10**

A Framework, Themes, and Ideas for Holy Week and Easter Sunday

This section provides ideas and information to inspire planning for worship and sermons. It is based on a suggested series—a framework for worship and preaching during this liturgical season. The series idea arises from the lectionary texts and aligns with the liturgical season. You may choose to lean into the series framework fully or not at all; these ideas and words for worship will be effective whether labeled by the series name or not.

This section includes commentary plus suggestions for themes and imagery for each week. In the next section, you'll find worship words for each part of the service—Gathering, Proclaiming, Thanksgiving, and Sending.

Disrupted: A Worship Series for Holy Week and Easter Sunday

> When Jesus enters into the heart—of the city, our politics, our religion, our lives—he disrupts every power in order to restore life.

Holy Week is not a gentle stroll toward resurrection. It is a collision course with every power that resists life. As Jesus enters Jerusalem in Matthew 21 and walks through the final days of his earthly ministry in the Gospel of John, he does not conform—he disrupts. He disrupts expectations, systems, and the very powers that hold us captive—in order to restore what is broken, to make us whole, to redeem the world.

Each movement in Holy Week reveals a layer of this disruption:

- **Palm Sunday: Disrupted City**—Jesus disrupts the city, not as a warlord but as the Prince of Peace, turning triumphalism on its head.
- **Holy Monday: Disrupted Markets**—Jesus disrupts the marketplace that has encroached upon the temple, revealing the inseparable link between worship and justice.
- **Holy Tuesday: Disrupted Authority**—Jesus confronts religious leaders exposing corrosiveness of their hypocrisy.
- **Holy Wednesday: Disrupted Loyalty**—Jesus disrupts conditional loyalty, confronting betrayal not to condemn but to absorb it into redemptive love.
- **Maundy Thursday: Disrupted Religion**—Jesus disrupts religion, redefining holiness through humility, and community through service.
- **Good Friday: Disrupted Power**—Jesus disrupts power itself, revealing that death's grip is temporary, and that sacrificial love is the true seat of authority.

- **Holy Saturday: Disrupted Hope**—Jesus lies silent in death, disrupting expectations of hope without the waiting or the grieving.
- **Easter: Daybreak**—As the first rays of sunlight break the terror of night, so too the resurrection of Jesus is the earthshattering disruption we desperately need.

Though Holy Week marks the end of the Lenten season, the events of the week mark such a significant shift in narrative focus and intensity that it merits its own attention. Worship leaders may use discretion, however, in maintaining the Lenten theme through Holy Week or shifting to the series as outlined here. Though what follows does not include commentaries for Monday through Wednesday or Saturday, liturgical resources are offered to encourage devotion and meditation throughout the week.

Where possible, lean into the experiential nature of the week, allowing the scripture and the liturgy to speak independent of preaching. Invite the congregation into prayer and ritual action—i.e., walking a labyrinth, prayer stations, stations of the cross, footwashing/handwashing, anointing.

For Good Friday, invite the people to write down the powers that bind them (fear, shame, addiction, injustice, apathy) and nail these to a rough wooden cross in silence. At the end, darken the sanctuary and carry the cross out, leaving the space stripped and empty. Or host a "Vigil of Waiting" for Holy Saturday, creating space for personal or communal vigil with candles, icons, and psalms of lament. Invite the people to write letters to God about the spaces in their lives where God seems silent or absent. These can be sealed and laid at the tomb (covered table or stone symbol).

Consider ways to lean into the experiential nature of this week:

- Labyrinth Walks
- Prayer Stations
- Stations of the Cross
- Foot or Hand Washing
- Anointing

During Good Friday worship:

- Invite people to record the powers that bind them; nail these to a cross.
- End service in darkness; carry cross out, leaving space empty.

During Holy Saturday worship:

- Create space for personal and/or communal vigil.
- Light candles, place icons, or pray psalms of lament.
- Invite people to write letters telling God about the spaces where God seems absent.
- Lay letters on a table or other structure representing the tomb.

Ultimately, Holy Week becomes a mirror: *What powers govern our hearts? Our churches? Our politics? Our hopes?* Jesus does not overthrow by might but by love, and his disruptions are always for the sake of resurrection. Let this be a week of holy unrest in your congregation—a sacred disruption that leads to Easter renewal.

Palm Sunday

Matthew 21:1-11 | Disrupted City

> **Key Images:** palms/cloaks creating a pathway, donkey, a city in turmoil
>
> **Themes:** humility and peace as disruption

> When he entered Jerusalem, the whole city was in turmoil,
> asking, "Who is this?" (Matthew 21:10)

Buzzing with Passover fervor, overrun with pilgrims, and politically tense—the city was ready for something to happen. It is into this fragile landscape that Jesus rides on a borrowed donkey. The scene is pregnant with both prophetic symbolism and satirical power—with strong allusions to Zechariah's prophecy (Zech. 9:9), announcing the arrival of a king who comes in humility and peace.

Jesus's entrance is a kind of in-your-face performance art that confronts the imperialist narrative that might is right. Matthew punctuates the disruption Jesus causes to the city with the word "turmoil" or "stirred" (σείω *seio*, to shake or agitate). This word is translated later in the gospel as "earthquake," each instance symbolizing another seismic disruption to the status quo.

The city, the center of political, religious, and economic power, is put on notice: the Kingdom of God has arrived—and it does not play by your rules.

> How do we welcome Jesus when he doesn't meet our expectations?
>
> What if his peace looks like confrontation—not with others, but with us?
>
> In what ways is Jesus still disrupting the cities we build—literal and figurative?

Maundy Thursday

John 13:1-17, 31b-35 | Disrupted Community

> **Key Images:** towel and basin, foot washing, images of hospitality and service
>
> **Themes:** love and service, new commandment, servant leadership

> Having loved his own who were in the world,
> he loved them to the end. (John 13:1)

In Greek, that last phrase means to completion or to the fullest extent. This statement sets the scene understanding what is happening at the table. Jesus is giving a master-class demonstration of unconditional, self-initiated and self-giving love. And while the other gospels highlight the meal itself as the pinnacle of what happens at the table, John's gospel highlights the foot washing.

In the ancient world of dusty roads and generally open-toed footwear, foot washing was a common practice of personal hygiene and hospitality upon entering a home. Yet, Jesus disrupts both the meal and expected norms by taking the role of both host and servant and washing the disciples' feet. Jesus literally lays aside (τίθημι tithēmi) his robe—in the same way he talks about laying down his life—and he dries their feet with a towel in the same way the woman who anointed his feet dries them with her hair.

Jesus demonstrates through disruptive servanthood this self-initiated, self-giving love for everyone at the table, including his betrayer. Jesus's love is undeterred by any of the physical or relational mess that any of them bring to the table but instead welcomes and accepts them for who they are, as they are, so that they all might be loved into life.

In the upper room, power is redefined as service, and the social hierarchy is upended. The new commandment is given—not as recorded law, but as the dynamic heartbeat of Christian identity and community.

> What might the world become if we were to love others and their mess so completely and unconditionally, to the fullest extent?

Good Friday

John 18:1-19:42 | Disrupted Power

> **Key Images**: symbols of crucifixion—the cross, crown of thorns, spear, nails
>
> **Themes**: the paradox of glory through suffering

Here every form of human power is paraded and exposed—religious, political, judicial, and military. And each character in the Passion account is trapped in the machinery of power: Judas by greed, Peter by fear, Pilate by compromise, the priests by self-preservation, the crowd by propaganda.

Yet, Jesus is calm. His silence is not surrender, but judgment. His crucifixion is not defeat, but enthronement. This is Jesus's hour of glory, not shame. The cross is a throne, the inscription "King of the Jews" is ironically true, and the final words—"It is finished"—are a victory cry. Jesus disrupts the very essence of power by turning every death-dealing instrument of empire into glory.

> Where do we still bow to powers that crucify the innocent?
>
> Are we willing to see the cross as revelation of a God who reclaims every power through love?

Easter Sunday

Matthew 28:1-10 | Daybreak

As the first rays of sunlight break the terror of the night, so too the resurrection of Jesus is the earthshattering disruption we desperately need.

> **Key Images**: empty tomb, spices, signs of an earthquake, large stone, angel
>
> **Themes**: the surprise of resurrection, new creation/paradigm, disrupting fear

The women come while it is still dark—bearing grief, not hope. Perhaps they are looking for closure. Or perhaps they are looking for one more piece of empirical evidence to confirm the end of the story. Perhaps they are trying to make sense of what happened and are uncertain about what comes next. Whatever the motivation, the women come anticipating and expecting something that can help them move forward.

They expect to find a sealed tomb and a lifeless body. But instead, the earth quakes, an angel descends, and the stone is rolled away. This is not gentle reassurance but cosmic disruption. The very ground shakes (from the same root word that describes the city's disruption in Matthew 21).

The resurrection is not a private spiritual victory but an act of divine upheaval, a new Genesis. As dawn breaks over the city still heavy with Roman power and religious betrayal, a different kingdom rises with the Son of God who is already on the move—disrupting despair, commissioning women as the first apostles, and sending his disciples into the world with good news that cannot be confined.

> What if resurrection is less about fixing everything instantly, more about setting a new world in motion?
>
> How might resurrection be trembling underfoot in our own lives—hidden but rising?

Words for Worship, Holy Week and Easter Sunday

Gathering

Call to Worship: Palm/Passion Sunday
(Heather Josselyn-Cranson)

Here we stand with the disciples,
Here we stand with the donkey and her colt.
We stand, holding palm branches and shouting,
"Hosanna to the Son of David!"
We stand on a road that begins with blessings and palms,
A road that ends with crucifixion and lament.
Let us set out on this road together,
A road that leads from passion to resurrection.

Call to Worship: Palm/Passion Sunday (Isaiah 50:4-9a and Psalm 31:9-16)
(Jo Ann Cooper)

Morning by morning, the darkness is disrupted by the opportunity of a new day.
We gather to praise God, who restores our hope.
Shame is disrupted by the resolve that comes from being known by God.
We gather to praise the Christ who restores our strength.
The whispers of truth and possibilities disrupt the desire to give in or give up.
We gather to praise the Spirit of God, who restores our purpose.

Call to Worship: Monday of Holy Week
(Jo Ann Cooper)

"Lazarus come forth"
The commands of Jesus disrupt our dead ends and restore hope.
"Leave her alone"
The commands of Jesus disrupt our self-serving intentions
and restore devotion.
We begin, yet again, the journey of passion and restoration.
May the commands of Jesus fill our hearts and minds
with the fragrance of love and devotion.

Call to Worship: Tuesday of Holy Week
(Jo Ann Cooper)

Light disrupts darkness.
The Lord is our refuge. Our hope is in God.
Curiosity disrupts judgment.
The Lord is our refuge. Our hope is in God.
Compassion disrupts loneliness.
The Lord is our refuge. Our hope is in God. Always.

Call to Worship: Tuesday of Holy Week
(Heather Josselyn-Cranson)

The hour has come for the Son of Man to be glorified!
Listen!
Let us believe in the light as Children of the Light!
Pay attention!
Jesus, lifted up, draws us to himself.
We are servants of Jesus: let us follow him.

Call to Worship: Wednesday of Holy Week
(Jo Ann Cooper)

Someone is called to share in the journey of the outcast.
Lord, is it I? Let us run with perseverance.
Someone is called to speak truth to the rumors of hate and fear.
Lord, is it I? Let us not become bogged down in sin.
Someone is called to offer bread to the hungry.
Lord, is it I? Let us not forget the hunger within us.
Someone is called to love as Jesus loves.
Lord, is it I? Let us fix our eyes on Jesus.

Call to Worship: Maundy Thursday
(Jo Ann Cooper)

When trust is disrupted by betrayal and denial,
We gather to receive restoration.
When joy is disrupted by pain,
We gather to receive healing.
When new commandments disrupt traditions,
We gather to receive love.
On this night we gather to receive,
So that we might share restoration, healing, and love with the world.

Call to Worship: Maundy Thursday
(Heather Josselyn-Cranson)

Let us call on the name of the Lord!
Let us lift up the cup of salvation!
Let us offer a sacrifice of thanksgiving,
And call on God's Holy Name!
Let us hear of the Holy Supper
And share the bread and the cup.
Let us follow Jesus's example
And love as he loves us.

Good Friday: Call to Worship
(Heather Josselyn-Cranson)

Behold!
The Prince of Peace . . . taken by violent hands. Behold!
The Only Begotten Son . . . forsaken on the cross. Behold!
The Holy One of Israel . . . crucified with criminals. Behold!
The Good Shepherd . . . like a lamb led to the slaughter. Behold!
The Light of the World . . . extinguished for our sake.
Let us behold the Love of God and let us follow that Love to the cross.

Opening Prayer: Palm/Passion Sunday
(Heather Josselyn-Cranson)

God of Steadfast Love, all times are in your hands, including this holy week. Sustain us with your grace to follow Christ on his path of humble obedience. Give us the same mind that was in Jesus, so that we may journey with him from Bethphage, to Jerusalem, to the Passover table, to Gethsemane, to Golgotha, to the tomb. And strengthen our faith as we hear and remember and pray, so that at every stage of the journey, we may confess that Jesus Christ is Lord. **Amen.**

Opening Prayer: Tuesday of Holy Week
(Heather Josselyn-Cranson)

Strong Fortress and Rock of Refuge, we come to you in need of help and hope. We come, listening yet again for your power and wisdom. We come, tripping on our own stumbling blocks. We come, for our cause and our reward are with you. Draw us near and fill our mouths with praise, for you are our hope and our trust, the Living God. **Amen.**

Opening Prayer: Wednesday of Holy Week
(Heather Josselyn-Cranson)

Sustainer of the weary, give us strength to persevere as we follow your only-begotten Jesus through Holy Week. Keep our eyes on him. Fill our hearts with your love. Move our wills to take up our own crosses. Shape our lives through the hearing of your Word. Increase our trust that the joy of Easter will come after the sorrow of Good Friday. Walk with us on this road. **Amen.**

Opening Prayer: Maundy Thursday
(Heather Josselyn-Cranson)

Merciful and Eternal God, we have come to this day of remembrance, when we recall Jesus's final meal with his friends. You have given us this day as a perpetual ordinance, so that we may experience his presence with us as we marvel at his love for his disciples and for all the world. Help us not to flinch from the intimacy of foot-washing, from the solemnity of gathering around the table, from the anticipated sorrow and mystery of these Three Days. Give us strength to follow the example that Jesus set for us. **Amen.**

Opening Prayer: Good Friday
(Heather Josselyn-Cranson)

Merciful God, on this solemn day when we remember Christ's death on the cross, be not far from us. Fortify us to remain at the cross in prayer and sorrow. Help us to see and feel the immensity of your love for all the world, and for us. Give us wisdom to comprehend the mysterious paradox of divinity subjected to humility and death. Fill us with the mercy and grace we need to testify to the truth in our worship and in our lives. **Amen.**

Confession: Palm/Passion Sunday
(Heather Josselyn-Cranson)

Compassionate One, we confess to you that we are fair weather friends: we find it easy to wave palms and sing Hosannas, yet we long to turn away when the time for sorrows and sighing comes. You call us to stay awake, but we would rather take our rest. Forgive us this shallow faith. Grow in us deep roots that help us to remain by the side of Jesus throughout this week. Even more—help us to see him in all of the suffering people around the world and let our faith in him move us to compassion for them. We pray this in the name of the one who emptied himself for our sake: Jesus, the Christ. **Amen.**

(The people are invited into a brief time for silent confession)

Hear these words of assurance: being born in human likeness, Jesus knows our frailty and failings. Submitting to death on a cross, Jesus took upon himself all of our sin. Trusting in his love and sacrifice, we find forgiveness and redemption. In the name of Christ, you are forgiven!
In the name of Christ, you are forgiven! Thanks be to God!

Monday: Prayer of Confession
(Heather Josselyn-Cranson)

Merciful God, as we follow our Lord Jesus this week to the cross, we see our own failings in the light of that cross. We come to you, aware of words misspoken, kind actions not taken, and love withheld from friend and stranger. We confess our sin to you, asking that you purify our conscience in your precious steadfast love. Take away our sin, and restore us to your light, that we may serve you all our days.
(followed by silence)
Hear these words of assurance: Christ, our High Priest, offered himself to obtain eternal redemption and to purify our conscience with his blood. Having been washed clean by Jesus himself, we are a forgiven people!

Prayer of Confession: Tuesday of Holy Week
(Heather Josselyn-Cranson)

Holy One, you formed us in the womb to be your servants, and yet we turn to other masters. We look for fulfillment in money and things, in human relationships, in our work, and we forsake you. **Forgive us, redeem us.**

Forgive our distraction with all that is not You. Keep Jesus before our eyes each day of this Holy Week, that we may remember and imitate his self-giving ways. **Forgive us, redeem us.**

Cleanse our hearts, restore us, and raise us up to serve and praise you all our days. **Amen.**

Hear these words of assurance: God chose what is weak in this world to shame the strong. Christ Jesus became for us righteousness, and sanctification, and redemption. Through him, we are forgiven. **Thanks be to God!**

Prayer of Confession: Maundy Thursday
(Heather Josselyn-Cranson)

Eternal Compassion, incline your ear to hear us as we confess to you.
Jesus showed us a life of generosity **and yet we hoard.**
Jesus showed us a life of inclusion **and yet we turn others away.**

Jesus showed us a life of compassion **and yet we remain distant.**
Jesus showed us a life of love **and yet we hesitate to reach out.**
Forgive us, Loving and Merciful One, for failing to take up the example that Jesus gave. Make us bold to follow his example in our love for one another and in our love for you. In the name of Jesus, we pray. . . . *(time for silent confession)*

Hear these words of assurance: Jesus himself loves us and washes us clean. We are his, beloved and cleansed. In the name of Jesus Christ, we are forgiven!

Good Friday: Prayer of Confession
(Heather Josselyn-Cranson)

Look down, loving Jesus, look down from the cross.
Look down at our sin, our transgressions for which you were wounded.
We confess to you our iniquity.
We confess that we are not the people you have called us to be.
You set us an example of perfect love, and yet we love ourselves more than others.
You have given us a beautiful world that satisfies all our needs, and yet we have disdained the earth, taking more than we need.
You have laid your path before us, and we have all gone astray.
Look down upon us, loving Jesus, and forgive us.
Forgive us and call to us again to follow in your steps.
Strengthen us to take up our own crosses and follow you.
Silence for individual reflection and confession.

Holy Saturday: Opening Prayer
(Heather Josselyn-Cranson)

Our Rock, Our Fortress, and Our Refuge, on this day Christ rested in the tomb, the pain of crucifixion ended but the joy of resurrection not yet arrived. Give us patience to wait with Christ this day. Help us refrain from all that distracts us. Let us not rush into mindless preparation or celebration, but help us to abide in these liminal hours. Grant us hope in your steadfast love and the slow but steady unfolding of your plan for salvation. In the name of the one who suffered and died for us, **Amen.**

Proclaiming

Prayer for Illumination (Philippians 2:5-11)

God of restoration, just as Jesus emptied himself for your glory, may we empty ourselves of all that keeps us from hearing the promises and freedom your grace offers. **Amen.**

Prayer for Illumination: Maundy Thursday
(Heather Josselyn-Cranson)

Loving God, your Son Jesus is our way, our truth, and our life. As we hear about his last days from holy scripture, fill our minds with your loving truth, fill our eyes with a glimpse of your way in the world, and fill our hearts with the desire to live as Jesus lived, to the glory of your Name. **Amen.**

Solidarity: Liturgy for Stations of the Cross
(Britney Winn Lee)

Jesus Is Condemned to Death.
REFLECTION:
Condemnation is the fruit of judgment; connection is the fruit of curiosity. Condemnation is the path to an irredeemable ending; connection is a path to resurrection.
Jesus's condemners prepare to strike the gavel and sentence him to no return; Love prepared to tear the veil and rewrite the story of God's people.
But in this breath-stealing moment, Easter had not yet been. And all that was known of death was damnation. When Jesus is condemned, the world asks if anything that felt true before was really ever true.
ACTIVITY:
Use the rope or string provided to tie and unravel knots as you consider the below meditation.
MEDITATION:
What in my life feels or has felt so final that everything I knew to be true seems/seemed as if it was unraveling?

The Cross Is Laid upon Him.
REFLECTION:
Once condemned, Christ is burdened with the journey of completing his own punishment— carrying unto death the instrument of his own execution.
The crowd that once waved their branches at his entrance are jeering violence toward his exit. How fast and severe the mob's mentality can turn.
Certainly, the wood is heavy on his bruised and aching body. But surely more so is the disheartening weight of witnessing how easily Love-made-humans misidentify love, label it criminal, and convict it to be crushed. When the cross is laid upon him, the world asks how humanity can get it so devastatingly wrong?
ACTIVITY:
Use the paper and pens provided to journal a response to the following meditation. Place your paper in the bucket of water, and know that God weeps, too.
MEDITATION:
What grief or confusion have you felt when hateful and violent things have been done in the name of love?

His First Fall.
REFLECTION:
Here, there is no question: God is a human. A human hurting, a human humiliated, a human humbled beneath the grain of the wood and the chants of the people.
Here, there is no question: God is with us. Jesus not only stands in solidarity with creation, he crumbles in solidarity with us, too—crouched and dirty, helpless and halted.
We are known. What it means to exist in this kind of place as this kind of person is known. The gasp that comes with stumbling, the slow-motion of falling, the feeling of eyes onlooking, the wounded wonder about whether or not you have it in you to rise. When Jesus falls for the first time, the world gets the sense that God understands.
ACTIVITY:
Using markers, write on the provided tile one word responses to the following meditation.
MEDITATION:
There are times in our lives when we physically, mentally, emotionally, and/or spiritually lose our footing. Think about some of those times for you. What words would you describe how it feels on the way down?

He Meets His Mother Mary.
REFLECTION:
Is there a more excruciating pain than to watch that which we birthed suffer and die while we can do nothing to stop it? Whether that which was birthed be a child, a home, a dream.
We pause with Mary here, and we bear witness longer than is comfortable to both the pain and its layers. God who birthed Mary was birthed by Mary to save Mary from death by going into death as Jesus.
God and humanity connect in this moment over what it means to birth life that can be loved and lost, to birth life worth dying for. Here, we have the most intimate and vulnerable connection—every parent or parent figure who has lost a child to disease or injustice, every person who has wished they could take the place of those who suffer, but can't. When Jesus meets his mother Mary, the world is met with the deepest empathy of the Divine Parent.
ACTIVITY:
Spend some time observing the provided pictures of the Madonna and child as you consider the following meditation.
MEDITATION:
What has been the history of my reactions to this kind of impossible pain or the fear of it? Do I run, avoid, self-medicate, distract, consume, fight, abandon, freeze? How does it feel to know that there is nowhere in the human experience that God hasn't gone, including here?

Simon of Cyrene Is Made to Bear the Cross.
REFLECTION:
Simon, how does this moment feel to you? Do you fear that you have somehow been declared guilty by association and will meet your end, too? Do you worry that you are now complicit in his killing?
Do you wish you had more in you to do more for him, for the world? Does it feel like this is a meaningless drop in the bucket of righting the wrongs of humanity? Your service was not nothing. We will remember your kindness. This moment was not nothing. For a few seconds, you helped love keep going. When Simon of Cyrene is made to bear the cross, the world asks if we have anything to offer?
ACTIVITY:
Use the next few minutes to send a text (or write a postcard using the paper provided) to someone who is carrying impossible grief or despair.
MEDITATION:
Do I believe that this moment is not nothing, that even for a few seconds it is worth it to help love keep going?

Jesus's Face Is Wiped by Veronica.
REFLECTION:
In the legend of the Stations of the Cross, Jesus is met on his journey to death by a woman of Jerusalem named Veronica who wipes the blood, sweat, and surely tears from his face.
She dignifies him amid his most undignifying moment, offers comfort though he is overwhelmed with pain, clears his sight when all that is ahead is Golgotha. Like care given at hospice bedsides and art made for war torn cities, it matters.
The story says the image of Christ's face was left marked upon her cloth. In honoring his worth in his very moment of extreme weakness, Veronica (her name meaning "true image") has shown us what it means to bear the image of God.
When Jesus's face is wiped by Veronica, the world asks if it is this image we also bear and this worth we also maintain no matter the extent of our pain or weakness?
ACTIVITY:
While feeling the textures of the provided cloth, spend some time reflecting in the mirror beside it and on the following meditation.
MEDITATION:
Do I believe that no matter what, no matter when, I bear the image of God and am worthy of love? Do I believe this of my neighbor, stranger, and enemy as well?

His Second Fall.
REFLECTION:
If his first fall threatened our minds, it is Jesus's second fall that threatens our spirits—our energy to believe in a comeback has been halved, our anxiety that God may be breaking down has been multiplied.

If the first fall threatens our momentum, it is the second fall that threatens our hope—we question if this is the pattern, the future, the way of things from here on out.

Those who have relapsed in recovery, received bad news in remission, or tried again every Monday and every January and every rock-bottom for years, know this gut-sinking feeling. When Jesus falls for a second time, the world asks if hope can convalesce, if it has a reason to.

ACTIVITY:
Look through the toolbox provided with tools labeled "people I can ask for help," "boundaries," "possible different endings," "self care," and "spiritual practices," "the Holy Spirit" while considering the following meditation.

MEDITATION:
When in my life have I experienced a second (third, fourth, 80th) fall? What tools do I need in my toolbox to keep going?

He Meets the Women of Jerusalem.

REFLECTION:
"Wail not for me, sisters, but for yourselves and for Jerusalem." Jesus, as the legend goes, has encountered his inconsolable followers, and for good reason they are destroyed by his suffering.

Is anything more difficult than zooming out from the acute pain of love threatened, lost, or destroyed? Does anything feel bigger or more important or deserving of our time, grief, and attention?

But here, Jesus invites the women into a deeper, holistic consideration—there is more going on. Love is not destroyed, love will keep going, love will win. But grieve for the humans who destroy themselves in their attempts to destroy love. When Jesus meets the women, the world is reminded who may need what we know of love when tragedy has passed.

ACTIVITY: Use the pictures of the sky below and consider the different ways you would respond to the following meditation depending on what picture's perspective you are taking.

MEDITATION:
From these different perspectives, how would I describe the sky? How does it change the more I zoom out? What does that make me think or feel about our perspectives of pain or of God?

His Third Fall.

REFLECTION:
This is the road's end. There's nowhere else to go, no one else to become, nothing else to give or try or say or grasp onto.

His disciples are in hiding. His mother is traumatized. His body has reached its limits, his beloved creation has made him the despised enemy.

Everything we thought he would bring, everything we needed him to be, all the freedom and peace and joy and love we hoped that God would realize in the Kingdom be talked about is on the ground. When Jesus falls for the third time, the world asks "was the Good News not good enough to last?"
ACTIVITY:
Blow out the candle in front of you and sit with the below meditation for a moment. Before you leave, light it again for the next person.
MEDITATION:
When have I felt hopeless, like the last thing I was holding onto had crumbled? What did I learn about myself and/or about God then?

He Is Stripped of His Garments.
REFLECTION:
It is one thing to be in pain, it is another to be exposed—pain on display is a whole new level of vulnerability. Jesus's has never been more vulnerable than now. But in tearing his clothes, two things take place. Not only is God humiliated—any ounce of dignity pulled apart and made into a game for soldiers—but his humiliators are also exposed.
With no covering, the crowd must come to terms with what they'd just done. We cannot harm another without something being harmed in us as well; when we kill, something in us dies. When Jesus is stripped of his garments, the world must face what it is capable of.
ACTIVITY:
Use the cloth to tear strips. As you tie them to the wire provided, consider the following meditation.
MEDITATION:
When have I no longer been able to hide my pain or the pain I have caused?

He Is Crucified.
REFLECTION:
Has the jeering subsided with the crowd falling away? Are they holding their breath wondering if they took it all too far?
Does something in them know that this is God, that he is good, that a mistake has been made? Is the abuse of power doubling down as its loyalists begin to waiver?
Is all that can be heard a pounding hammer? An uncontrollable sniffle? The groans of the criminals dying above him? The thud of the wood sliding into place? The haunting howl of a man executed by the state? When Jesus is crucified, the world stops.
ACTIVITY:
Use the hammer and wood provided to beat a rhythm into the space as you think about the meditation below.

MEDITATION:
Can I close my eyes and imagine I'm there? What are the sounds, smells, sights? What do I feel in my body and spirit?

He Dies on the Cross.
REFLECTION:
It is finished. It is finished. Forgive them, Father, and today you'll be with me in paradise, and you're each others' family now, and God why have you forsaken me, and I'm thirsty, and . . .
It is finished. It's finished? Surely not. Surely we'll wake up from this nightmare. Surely this is a part of it all. Surely his chest will rise any second now. Any second now . . . any second . . .
But it doesn't. It's over. It's all . . . over. When he dies on the cross, the world asks if death is the end? If it is the point?
ACTIVITY: Close your eyes and breathe deeply.
MEDITATION: No prompt, just be.

His Body Is Taken Down from the Cross.
REFLECTION:
In entering this world as a refugee, Christ is birthed into a borrowed manger. In leaving this world through public lynching, Christ is laid into a borrowed tomb. Creator-made-vulnerable has now received the sweetest expressions of human hospitality and the vilest versions of our rejection. Emmanuel, God-with-us, has indeed been.
Like prayers at an unmarked migrant's grave, pilgrimages to the Tallahatchie River, vigils after bombings, and liturgies written for everyday injustices and forgiveness—when his body is taken down from the cross, the world practices resistance in honoring our dead and declaring that another world must be possible.
ACTIVITY:
Use the stones provided to make an "altar of remembrance" while meditating on the words below.
MEDITATION:
Can I bring to mind a person or people group whose lives were stolen by the hands of injustice? Can I honor the image of God in them; can I ask for strength to honor the image of God in their oppressor, as I acknowledge and offer mercy to both the wounder and wounded within me?

His Body Is Laid in the Tomb.
REFLECTION:
One last offering—let's imagine what that might have been like. One last offering of cloth and herb, oil and water.

They didn't know what would come next. And yet they knew that it mattered to die well. To meet death (even a traumatic and devastating one) with space, ritual, beauty, care, time, company, nurture, and love. To give what we could until we couldn't give anymore.

To posture ourselves with the trust that even if this is in fact the end, we will make sure that the end will have meaning and be rooted in relationships. When his body is laid in the tomb, the world is shown what it means to help someone or something die well.

ACTIVITY:
Opening your palms and closing your eyes, rest in the words below for as long as you need.

MEDITATION:
Where in my life have I seen a beautiful death? What in my life is difficult to let "die well?" Can I offer it to God today?
Because death is not the end. See you Sunday.

Thanksgiving

Monday: Intercessions
(Heather Josselyn-Cranson)

Let us lift our thanks and our petitions to God, praying:
We take refuge in the shadow of your wings.
We give thanks, Loving God, for the eternal redemption
you offer us through your Son Jesus:
We take refuge in the shadow of your wings.
We ask that, in your merciful grace, you would pour your light
into our hearts so that we can better imitate Jesus's self-giving love:
We take refuge in the shadow of your wings.
We pray for family, friends, and members of this congregation
who suffer and are in need of your healing touch:
We take refuge in the shadow of your wings.
We pray for the Church, that you would fill it with
the fragrance of your holiness and truth:
We take refuge in the shadow of your wings.
We pray for the nations of the world, where people wait for your justice and mercy:
We take refuge in the shadow of your wings.
We pray for all who have gone before us, whose lives we remember, whose love we imitate, and who are now restored in the eternal river of your delight:
We take refuge in the shadow of your wings.
Finally, we pray to you the prayer of our Brother Jesus, who lived as a servant and taught us to pray, saying
Our Father. . . .

Monday: Offertory Prayer
(Heather Josselyn-Cranson)

Eternal God, you are always working in the world to bring light, and justice, and everlasting redemption to all. We thank you that you invite us to participate in this work. We offer you these gifts, praying that you would make our offering a greater and more perfect means for doing your work. In addition to this financial gift, we offer you our lives, following the one who offered himself without blemish to you. In his name we pray: **Amen.**

Wednesday of Holy Week: Intercessions
(Heather Josselyn-Cranson)

Lord God, our Help and Deliverer, we pray to you, **Do not delay!**
Remember the least and lost, and all who cry to you for help: **Do not delay!**
Speak peace into the hearts of all who lead: **Do not delay!**
Touch the ill and hurting with your healing hands: **Do not delay!**
Bring the lonely into community where they can find love and joy: **Do not delay!**
Give guidance and courage to the young: **Do not delay!**
Give wisdom and acceptance to the aged: **Do not delay!**
Move in the hearts of all your followers, to act in ways that spread your reign throughout the world: **Do not delay!**
Hear the cries of our hearts and the prayers of our lips, O Lord God, our Help and Deliverer. **Do not delay!**

Good Friday Intercessions
(Heather Josselyn-Cranson)

Crucified God, hear our prayers:
We pray for the strength and maturity to walk Jesus's way of forgiveness, letting go of hurts and grievances and entrusting all to your divine justice which is always tempered by mercy.
Father, forgive them for they know not what they do.
We pray for all those who are imprisoned, oppressed, alone, and afraid. We pray for those in need who do not see an end to the violence and misery in which they live.
My God, my God, why have you forsaken me?
We pray for the loving kindness to walk Jesus's way of compassion, that we would see all people are members of our family, and that we would extend your love to them.
Woman, here is your son. Here is your mother.
We pray for the understanding to walk in Jesus's way of wisdom, turning to you for guidance in all things.
Father, into your hands I commend my spirit!
We pray for those who lack healthy food, clean water, and safe shelter. We pray that those with too much would learn to live with less, that there could be enough for all.
I am thirsty.

We pray for all who have come to the end of their time on earth: those who have died surrounded by family and those who have died alone, those who have died full of days and those who have died far too young.
It is finished.
We pray, even on this solemn day, for the hope that you promise us: the hope of abundant life, of steadfast love, and of resurrection. We thank you for this hope and pray that we may be bearers of hope to all those around us. Finally, we pray in the hope that we will one day dwell with you, in the heavenly Jerusalem.
Truly, I tell you, today you will be with me in Paradise. Amen.

Holy Saturday: Intercessions
(Heather Josselyn-Cranson)

Refuge of Love, hear our prayers:
We call and cry for help!
We see friends and family who are sick and suffering *(pause to lift up individual names)* . . . touch them with your healing grace.
We call and cry for help!
We see communities where some are marginalized and mistreated *(pause for specific situations)* . . . bring your justice upon the earth.
We call and cry for help!
We hear of war and violence where too many innocent people die *(pause for specific locations)* . . . let your reign of peace begin.
We call and cry for help!
We live in a society that promotes selfishness and short-sightedness *(pause for particular concerns)* . . . put your own Spirit within us.
We call and cry for help!
We repeat the cruelty that Christ suffered, having learned nothing from his life and his death *(pause)* . . . open our ears and our hearts to his Passion, that we would be changed by his love and sacrifice.
We call and cry for help!
Remembering him, and all that he taught us, we dare to lift up to you, O God, the words he taught us to pray:
Our Father . . .

The Great Thanksgiving for Holy Week
(Jo Ann Cooper)

The Lord be with you.
And also with you.
Lift up your hearts.
We lift them up to the Lord.
Let us give thanks to the Lord our God.
It is right to give our thanks and praise.

It is right, and a good and joyful thing, always and everywhere, to give thanks to You, Almighty God, Creator of heaven and earth. In the tension of what has been and what will be, you meet us in this moment. While our minds reel from all that disrupts our comfort, you remind us that we are created in your image. You replace our comfort with courage and bring peace to the tension. Just as Jesus knew his purpose was to love fully, you provide your love for us.

And so, with Your people on earth and all the company of heaven, we praise Your name and join their unending hymn: **Holy, holy, holy Lord, God of power and might, heaven and earth are full of Your glory. Hosanna in the highest. Blessed is the One who comes in the name of the Lord. Hosanna in the highest.**

Holy are You, and blessed is Your Son, Jesus Christ, who disrupts our traditions with the invitation to notice the needs around us. As Jesus washes the feet of his disciples, he teaches us to show our love for one another in intentional ways. He reminds us that when we welcome one another, it is as though we are welcoming him. It is how we love with the love of Jesus.

It is because of such love Jesus left the Upper Room that night and humbled himself in obedience to your will by freely accepting death on the cross. By the baptism of His suffering, death, and resurrection, You gave birth to Your Church, delivered us from slavery to sin and death, and made with us a new covenant by water and the Spirit.

On the night in which he gave himself . . .
[*continue as printed in UMC Book of Worship*]

Great Thanksgiving for Palm/Passion Sunday
(Heather Josselyn-Cranson)

The Lord be with you.
And also with you.
Lift up your hearts!
We lift them up to the Lord.
Let us give thanks to the Lord our God.
It is right to give our thanks and praise.

It is right to give thanks and praise, to sing our Hosannas and raise our palm branches to you, Creator of all that is and Sustainer of all who live. You made all people in your image and open to us the Gates of Righteousness. Again and again, we turn away to other roads, and again and again, you set our faces in the right direction. For your eternal compassion, for the never-ending grace that you offer

us, and for the way you have shepherded your people throughout time, we raise our voices with your children across the centuries and around the world, singing:
Holy, holy, holy Lord, God of power and might,
Heaven and earth are full of your glory.
Hosanna in the highest.
Blessed is he who comes in the name of the Lord.
Hosanna in the highest.

Holy are you, and blessed is the One who came in your name, Jesus Christ.
Born in humility, he taught obedience in word and deed:
Gathering with fishermen rather than princes,
Riding on a donkey rather than a war horse,
Preaching selflessness rather than greed,
Embracing death on a cross rather than life on a throne.

At table with his friends, on the night when he was betrayed by one of them,
Jesus took a loaf of bread, and after praying to you and blessing it, he broke it,
Gave it to his disciples, and said "Take, eat, this is my body."

Then he took a cup, and after giving thanks to you, he gave it to his friends, saying, "Drink from this, all of you, for this is my blood of the covenant, which is poured out for many for the forgiveness of sins."

Remembering his life of humility, his love and teaching,
his final meal with his disciples, and his sacrifice for our sake,
We offer you these gifts of bread and cup,
And we offer you ourselves, just as we are,
Singing the tremendous mystery we have been taught:
Christ has died; Christ is risen; Christ will come again!

Pour down, loving God, your Holy Spirit on this bread,
on this cup, on these people.
Feed us now with the very body and blood of your Son,
Just as you make us into the body of Christ which can feed
a hungry and hurting world.
Knit us together in communion with you, with one another, and with all creation,
singing our Hosannas in expectation of that coming Day
when all people will dwell with you,
And death and mourning and crying will be no more.
Hosanna to the Son of David!
Hosanna to the God of Justice and Love!
Hosanna! Amen!

(to be followed by the Lord's Prayer, Breaking of the Bread, and giving of the elements to the people)

Great Thanksgiving for Maundy Thursday
(Heather Josselyn-Cranson)

The Lord be with you.
And also with you.
Lift up your hearts!
We lift them up to the Lord.
Let us give thanks to the Lord our God.
It is right to give our thanks and praise.

It is right to give thanks to you, Loving God, at all times and places,
for you have created, nurtured, and saved your people time and again:
When we were enslaved in Egypt, you gave us the Passover Feast
and rescued us from bondage.
When we were hungry in the wilderness, you sent down manna to feed us.
When we were exiled from home, you invited us to delight ourselves in rich food.
Whenever we find ourselves in need, you prepare a table for us and comfort us.

And so, for your never-ceasing compassion and care-taking,
we sing as we gather around this table:
Holy, holy, holy Lord, God of power and might,
Heaven and earth are full of your glory.
Hosanna in the highest.
Blessed is he who comes in the name of the Lord.
Hosanna in the highest.

Blessed are you, and blessed is your son Jesus.
He shared meals with his disciples on the shore and in the home.
He told parables comparing the Kingdom of God to a banquet.
He taught us that he is the source of our nourishment and promised us freedom
from hunger and thirst.
At his last meal with his disciples, celebrating a supper together before the Passover,
Jesus shared the bread and the cup with his beloved friends. They remembered his
words to them: "The bread of God is that which comes down from heaven and
gives life to the world . . . I am the bread of life." *(raise the loaf)* "I am the true vine
. . . as the Father has loved me, so I have loved you; abide in my love." *(raise the cup)*

Remembering his love, his meal, his sacrifice, and his glory, we offer you, O God,
this sacrifice of thanksgiving as we proclaim our Lord's death until he comes again:

Christ has died, Christ is risen, Christ will come again!

Eternal God, whose son commanded us to love one another, we pray that you
would anoint this celebration with your own Spirit, that this would truly be a
communion of love. In this holy meal, knit us together in love and fellowship.

Feed us with the body of your Son so that we may be his body for the world, ready to share his love with all in need.

Glory to you, God of Love, and glory to your Son, whose meal we share together, and glory to the Spirit—One God, now and forever. **Amen.**

(to be followed by the Lord's Prayer, Breaking of the Bread, and giving of the elements to the people)

Sending

A Week Where Transformation Will Meet You (A Holy Week Benediction)

And now, my friends, go forth
To a week where transformation
Will meet you and guide you.
Do not hide when they recognize you,
Do not doubt when you see Christ,
Do not deny when you are confronted.
Do not stop until you are at the cross
And there you will see the light
And the burdens of your heart will roll away.
Until then God be with you! Amen.
—B. Kevin Smalls, *Africana Worship Book, Year B*

Maundy Thursday: Low Enough to Wash Dirty Feet

As you depart, remember Jesus Christ, who bent down low enough to wash dirty feet and gave his disciples a new commandment to love one another. May all glory, honor, and dominion be his in this world and in our lives, now and forever more. Amen.
—Kwasi I. Kena, *Africana Worship Book, Year B*

A Sending

The Lord who heals all your iniquity bless and keep you;
    the face of the Lord who heals all your afflictions
        shine upon you and be gracious to you;
    the light of the countenance of the Lord who redeems your life
        be lifted upon you and give you peace. Amen.
—*The United Methodist Book of Worship*

EASTERTIDE

Year A Lectionary Texts

Redemption Songs	Acts 2:14a, 22-32	**Psalm 16**	1 Peter 1:3-9	John 20:19-31
Redemption Songs	Acts 2:14a, 36-41	**Psalm 116:1-4, 12-19**	1 Peter 1:17-23	Luke 24:13-35
Redemption Songs	Acts 2:42-47	**Psalm 23**	1 Peter 2:19-25	John 10:1-10
Redemption Songs	Acts 7:55-60	**Psalm 31:1-5, 15-16**	1 Peter 2:2-10	John 14:1-14
Redemption Songs	Acts 17:22-31	**Psalm 66:8-20**	1 Peter 3:13-22	John 14:15-21
Redemption Songs	Acts 1:1-11	**Psalm 47**	Ephesians 1:15-23	Luke 24:44-53
Redemption Songs	Acts 1:6-14	**Psalm 68:1-10, 32-35**	1 Peter 4:12-14; 5:6-11	John 17:1-11

A Framework, Themes, and Ideas for Eastertide

This section provides ideas and information to inspire planning for worship and sermons. It is based on a suggested series—a framework for worship and preaching during this liturgical season. The series idea arises from the lectionary texts and aligns with the liturgical season. You may choose to lean into the series framework fully or not at all; these ideas and words for worship will be effective whether labeled by the series name or not.

This section includes commentary plus suggestions for themes and imagery for each week. In the next section, you'll find worship words for each part of the service—Gathering, Proclaiming, Thanksgiving, and Sending.

Redemption Songs: A Worship Series for Eastertide

> When resurrection dawns on the weary, songs of hope announce the arrival of a better story, a better life, a new creation.

Won't you help to sing these songs of freedom?
'Cause all I ever have—redemption songs . . .
—Bob Marley, "Redemption Song"

The enduring legacy and power of Marley's song lies in its timeliness and relevance. Written near the end of his life, and in view of both personal and systemic oppression, the song speaks of both a longing for freedom and power to attain it. This power lies in the community's willingness to sing the *songs of freedom*. The singing itself becomes both resistance and redemption.

In the glow of the empty tomb, the Psalms become songs of freedom—giving melody to a new kind of life made possible by the resurrection. They are redemption songs—poetic witnesses to God's enduring faithfulness, compassion, and renewal. They carry the tension of lament and praise, yearning and fulfillment, weariness and wonder. These ancient songs don't just remember past deliverance; they proclaim a better future breaking in. We are to be more than readers, but singers joining the chorus of the redeemed.

Focusing exclusively on the psalm readings for the Easter season, the series seeks to uncover how each Psalm sings of hope rising among the ruins, of a world being remade, and of people learning to trust joy again. Rather than naïve praises, they are hard-won hallelujahs, grounded in suffering and resurrected in love.

Take care to contextualize the Psalms for your community:

- Invite artists to participate, and provide support for their work.
- Include artists who are not regularly part of a church.
- Host a concert or exhibit featuring the artists.
- Facilitate singing these songs of freedom for your community.

In keeping with the theme, each lection is intentionally paired with a more secular song. The hope is that the series awakens the ability to find *redemption* everywhere—thus widening the scope of the possible. That said, care should be taken for how these songs may need to be contextualized for your community, musically or pastorally. Use the popularity of some of the songs as an opportunity to invite and support artists from your surrounding community—especially those who may not regularly participate in Christian worship. Consider hosting a concert featuring these artists at the close of the series—whether as a benefit concert for some mission or a paid concert to support the local artist community. However it happens, the key is to galvanize the communal call to *sing these songs of freedom.*

This Easter, let the Psalmist lead, as resurrection begins to reorient us toward God's unfolding new creation.

Week One (Second Sunday After Easter)

Psalm 16 | Redemption Songs: Fix You

> **Key images**: lights lighting a path, hands open in surrender, a sunrise
>
> **Themes**: God as refuge and steady joy, trust in God

> You make known to me the path of life; in your presence
> there is fullness of joy. (Psalm 16:11)

The verses of "Fix You" by Coldplay provide an emotional reflection on what it feels like to walk in the dark—*When you feel so tired, but you can't sleep, stuck in reverse.* Written for someone in the throes of grief, it gives voice to the anguish of waiting to feel better. In turn the chorus gives answer with a glimmer of hope to a weary soul—*Lights will guide you home, and ignite your bones, and I will try to fix you.* With repetition the chorus moves from a glimmer into an anthemic declaration.

So too, Psalm 16 is a quiet declaration of confidence—a kind of resurrection vow—for someone who has walked the edge of despair and chosen to trust God anew. It functions liturgically as a "night song," grounding joy in God's faithful presence in the dark.

Resisting the anxiety of self-reliance, the psalmist confesses: *You are my* Lord; *I have no good apart from you* (v. 2). The word "good" (טוֹב *tov*) carries the Genesis resonance of God's creative verdict—life as it was meant to be. Resurrection reawakens the *tov* of creation.

In verse 9 the phrase for "my body also rests secure" includes the word *betach* (בֶּטַח), meaning to dwell in confident safety. This is not mere survival but resurrection rest. Resurrection doesn't remove every shadow—but it changes how we walk through the night.

| What are the lights guiding you home?

Week Two (Third Sunday After Easter)

Psalm 116:1-4, 12-19 | Redemption Songs: No Love Dying Here

> **Key images**: Hands raised with a cup; thread or rope frayed and broken; an ear listening attentively
>
> **Themes**: gratitude for God's mercy, testimony and witness

I love the LORD because he has heard my voice and my supplications. (Psalm 116:1)

Written as a defense of the staying power of love, the song "No Love Dying Here" narrates all the little ways in which the specter of death creeps into ordinary life. Yet, defiantly Porter reframes each slight and pang into a declaration: *Well the death of love is everywhere, but I won't let it be / There will be no love that's dying here for me.* Love known, experienced, and shared provides the lens to see that all is never lost.

Psalm 116 is a testimony of survival, voiced by someone who faced death and lived to tell of God's mercy. It is raw, remembered, yet relit with gratitude. The opening verb, *ahav* (אָהַב), usually reserved for deep relational love, signals a personal transformation. God didn't just act—God heard.

Though not included in the reading, verse 7 provides a grounding for gratitude. *Return, O my soul, to your rest* is both a command and a confession. It implies that the soul wandered in turmoil, disoriented by suffering or fear. Yet the word for "rest" (מְנוּחָה *menuchah*), evokes not sleep, but soulful settledness—a return to the deep center where we remember that God has not abandoned us.

This moment of rest comes not from resignation but from realization: *"for the LORD has dealt bountifully with you."* The word translated "dealt," refers to how one deals with a child—nurturing, weaning, bringing to maturity. It connotes kindness measured over time. This is not merely rescue; it is the re-training of the soul in how to live again.

This psalm is a resurrection of the nervous system, not just of the spirit. It gives permission to breathe again, and to believe that joy doesn't require urgency—it can be still.

> What personal or communal testimony are we being called to share this Easter season?
>
> Where and in what ways do we need to proclaim there will be no love dying here?

Week Three (Fourth Sunday After Easter)

Psalm 23 | Redemption Songs: Safe and Sound

> **Key images**: A shepherd's crook; a table set in wilderness; shadow giving way to light
>
> **Themes**: God's presence and providence

> Even though I walk through the valley of the shadow
> of death, I will fear no evil (Psalm 23:4)

This beloved psalm needs no embellishment; yet within the context of Easter, it takes on heightened depth. The shepherd imagery invites reflection on God as both protector and presence. The phrase traditionally rendered as *shadow of death* (צַלְמָוֶת *tsalmawet*) can also mean deep darkness. More than mortal danger, it speaks to every form of despair.

Redemption here is not loud or flashy—it is the quiet comfort of being known, accompanied, and fed. The song "Safe and Sound" by Taylor Swift offers a fitting reflection:

> Just close your eyes, the sun is going down
> Come morning light, you and I'll be safe and sound

> Who walks through shadows right now and needs to hear "you'll be alright, no one can hurt you now"?

Week Four (Fifth Sunday After Easter)

Psalm 31:1-5, 15-16 | Redemption Songs: Let It Be

> **Key images**: open hands painted or sculpted, a fortress or rock of refuge
>
> **Themes**: Trusting God, worry and anxiety

> Into your hand I commit my spirit. (Psalm 31:5)

This psalm is a raw and reverent act of trust amid pain. Threatened, cornered, and anxious—the psalmist carries the voice of one stretched thin between peril and praise. Yet their response is not despair, but release. In verse 5, the Hebrew word *aphqid* (אַפְקִיד "I entrust/commit") is the same used for placing something in safekeeping—a conscious, willing release of what one cannot control. Similarly, the phrase "into your hand," implies radical surrender—not resignation, but entrusting. This is a redemption song sung in real time, where nothing is wasted when it is entrusted into God's care.

The classic song "Let It Be" by The Beatles captures this spirit. Written as a response to an anxiety-riddled dream, the words "Let it be" became a phrase not of resignation, but of trustful surrender in a time of personal and cultural crisis. This not a passive giving-up, but a prayerful openness to something beyond us—a wisdom that comes when striving ceases and grace is allowed to speak.

Psalm 31 and "Let It Be" both speak to the human impulse to cling tightly in crisis. But they invite us into a better posture: open hands, open hearts. Such openness is an act of hope, not hopelessness.

> How does your community discern the difference between passive resignation and spiritual release?
>
> What does it mean to place our spirit, our life, our time into God's hands?

Week Five (Sixth Sunday After Easter)

Psalm 66:8-20 | Redemption Songs: Rise Up

> **Key images**: symbols of praise and celebration, communal footprints, flames and waves
>
> **Themes**: testimony and witness, deliverance and rescue, gratitude

> . . . we went through fire and through water; yet you have brought us out to a spacious place. (Psalm 66:12)

Psalm 66 is communal testimony. It is a shout of collective deliverance, grounded in memory. The phrase "fire and water" recalls Exodus imagery and evokes collective trauma overcome. "A spacious place" (רְוָיָה *revaya*) is perhaps more literally translated as "saturation that results in overflow." It is the same word used in Psalm 23:5—"my cup overflows." Redemption leads not just to relief, but to absurd abundance.

This communal abundance enables the shift from "we" to "I" in v. 13, signaling personal witness born out of shared history. The community's praise and experience of God's faithfulness emboldens and encourages the psalmist's own faith—[*God] has not rejected my prayer or removed his steadfast love from me*. Such is the power of communal testimony.

Andra Day's song "Rise Up" echoes this power:

> All we need, all we need is hope
> And for that we have each other . . .

How can the church bear witness to resurrection hope beyond these walls?

Are we giving space to name both the "fire and water" and the God who brought us out?

The Ascension of the Lord

Psalm 47 | Redemption Songs: Higher Love

Key images: trumpet blasts, festival images, clapping hands, released balloons

Themes: The reign of God, Christ's ascension

God has gone up with a shout, the LORD with the sound of a trumpet (Psalm 68:5)

This royal enthronement psalm is a jubilant hymn to God's reign over all nations. It is structured around a call to praise (vv. 1–2), a description of God's absolute rule (vv. 3–4), a liturgical exclamation of ascent (v. 5), and a universal invitation to praise (vv. 6–9). The repetition of the verb "sing praises" (זַמְּרוּ *zammeru*) five times in verses 6–7 creates a crescendo of joyful acclamation. The final stanza shifts from Israel-centered language to a more universal frame, indicating an expansive theological vision.

The psalm functions as a theological pivot—declaring that the joy of redemption is not private, but points to God's rightful reign over all creation. It invites the worshiping community to expand its vision—from soul-level peace to global, joyful submission to God's rule. This psalm reminds us that redemption is not just about being saved from distress but about participating in a new order—one defined by worship, joy, and God's reign *on earth as it is in heaven*. As the song "Higher Love" declares:

> Bring me a higher love . . .
> Where's that higher love, I keep thinking of?

How do our lives "sing praises" in a world that often resists joy?

Where are we being sent now that Christ has ascended and sent us in his name?

Week Six (Seventh Sunday After Easter)

Psalm 68:1-10, 32-35 | Redemption Songs: Glory

> **Key images**: Mountaintop clouds, a throne of mercy, rain falling gently on dry ground.
>
> **Themes**: justice, joy and generosity, reign of God

You ascended on high, leading captives in your train (Psalm 68:18)

Psalm 68 is another enthronement hymn, thunderous in tone. It portrays God as a victorious warrior-king, but also as "father of orphans and protector of widows" (v. 5). The paradox is powerful: God's strength is expressed in care for the vulnerable. This is reinforced in verse 9 with the image of God raining down abundance (נָטַף *nataph*, meaning to drip or distill)—a poetic picture of divine generosity.

Paul will later quote verse 18 in Ephesians 4:8 as both prophecy of Christ's ascension and confirmation of resurrection's impact on everyday life. The One who ascends also descends in order to *fill all things*—all peoples—with gifts of grace. There is no separation here between God's transcendence and tenderness.

Psalm 68 is a redemption song of a people who have been lifted, gathered, sheltered, empowered. It ends with an invitation: "Sing to God, O kingdoms of the earth." The vision and its implications are more than just personal salvation—it is a cosmic uprising of justice, praise, and joy.

The song "Glory" from the motion picture *Selma* captures this intersection of justice, praise, and joy:

> And we'll fight on to the finish, then when it's all done
> We'll cry glory, oh glory

> Where do we see God "rising" in the world today—not in domination, but in liberation?
>
> Who in our community needs the "rain of generosity" today?

Words for Worship, Holy Week and Eastertide

Gathering

Call to Worship (2nd Sunday of Easter)
(Felicia Patton)

Bless the Lord who gives us counsel! Jesus calls us to be at his right hand for, in him, there are pleasures forevermore. Let us worship in Christ today! Amen

Call to Worship (2nd Sunday of Easter)
(John Thornburg)

As we gather today, we face a choice.
We have said that God is our choice.
We have said that in God's presence there is always joy.
We have said that God is our truest guide.
Now we must ask, "Do we mean it?"
We must see how serious we are.
With confidence, let us explore just how good God is;
And in doing that, may we experience real joy.

Call to Worship (3rd Sunday of Easter)
(Felicia Patton)

Lord hear us as we call on your name! Let our praise ring up to you and never cease! As we join in worship, may your matchless name be lifted high. Amen

Call to Worship (3rd Sunday of Easter)
(John Thornburg)

God's ears are always turned toward us.
God listens every moment, every hour, every day.
So, if we cry out, God will hear us and come to our aid.
What can we possibly do to show our gratitude?
Here and now, in each other's presence, we can express our love to God.
Here and now, we can promise to be the people God is calling us to be.
The time is now.
The time is now!

Call to Worship (4th Sunday of Easter)
(Felicia Patton)

The Lord is our shepherd. Open the gates to salvation through your sacrifice on the cross. We offer you unending praise for we are healed by your wounds. On the cross you delivered us. Amen.

Call to Worship (4th Sunday of Easter)
(John Thornburg)

Friends, God is our shepherd.
God provides us with food to eat and water to drink.
God is our shepherd.
God gives us shelter.
God is our shepherd.
God gives us life itself. We lack nothing.
Life is not a reward we have earned.
It is the pure gift of the God who loves us.
As we worship today, let us look for ways to love like God loves.
We will be watching and listening.

Proclaiming

Prayer for Illumination (2nd Sunday of Easter)
(Felicia Patton)

Ever-present God; You are our protection from dangers seen and unseen. You are our refuge. Show us the path that we must take in life. Stay beside us, guide us, and keep us so we never depart from your joy. We thank you for your goodness and faithfulness. Amen.

Prayer for Illumination (2nd Sunday of Easter)
(John Thornburg)

Eternal God, as we listen for your word,
even in the midst of life's endless distractions,
capture us; convict us; convert us; surprise us; and renew us. Amen.

Prayer for Illumination (3rd Sunday of Easter)
(Felicia Patton)

Lord, hear our prayers. Hear our cries as we lift up to you all that entangles us. Free our minds from the overwhelming cloudiness of distress and despair. Listen to our voices as we cry out to you, Lord save us. You are where we find peace and mercy. Let your presence be the solace to our pain. Amen.

Prayer for Illumination (3rd Sunday of Easter)
(John Thornburg)

Eternal God, as the scriptures are read, help us listen the way you listen. Help us hear what you are really saying; not what we wish you were saying. Give us true ears to hear your truth. Amen.

Prayer for Illumination (4th Sunday of Easter)
(Felicia Patton)

Lord, as our shepherd you lead us. Open the gates to your will for our lives. Restore our souls and lead us on your righteous path. Lead us through your gates, where salvation lies. May we never enter the gates of thieves and robbers and join you in salvation.
Make the pathway straight. May we dwell in your house forever. Amen.

Prayer for Illumination (4th Sunday of Easter)
(John Thornburg)

Life-giving God, as we listen for your word,
sharpen all of our senses,
so that with every cell of our being,
we can understand what you are saying to us today. Amen.

Thanksgiving

Offertory Prayer (2nd Sunday of Easter)
(Felicia Patton)

Lord, we give thanks for the gifts you have provided for us. Please bless the gifts we give back to you. You are our portion. You gave your life in sacrifice to us on the cross, and now we sacrifice in order to enrich your kingdom on Earth. The gifts we give are but a portion of what you have sacrificed to us, and through this, your goodness will be spread amongst the least of these. We give these gifts freely as you have given all of yourself to us. Amen.

Offertory Prayer (2nd Sunday of Easter)
(John Thornburg)

Life-giving God, you are the source of every good thing we have. We do not want to think about life without you. Your love is hope-producing and despair-crushing. In you, we feel secure, even when we are surrounded by cloudy, threatening skies. As we bring our gifts to you, fill us with the gladness that we are returning something to you. Help us search our hearts for how to be more and more generous, so we can be more like you. Amen.

Offertory Prayer (3rd Sunday of Easter)
(Felicia Patton)

What shall I return to the Lord for all his goodness to me? This sacrifice is but a portion of what you sacrificed for me on the cross. Through your sacrifice, the chains of sin have been lifted off of me, and I am free through your death and resurrection. I vow to you, O Lord, to give you a sacrificial offering of thanks in the presence of your people. With joy in my heart, I will fulfill my vow to you. Praise the Lord! Amen.

Offertory Prayer (3rd Sunday of Easter)
(John Thornburg)

Life-giving God, the story of your generosity is infinite, deep, and awesome. We want to reach toward others the way you reach toward us. We know that your love is sacrificial, and that is what we want ours to be. Remove whatever separates us from being as generous as you. Break open our hearts so we can hear and love the broken-hearted among us, just as Jesus did. We pray in Jesus's name. Amen..

Offertory Prayer (4th Sunday of Easter)
(Felicia Patton)

Lord, through your sacrifice on the cross, we feel your unyielding love and devotion to us. You have led us into your gates where we shall not want. It is now our chance to be a channel for your love. May we devote our lives to cheerful giving to others and praising your name. Create in us a clean heart, protect us, and guide us in your way. May we give to those in need, as you have given to us. Amen.

Offertory Prayer (4th Sunday of Easter)
(John Thornburg)

Gracious and Eternal God, you give us everything we need, and in our better moments, we remember that and give you thanks. But when we are in our hardest moments, we often forget that you are still present; still feeding and anointing us.

Give us the insight, the wisdom and the courage to believe that you are the source of everything in every moment and make us more steadfast in our generosity. Amen.

Ritual of Healing for Isolation
(Lisa Hancock)

So often, we think of rituals of healing as addressing specific physical or mental health challenges. The following healing ritual draws on "A Service of Healing I" from The United Methodist Book of Worship with a focus toward the healing of isolation in congregations and communities. Depending on the logistics of your space, **consider whether you want to include anointing with oil with the laying on of hands** as congregants come forward during the ritual. A blessing is included for both possibilities. Since this is a ritual for healing isolation, **have two leaders— either clergy or laypersons—at each station** so that more than one person is involved in the laying on of hands/blessing of each congregant. During the closing blessing, **encourage congregants to hold hands with their neighbors** in the pews or **look at one another while reading the closing blessing** as a way of embodying support and togetherness as healing antidotes to isolation.

Invitation to Healing

Beloved children of the Good Shepherd,
we come knowing that something is not right.
We live in a world that isolates us from one another,
that tells us it's everyone out for themselves.
We feel forced to carry our burdens alone,
to not name what we need,
or to feel shame when we acknowledge our vulnerability.
We have been scattered not just from our Shepherd,
but from the flock.
And so, let us come together now
to seek God's healing touch.
Let us gather in this space like a family
gathering around the table to bless one another
and reclaim our place in the flock
of Jesus Christ, our Shepherd and Guardian.

Prayer for Communal Healing

Healing God,
In the midst of our busy lives,
the stresses, burdens, and challenges
we face day in and day out,
we miss the silent wounds that we carry

from our lack of connection to one another.
Heal us, God, from disconnection and isolation.
Bind us together and build in us a community
of support and encouragement.
Help us be for one another the Body of Christ,
tending one another as we are tended by you.
Amen.
If you are not using oil, skip to Prayers for Healing.

Thanksgiving over the Oil
Merciful God,
We give thanks to you for the gift of oil.
As your apostles anointed many who were sick and healed them,
pour out your Holy Spirit on us and on this gift,
that in turning away from isolation and toward belonging as
family in Christ, the wounds of our disconnection may be healed;
through Jesus Christ our Lord. **Amen.**

Prayers for Healing
Invite congregants to come forward for anointing or laying on of hands at one of the stations provided. Include two people at each station. If possible, allow enough space for congregants to pray at the altar after receiving anointing or blessing.

Consider singing one or more of the following hymns as people come forward for anointing/blessing: "Lord Jesus Christ, your light shines," (Worship and Song 3137); "My Shepherd Will Supply My Need," (Psalms for All Seasons 23A, Glory to God 80); "O Christ, the Healer" (United Methodist Hymnal 265).

Prayer for Anointing
For each congregant receiving anointing, one person lays a hand on the congregant's shoulder while the other anoints the individual, saying:
I anoint you with oil
in the name of the Father, and of the Son, and of the Holy Spirit.
May God heal your wounds of isolation so that you may find your home
in the love of God and the fellowship of the Body of Christ. Amen.

Prayer for Laying on of Hands
For each congregant who comes forward, each person at the station lays a hand on the individual's shoulder, while one says:
We lay our hands on you
in the name of the Father, and of the Son, and of the Holy Spirit.
May God heal your wounds of isolation so that you may find your home
in the love of God and the fellowship of the Body of Christ. Amen.

Prayer after Anointing/Laying on of Hands
Once all who came forward have returned to their seats, invite congregants to either join hands or look one another in the eye as you say this prayer together.
Almighty God,
We pray that each of us may be comforted in our suffering
and made whole.
When we are afraid, give us courage to reach toward one another;
when we feel weak, grant us the strength to name our vulnerability;
when we are afflicted, help us persevere together;
when we are lost, show us how to offer one another hope;
when we are alone, move us to come alongside one another.
In the name of Jesus Christ, we pray. Amen.
—adapted from "A Service of Healing I," "Thanksgiving and Communion," "Dismissal with Blessing"

Sending

Benediction
(Lisa Hancock)

Remember this: the world will tell you the best response to suffering is to turn away. Yet the Guardian of our souls came near to our suffering and calls us to do the same. As you leave this place, how will you be a healing companion with your neighbors who are suffering, isolated, and struggling? May you go in peace to bring peace to all you meet. **Amen.**

Pentecost and Trinity Sunday

Year A Lectionary Texts

| So Come | Acts 2:1-21 | Psalm 104:24-34, 35b | 1 Corinthians 12:3b-13 | John 7:37-39 |
| So Come | Genesis 1:1-2:4a | Psalm 8 | 2 Corinthians 13:11-13 | Matthew 28:16-20 |

A Framework, Themes, and Ideas for Pentecost and Trinity Sunday

This section provides ideas and information to inspire planning for worship and sermons. It is based on a suggested series—a framework for worship and preaching during this liturgical season. The series idea arises from the lectionary texts and aligns with the liturgical season. You may choose to lean into the series framework fully or not at all; these ideas and words for worship will be effective whether labeled by the series name or not.

This section includes commentary plus suggestions for themes and imagery for each week. In the next section, you'll find worship words for each part of the service—Gathering, Proclaiming, Thanksgiving, and Sending.

So Come: A Worship Series for Pentecost and Trinity Sunday

> The Holy Spirit confirms the great promise through Jesus that "God is with us." So, come and step into the life of the Spirit.

At the intersection of Pentecost and Trinity Sunday, the Church pauses to consider both the power of God's presence and the pattern of God's nature. We sit in the holy tension between inviting God's Spirit and responding to Christ's call. These moments are not separate—they are two sides of one divine rhythm: the Spirit comes, and we come alive; the Triune God sends, and we are drawn into mission.

In "So Come," we explore the holy rhythm of invitation: we call upon the presence of the Living God, and we hear Christ's invitation to come and be sent. As the Spirit descends and the Triune God commissions, we are drawn into a grace-filled movement of presence and participation—God with us, and us with God—for the sake of the world.

The phrase "So Come" becomes a prayer, a summons, and a commission:

- *So come, Holy Spirit*—as thirst meets Living Water.
- *So come, follow me*—as worship turns into witness.

Rooted in John 7:37-39 (Pentecost) and Matthew 28:16-20 (Trinity Sunday), the series speaks to our deep spiritual thirst, the transforming presence of the Spirit, and the commissioning call of the risen Christ. Worship leaders should consider ways to invite worshippers to name their thirsts—as individuals and as a community. Consider creating a prayer wall or station where people can write a one-line invitation: "Come, Holy Spirit, into _____." This could be done prior to worship or during the prayers of the people. Or consider offering a time for people to come forward to a central bowl or fount of water, touch it, and whisper a personal "So come . . ." prayer.

Likewise, highlighting the Spirit's empowerment for ministry, commission everyone as "Sent Ones" at the end of worship. Perhaps lay hands on one another in pews or offer anointing with oil or water to "go in the name of the Triune God." This could also be done to highlight and bless ongoing ministries of the congregation, specific mission partnerships, or other community partners.

Taken together, the texts for both Sundays bookend a movement from inward longing to outward sending—from spiritual empowerment to holy responsibility. They reveal the generous heart of

---

Invite worshippers to name their thirsts:

- Create a prayer wall or station where people can write a one-line invitation: "Come, Holy Spirit, into _____."

- Invite people to come to a central bowl of water, touch it, and offer personal prayer.

God, who not only dwells with us but draws us into divine relationship and purpose. In a world fractured by disconnection, anxiety, and a crisis of meaning, the Church must become a community that thirsts for the Spirit and responds to Christ's call with boldness. "So Come" is both our longing and our mission—it names the relationship between the Spirit who dwells within and the Christ who calls us beyond ourselves. *So come, Holy Spirit. So come, Church.*

Highlight the Spirit's empowerment for ministry:

- Commission all as "Sent Ones."
- Lay hands on one another in pews.
- Offer anointing with oil or water to "go in the name of the Triune God."

Highlight and bless ministries, mission partnerships, and other community partners.

Pentecost Sunday

John 7:37-39 | So Come and Receive

> "Let anyone who is thirsty come to me, and let the one who believes in me drink. As the scripture has said, 'Out of the believer's heart shall flow rivers of living water.'" (John 7:37-38)

This passage takes place during the Festival of Tabernacles, a time when the Jewish people celebrated God's provision in the wilderness and prayed for future rains. On the last day of the festival, the high priest would pour water—often from the Pool of Siloam—onto the altar as a libation, symbolizing both past provision and the hope of the Spirit's outpouring in the age to come.

Jesus interrupts this ritual, declaring Himself as the true source of living water—the fulfillment of what the festival anticipated. In ancient Jewish thought, "living water" (ζῶν *zōn*, meaning "living, active, life-giving") referred to flowing, fresh water (as opposed to stale, stagnant). Jesus's words are bold—he doesn't just point to the ritual; he fulfills it. He invites all who are thirsty to come to him and drink. And this living water is not just for personal refreshment—it will flow out of believers to quench the thirst of the world *(see 1 Corinthians 12)*.

Verse 39 clarifies that this is about the Holy Spirit, whom Jesus's followers would receive after his glorification. Pentecost is the fulfillment of this promise—the moment when the Spirit is poured out like a rushing river, filling and transforming the Church *(see Acts 2)*. And key to this transformation is Jesus's invitation to *come to me* (erchesthō pros me), meaning "be moving continuously toward me, for me". Pentecost is not a one-time event. Instead, we are called to continually come to Jesus for the Spirit's renewal, so that through Jesus we might participate in the renewal of the world.

In this way, the Holy Spirit is not an abstract presence—it is living water, flowing to and through believers, renewing and refreshing all who receive it. Jesus invites us to come and drink deeply, so that we might also become sources of life for others. In his *Meditations of the Heart,* Howard Thurman expounds on the water metaphor to crystalize how we might engage with the Spirit:

> The dominant trend of a (person's) life may take on the characteristics of a canal, reservoir or swamp. The important accent is on the dominant trend. There are some lives that seem ever to be channels, canals through which things flow . . . If you are a canal, what kind of things do you connect?
>
> Or are you a reservoir? Are you a resource which may be drawn upon in times of others' needs and your own as well? Are you a swamp? Are you always reaching for more and more, hoarding whatever comes your way as your special belongings? If so, do you wonder why you are friendless, why the things you touch seem ever to decay? A swamp is a place where living things often sicken and die. The water in a swamp has no outlet. Canal, reservoir, or swamp—WHICH?

Trinity Sunday

Matthew 28:16-20 | So Come and Go

> And Jesus came and said to them, "All authority in heaven and on earth has been given to me. Go therefore . . ." (Matthew 28:18-19)

This passage, often called "The Great Commission," is both a sending and a promise. The disciples are commanded to go—to make disciples, baptize, and teach—but their going is anchored in the assurance that Jesus is with them.

Of note is the action that happens in this passage. It is not a static scene, rather it is marked by the movement of discipleship. Just as the disciples come to meet Jesus in v. 16, Jesus draws near to them in v. 18 and commands them in v. 19 to keep going (Πορευθέντες, poreuthentes, meaning "as you go" rather than a one-time command). Thus is the way of discipleship—the seamless flow of coming and going centered, grounded and empowered by the presence of Jesus. And so, the disciples are commissioned to both a practice and a task: instruct other apprentices in this way.

The ground of Christian hope and the dynamism of the church lies within the sure and real promise of the presence of God through Christ Jesus by the Holy Spirit. And the church's witness is emboldened because the presence of the Lord is undeterred, uncontrolled and unrepressed by neither our worship nor our doubt. Whereas Pentecost Sunday emphasizes coming to drink of the Spirit, Trinity Sunday emphasizes going in the power of the Spirit. The Christian life is both a receiving and a sending through the Spirit.

In your community, how have you seen the Holy Spirit as both an indwelling presence and an outflowing power?

In what ways might you need to step into this flow of discipleship—of receiving and giving, of coming and going?

So come, Holy Spirit. So come, Church.

Words for Worship, Pentecost and Trinity Sunday

Gathering

Call to Worship for the Day of Pentecost
(C. Scott Maderer)

How many are your works, Lord!
Your works are beyond number!
All look to you.
Your gifts are beyond number!
ALL: May the glory of the Lord endure forever

Pentecost Call to Worship
(Scot Bontrager)

Rivers of living waters will flow from the hearts of Believers!
Come, Holy Spirit, Come!
Let all who are thirsty come to the font!
Come, Holy Spirit, Come!
We who are one in the body of Christ, we share in the One Spirit!
Come, Holy Spirit, Come!
So Come, all who believe! Come, worship the one who gives us life!
Come, Holy Spirit, Come!

Call to Worship for Trinity Sunday
(C. Scott Maderer)

When we were children we talked, thought, and reasoned as children.
But we are not called to remain children.
We are called to put our childhood behind us and know fully.
Because Love is the greatest gift of all.

Opening Prayer for Pentecost
(Eleanor Colvin)

Come, Holy Spirit come,
Come when we welcome you. Come when we desperately beckon you.
Come when you are uninvited and interrupt us.
Come Spirit and disrupt us.

Pour over us,
Pour into us,
Such wind and fire
That people will wonder what new wine we are drinking.
Come Holy Spirit, inspire our thinking.
Until we think as you think.
Come Holy Spirit, enliven our actions.
Until we act as you act.
Holy Spirit, you are welcome here.
Amen.

Opening Prayer for the Day of Pentecost
(C. Scott Maderer)

O God, we come to worship you.
We gather as those who are thirsty.
O God, we come to worship you.
We gather as those who seek your living water.
O God we come to worship you.
We gather together to receive your Spirit.
O God we come to worship you.
We gather together to pour out your Spirit.

Opening Prayer for Trinity Sunday
(C. Scott Maderer)

Father God when you call us to the mountain we worship you even as we doubt.
We recognize that you have authority given to you even as we doubt.
You challenge us to GO and make disciples even as we doubt.
You are with us even as we doubt.

Confession and Assurance for the Day of Pentecost
(C. Scott Maderer)

God of flowing water. You provided water for the Israelites in the wilderness. But we thirst again. You provided manna from heaven for the Israelites in the

wilderness. But we grow hungry again. You promise us to give us the bread of heaven through the gift of the Spirit. Yet we still find ourselves when receiving the great gifts you give us hoarding them selfishly. Not allowing the river of living water to flow through us, but rather becoming a dam that holds back the flow of your Spirit to others.
Hear this good news Jesus said. "Let anyone who is thirsty come to me and drink." we but have to ask to receive the living water.

Confession and Assurance for Trinity Sunday
(C. Scott Maderer)
Lord God, you know our hearts and minds better than we know ourselves. Lord when we are but children in your eyes let us recognize and put that childhood behind us. Let us be honest to ourselves and others and have the courage to recognize what you call us to in our relationship with you. Let us have to courage to live a life of love that calls others to you. Be patient with us as we struggle without our doubts and fears. We pray this in your holy name, Amen.

Beloved of God hear the good news: Even when you doubt Christ is with you always, to the very end of the age.

Proclaiming

Prayer for Illumination
(C. Scott Maderer)
Lord, all too often we fail to allow the Spirit to act through us to spread your living water. Let us open our eyes, our ears, and most of all our hearts to allow your Spirit to act through us so we can hear your Word today. Amen.

Prayer for Illumination
(C. Scott Maderer)
Lord, let us receive your Word today with the confidence to walk with you in all things. Let us have ears to hear, eyes to see, and the courage to follow you.

Thanksgiving

Pentecost Offertory Prayer
(Scot Bontrager)
Sister Holy Spirit, Lord, Giver of Life, you have given us innumerable gifts. Some you have called to be pastors and overseers, others you have called to be teachers, prophets, and interpreters. You have filled us with faith, hope, and love. You have

inspired us, breathed through us, and stirred us to action. We cannot know where you will blow, or what you will do next, but we stand ready to be a part of your mighty works in the world. Inspire us once again. Give us the gifts we need for your mission today. Unite us into one body.

We ask that you bless the offering that we are about to receive. Inspire us with your spirit of generosity and abundance. Help us to give as freely as you give to us. Awaken in us a sense of your abiding presence in our lives, removing all doubt that you are working in and through us. Cast aside our fears and let your love flow through us as we work share your mighty presence with the last, the lost, and the least in the world.

Offertory Prayer
(C. Scott Maderer)

Heavenly Father, receive these gifts that we lift up to you. Let each of us give over our gifts for the common good. Though there are different kinds of gifts, there is but one Spirit. Though there are different kinds of service, there is but one Lord.

Offertory Prayer
(C. Scott Maderer)

Heavenly Father, accept these gifts as we bring them before you with hearts filled with the Holy Spirit. Use these gifts to continue to let us go and make disciples of all nations. Amen.

Pentecost Great Thanksgiving
(Scot Bontrager)

The Lord be with you.
And also with you.

Lift up your hearts.

The pastor may lift hands and keep them raised.

We lift them up to the Lord.

Let us give thanks to the Lord our God.
It is right to give our thanks and praise.

It is right, and a good and joyful thing,
always and everywhere to give thanks to you,

Father Almighty (almighty God), creator of heaven and earth.

When all things were formless and void, your Holy Spirit brooded over the deep waters. In a breath all things came into being. With a word, you proclaimed them good and very good.

You loved us into existence. You showed us how to love. Your love sustained us as we grew. But we turned away and our love failed. Your love remained steadfast, burning ever brighter for our salvation.

You sent prophets filled with your Spirit to call us home.
In fire and wind you made covenant. In silence you spoke the truth. You sent Miriam to sing inspired songs that led your people to the land. You empowered Deborah to judge Your people and give the land rest.

And so, with your people on earth and all the company of heaven, we praise your name and join their unending hymn:

The pastor may lower hands.

Holy, holy, holy Lord, God of power and might,
heaven and earth are full of your glory. Hosanna in the highest. Blessed is he who comes in the name of the Lord. Hosanna in the highest.

The pastor may raise hands.

Holy are you and blessed is your Son, Our Lord, Jesus Christ, the one who was filled with the power of the Holy Spirit. The one with whom you are well-pleased.

In the power of the Spirit he fed the hungry, healed the sick, gave sight to the blind, and proclaimed release to the captives. His love flowed forth like a river. He showed us true justice and compassion. He perfected the law. And with his light yoke, he gave us rest.

By the baptism of his suffering, death, and resurrection you gave birth to your Church, delivered us from slavery to sin and death, and made with us a new covenant by water and the Spirit.

The same Spirit which filled him filled his disciples, empowering them to do the same mighty acts. She filled the early Church, sending Mary to proclaim the resurrection, Priscilla and Chloë to judge the congregations, and Lydia to lead the leaders.

The pastor may hold hands, palms down, over the bread, or touch the bread, or lift the bread.

On the night in which he gave himself up for us, he took bread,
gave thanks to you, broke the bread, gave it to his disciples, and said:
"Take, eat; this is my body which is given for you.
Do this in remembrance of me."

The pastor may hold hands, palms down, over the cup, or touch the cup, or lift the cup.

When the supper was over he took the cup,
gave thanks to you, gave it to his disciples, and said:
"Drink from this, all of you; this is my blood of the new covenant,
poured out for you and for many for the forgiveness of sins.
Do this, as often as you drink it, in remembrance of me."

The pastor may raise hands.

And so, in remembrance of these your mighty acts in Jesus Christ,
we offer ourselves in praise and thanksgiving,
as a holy and living sacrifice, in union with Christ's offering for us,
as we proclaim the mystery of faith.
Christ has died; Christ is risen; Christ will come again.

The pastor may hold hands, palms down, over the bread and cup.

Pour out your Holy Spirit on us gathered here,
and on these gifts of bread and wine.
Make them be for us the body and blood of Christ,
that we may be for the world the body of Christ, redeemed by his blood.

The pastor may raise hands.

By your Spirit make us one with Christ,
one with each other, and one in ministry to all the world. Inspire and enflame us.
Fill us with love. Empower us to do the work that is before us, until Christ comes
in final victory, and we feast at his heavenly banquet.
Through your Son Jesus Christ, with the Holy Spirit in your holy Church, all honor
and glory is yours, almighty Father (God), now and forever.
Amen.

Sending

Who Will Go?

When Jesus says "Follow me," who will go?
Here am I! Send me!
When the Spirit summons, who will go?
Here am I! Send me!
When the Lord calls who will go?
Here am I! Send me!
Here am I! Send me!
—Tony Peterson, *Africana Worship Book, Year B*

A Sending

Now to him who by the power at work within us
is able to accomplish abundantly far more
than all we can ask or imagine,
to him be glory in the church and in Christ Jesus
to all generations, forever and ever. Amen.
—Ephesians 3:20-21 NRSVue

After Pentecost

Year A Lectionary Texts

I Will	**Genesis 12:1-9**	Psalm 33:1-12	Romans 4:13-25	Matthew 9:9-13, 18-26
I Will	**Genesis 18:1-15**	Psalm 116:1-2, 12-19	Romans 5:1-8	Matthew 9:35-10:8, (9-23)
I Will	**Genesis 21:8-21**	Psalm 86:1-10, 16-17 or Psalm 17	Romans 6:1b-11	Matthew 10:24-39
I Will	**Genesis 22:1-14**	Psalm 13	Romans 6:12-23	Matthew 10:40-42

A Framework, Themes, and Ideas for After Pentecost

This section provides ideas and information to inspire planning for worship and sermons. It is based on a suggested series—a framework for worship and preaching during this liturgical season. The series idea arises from the lectionary texts and aligns with the liturgical season. You may choose to lean into the series framework fully or not at all; these ideas and words for worship will be effective whether labeled by the series name or not.

This section includes commentary plus suggestions for themes and imagery for each week. In the next section, you'll find worship words for each part of the service—Gathering, Proclaiming, Thanksgiving, and Sending.

I Will: A Worship Series for After Pentecost

> God's promises evoke the daring of faith in Abraham, Sarah,
> Hagar, Ishmael, and Isaac—and in each of us.

What really is the strength of a promise if not the strength of the relationship between the giver and receiver? That distance between the two is spanned by an intricate web of vulnerability and trust—the necessary infrastructure of any promise spoken or expected. A promise is an act of self-giving sacrifice that ultimately leaves the giver vulnerable. For the receiver, a promise is a dare to reject other potential sources of provision to trust the giver, itself an act of vulnerability. The stronger the promise, the stronger the vulnerability.

Following the semi-continuous pattern for the lectionary, the Old Testament readings for the 2nd-5th Sundays after Pentecost narrate from Genesis the foundational stories of the Abrahamic covenant—the call of Abram, the promise of Isaac, a blessing for Hagar and Ishmael, and the binding of Isaac. The tension in each of these stories is both heightened and resolved by God's promise as expressed by the repeated phrase "I will." And in each instance, it is God's "I will . . ." that enables the others' response of the same.

Is this not God's economy of grace—God moves towards us, and we respond by moving toward God and others? And it is within the crucible of the improbable—where the strength of God's promise meets the truth of our vulnerability—that transformation occurs and blessings are born.

Worship leaders should lean into the wordplay of "I Will," which raises questions about faithfulness and trust—whether in God or each other. Consider reframing each "I Will" statement for each character, for example:

Lean into the wordplay of "I Will":

- Create a pattern of reframing God's "I Will" statements

- Offer an "I Will" statement for each character in response to God's promises

- Genesis 12 | "I will bless you." (God)—
  "I will go to bless others." (Abram/Sarai)

- Genesis 18 | "I will surely return." (God)—
  "I will trust and believe." (Abraham/Sarah)

- Genesis 21 | "I will hear you." (God)—
  "I will cry out for justice." (Ishmael/Hagar)

- Genesis 22 | "I will be faithful." (God)—
  "I will surrender." (Abraham/Isaac)

To aide in enlivening the complexities of each story, consider having one or two persons act out the text while it is read. These could be persons of any age who, with minimal yet intentional preparation, could help dramatize the text with emotional expression that can better demonstrate the nuances of each text. Likewise, it may be helpful to focus on a particular character in each story—named or unnamed—and use their perspective to engage the scripture afresh.

Throughout these readings, we see a pattern: **God's promises evoke faith. But faith is not static; it is daring, sometimes difficult, and always transformative**. And so, Abram believed, Sarah laughed, Ishmael cried, Hagar persisted, and Isaac questioned—all entrusting themselves to a promise made strong through vulnerability. Lord, teach us the strength of your promise!

To enliven the complexities of each story, dramatize the text:

- One or two persons may act out the text while it is read.
- Actors express the emotional nuances.
- Focus on a particular character in each story.
- Use their perspective to engage the text in new ways.

Week One

Genesis 12:1-9 | "I will bless you."

> **Key Images**: tent, travel implements, caravan, altar, an oak tree
>
> **Themes:** calling, leaving, trust, obedience, uncertainty, promise, blessing, offspring

> I will make of you a great nation, and I will bless you and make your name great, so that you will be a blessing. I will bless those who bless you, and the one who curses you I will curse, and in you all the families of the earth shall be blessed." (Genesis 12:2-3)

We are not given a whole lot of detail about Abram's life upfront, suggesting he is an average, unremarkable person whose life is interrupted when God calls him into a new life in a new land with a new purpose. The call is to "go" (לֶךְ־לְךָ *lekh-lekha*), an emphatic phrase implying a sense of urgency to the need and command to get going. And notice that before a destination is given, God emphatically tells him what he must leave behind: . . . *your country and your kindred and your father's house* . . .

God invites Abram into a relationship of trust and radical obedience that becomes the paradigm for faithful discipleship. The implication is that blessing requires absolute dependence upon God alone. And God's promise is that the going in faith will be greater than the leaving of certainty.

God gives Abram six interrelated promises (v.2-3), all connected by the concept of "bless" (ברך *barak*) which implies divine favor that results in flourishing. The Divine plan and impetus for Abram's call is for blessing to so define his life that everyone—literally, all the people of the earth—will be blessed through him. God's call and invitation to Abram is to leave the world he knows behind to envision and establish a new world marked by blessing.

It's worth noting that Abram's father, Terah, had apparently tried to do this earlier (see Genesis 11:31-32). While there is no reason given and no divine mandate, we are left to assume that for whatever reason Terah became convinced that where they were was not the place they needed to be and that the land of Canaan was a better country to call home. And so, Terah packs up the family and heads to Canaan—but something happens, and he settles.

Maybe the journey was too long or the road too difficult. Maybe the resources were running out. Maybe others around him convinced him the struggle wasn't worth it. Maybe he began to doubt whether a new start for a new life was possible.

This our story too. Like Terah, though we may catch a glimpse of a better place of possibility—figurative and literal, as soon as we start the journey, we are confronted with all the reasons why we should just settle for where we are. Yet like Abram, God invites us into a daring of faith that leads to the kind of blessing that is not just personal but extends to the world.

| God will lead. Will we trust?

Week Two

Genesis 18:1-15 | "I will surely return."

> **Key Images:** oak tree, bread, milk, tent, meal preparation, table setting
>
> **Themes:** hospitality, trust, doubt, laughter, promise, fertility, blessing, impossibility, covenant

> The LORD said to Abraham, "Why did Sarah laugh and say, 'Shall I indeed bear a child, now that I am old?' Is anything too wonderful for the LORD? At the set time I will return to you, in due season, and Sarah shall have a son." (Genesis 18:13-14)

The passage opens with another theophany, this time at the "oak of Moreh" in Shechem, likely a sacred site of divine revelation for the Canaanites which has been appropriated now for the Abrahamic story (see Genesis 12:6). Though Abraham recognizes the three men collectively as God, it is uncertain if one of them is the Lord and the others mere angels. Regardless, Abraham's actions in v. 2-8, highlight the Ancient Near Eastern sacred duty of hospitality. The food prepared is a lavish feast—some estimate three seahs to approximate 22 gallons—highlighting the extravagance of the hospitality. This will be sharply contrasted with the inhospitality of Sodom in Genesis 19.

As their story unfolds it becomes clear that the expected sign and proof of God's faithfulness, and consequently the most profound tension in their story, consists entirely in the improbable birth of children to this otherwise old couple. In this way, Abraham and Sarah stand as archetypes for everyone who feels that the most promising thing in life is also what causes the most tension and conflict. Perhaps the issue of children for these would-be parents isn't merely a question of biological possibilities but more so of adequacy, capacity and faith. Instead of trusting the power behind the promise, they are fixated on the probability of the problem.

In v. 9 the visitors make it clear that they have come for Sarah, emphasizing that this story of covenant promise and faithfulness has always been about both Abraham and Sarah. Sarah has been central to the divine plan to literally and figuratively birth both a nation and a promise. Like Hagar and all the women that follow in this story of God and God's people, Sarah is as much a recipient and progenitor of God's blessing and covenant as Abraham.

Though the differences between chapters 17 and 18 may reflect differing editorial priorities, the narrative juxtaposition is striking, as Abraham is the first to laugh—specifically, at the notion that God would also bless Sarah (see Genesis 17:17-18). Not only does he laugh but he insists that God should not bless Sarah but rather Ishmael—presumably because Sarah is not worth the time or effort. It seems that Abraham doesn't believe in Sarah or, perhaps worse, he doesn't believe that God could use Sarah to fulfill the covenant promise. Could Abraham's lack of faith in her be the reason why she also laughs? Afterall, she considers herself "old" (בָּלָה, balah), a term meaning "worn out, decayed, or used up."

> "I will return to you . . ." is God's promise to every Sarah who feels left out or forgotten in their own story. And if God shows up for her—or you, or me—whom else would God show up for?
>
> Who will I show up for?

Week Three

Genesis 21:8-21 | "I will hear you."

Key Images: feast, celebration, laughter, wilderness, weeping, water

Themes: laughter, rejection, promise, provision, blessing, covenant, compassion

> Come, lift up the boy and hold him fast with your hand, for
> I will make a great nation of him. (Genesis 21:18)

This is now the second telling of the blessing of Hagar and Ishmael (see Genesis 16), which functions narratively as a kind of part two to the story. And while the combined accounts provide an origin story for the Ishmaelites, there are striking resemblances between Hagar's story and the subsequent Exodus story. Here the progenitors of the soon-to-be Hebrew nation have enslaved an Egyptian, and when an issue arises over the slave's fertility, her masters respond harshly to keep her in her place and eventually sends her away because their children are threatened by her child. In the opening chapters of Exodus, you find almost the exact scenario—only it's the Hebrews who are being oppressed by the Egyptians and later driven out to wander in the desert.

The conflict starts when Sarah sees Hagar's son "Isaac-ing." The verb צָחַק (*tzachaq*, "to laugh") is the same root as Isaac's name (יִצְחָק, Yitzchaq), and can mean either innocent laughter or mockery. The text is silent about the intent, but Sarah's perception is that laughter from the son of the slave woman is a serious threat to status, power, and privilege. Sarah's order to "cast out this slave woman with her son" uses the verb גָּרֵשׁ (*garash*, "drive out/banish") which is also used to describe the expulsion from Eden and the exodus from Egypt.

Though Abram is indifferent to Hagar's harsh treatment at the hands of Sarah in chapter 16, here in Genesis 21 Abraham is distressed. Perhaps his evolution of empathy is in response to God's promise of blessing for Ishamel in Genesis 17:20, or perhaps his exchange with the Lord about the judgment of Sodom (see Genesis 18:16-33) changed his priority for compassion and his practice of justice. Whatever the case, God reaffirms to him the promise of Genesis 17:20, and this time, instead of leaving Hagar to run away on her own (16:6), Abraham rises early to give her provisions and superintend her departure (21:14).

Here again God hears and responds to Hagar's plight. Just as God will later hear the cry of the Israelites in Egypt, so now "God heard the voice of the boy" (v.17). Considering the name Ishmael (יִשְׁמָעֵאל Yishma'el) means "God hears," this wordplay emphasizes God's attentiveness to the oppressed. Responding to the cries of Ishmael, God comes to Hagar and gives the slave woman the same covenantal promise and blessing which was given to Abraham—I will make a great nation of him (v. 18). God will be with her child and will bless her child with a future and hope.

Hagar's story emphasizes that God will bless all, not some. This is grace for the marginalized. Will we open our eyes to such grace?

Will we open our ears to hear the cries of those unheard?

Week Four

Genesis 22:1-14 | "I will be faithful."

> **Key Images**: journey, wood, mountain, altar, sacrifice, fire, ram, angel
>
> **Themes**: faith, obedience, testing, provision, worship

Isaac said to his father Abraham, "Father!" And he said, "Here I am, my son." He said, "The fire and the wood are here, but where is the lamb for a burnt offering?" Abraham said, "God himself will provide the lamb for a burnt offering, my son." And the two of them walked on together. (Genesis 22:7-8)

After no less than six iterations of God's promise to Abraham (Genesis 12:2-3, 15:5-6, 16:10-16, 17:2-8, 18:13-14, 21:12-13), now God tests (נָסָה nasah, meaning "to try, to prove or refine") Abraham's faith. Isaac is the tangible sign that *proves* that God is faithful to the promise, but this test asks Abraham to believe even if the tangible sign is removed. The terms used in v.2 to describe Isaac—*your son, your only son, the one whom you love*—further intensify the sting of the demand.

And just as Abram unquestioningly obeyed the earlier call to leave (see Genesis 12:4), so now Abraham *rises early in the morning* to fulfill his duty (v.3). Similarly, God instructs Abraham to go to a mountain *that I will show you* in the land of Moriah, a name that is possibly derived from the root רָאָה ra'ah, meaning "to see" or "provide." Perhaps this both alludes to the provision Abraham experienced in answering his first call from God and foreshadows his experience of provision on the mountain.

In considering the horror of the task, one cannot escape the normative worship practice of human sacrifice in the Ancient Near East. Neither can faithful interpretation escape the frequent condemnations of the practice throughout the Old Testament. Nevertheless, the point of the narrative is squarely on Abraham's absolute obedience to what God asks of him—a reflexive faith that has been honed and proven over time. A reflexive faith that immediately responds, "I will" to God's "I will." Abraham's reflexive faith occurs twice in this passage: once when God tells him to sacrifice his son and again when God tells him to stop.

The exchange between father and son in v. 18 is tender and poignant, heightening the drama and the emotional tension of the text. Abraham's response—*God himself will provide*—becomes the pivotal answer to this test of faith and the focus of faithful worship. Despite the moral dilemma it raises, this test confronts the would-be worshiper with the claims that God wants it all—everything we are and everything we have—and God provides. This duality is the heartbeat of worship and emphasizes both the strength and vulnerability inherent in God's actions toward us. Perhaps part of the interpretive task is to wrestle with this God who promises the impossible and demands the impossible, who leads through the impossible and provides for the impossible.

It requires vulnerability and trust, because the stronger the promise, the stronger the vulnerability.

Words for Worship, After Pentecost

Gathering

Call to Worship for Genesis 12:1-9
(Joe Kim)

God calls us to move into the unknown, trusting in divine promises.
We come with faith, like Abraham and Sarah, daring to follow where God leads.
God speaks, "I will bless you and make your name great, so that you will be a blessing."
We gather to receive God's blessing and to be a blessing in this world.
Let us worship the God who journeys with us.
We journey in faith, trusting the One who calls us by name.

Call to Worship for Genesis 18:1-15
(Joe Kim)

God appears in unexpected moments, speaking hope into impossible situations.
We come with open hearts, ready to hear the promises of our faithful God.
To Sarah, God said, "Is anything too wonderful for the Lord?"
With laughter and wonder, we proclaim the God of the impossible.
Let us worship the God who brings joy and life out of despair.
We worship in faith, trusting God's eternal promises.

Call to Worship for Genesis 21:8-21
(Joe Kim)

God hears the cries of the vulnerable and knows those cast aside.
Like Hagar and Ishmael, we trust in God's care and provision.
The angel of God calls, "Do not be afraid; for God has heard the voice of the boy."
We come to the well of God's mercy, where there is water for our thirsty souls.

Let us worship the God who provides in the wilderness and restores the weary.
We worship the One who is ever present in the lives of God's All.

Call to Worship for Genesis 22:1-14
(Joe Kim)

God calls us to places of trust, even when the path is unclear.
Like Abraham, we respond, "Here I am," trusting in God's faithfulness.
On the mountain, God provided a ram in place of Isaac.
In all of our journeys, we trust that God will provide for us, too.
One: Let us worship the God who provides.
We worship with faith, surrendering to the God of promise and provision.

A Prayer of Confession (Genesis 18:1-15)

Our Lord and our God, in the name of Jesus,
we come, today, confessing our sin before you.
It is what it is.
You see it (sin) for what it is.
Forgive us this day we pray.

Like Sarah, God, we've doubted you,
disbelieving that all things are possible with you.
It is what it is, God.
You see it (sin) for what it is.
Forgive us this day we pray.

Like Sarah, God, we've laughed at you,
thinking that your miracles have little chance of lifting our hopes.
It is what it is, God.
You see it (sin) for what it is.
Forgive us this day, we pray.

Like Sarah, God, we've lied to you, O God.
Lied to you, lied to our loved ones,
lied to co-workers, church members and strangers.
Yes, we've denied truth, even while we are standing face to face with your truth.
It is what it is, God.
You see it (sin) for what it is.
Forgive us this day, we pray.

And help us to know day after day that nothing is too hard for you, Lord.
Fixing our broken relationships is not too hard.

Finding a good paying job is not too hard.
Filling an empty heart is not too hard, God.
All things are possible for you.
And we thank you that at this appointed time you forgive us.
It is what it is, but it doesn't have to stay that way.
Thank you for making a way out of no way.
In Jesus's name we pray. Amen.
—Joseph W. Daniels, Jr., *Africana Worship Book, Year A*

A Prayer of Confession (Genesis 18:1-15)

God, we gather ourselves before you this morning as the family of faith,
in need of your grace in rebuilding and repairing our broken families.

Lord, we confess:
That we have contributed to family dissension and division,
family despair and disappointment . . .
(Silence)
That, we have fathered and mothered children
by women and men other than our own spouses . . .
(Silence)
That, we have allowed jealousy to destroy and disintegrate relationships . . .
(Silence)
That, we have dismissed family members,
intending to never see them or speak to them again . . .
(Silence)
Lord, we have banished family members to unknown places . . .
where their cries could only be heard by you . . .
(Silence)

Forgive us, God, we pray.
Use us today to be agents of reconciliation.
Use us today to provide for loved ones when and where we can.
Grant us the faith to know that where we have failed,
you are more than able to make things right.
Please, O God, bless the family members we have banished,
and move in our hearts so that me may love them unconditionally,
as you so generously and unconditionally love us.
In the name of Jesus, the Christ, who makes this all quite possible, **Amen.**
—Joseph W. Daniels, Jr., *Africana Worship Book, Year A*

O Gracious Power: A Confession (Genesis 12)

O Gracious Power,
You made us in your image
to be one human family
gathered in one house of faith
with one spirit of peace and joy.

But we have ignored your intention.
We have built a wall between the nations,
a wall between women and men,
a wall between the rich and poor,
a wall between the strong and weak,
a wall between the races,
a wall between people like us
and those who are different.

Give us a vision of your inclusive love,
that by the ministries of music and word,
sacrament and service
we may dismantle the walls of division
and live as one family in the household of faith.
—Thomas Troeger, *Borrowed Light: Hymns, Texts, Prayers, and Poems*

Proclaiming

Prayer for Illumination (for the Second Sunday after Pentecost)

God of compassion, you have opened the way for us and brought us to yourself. Pour your love into our hearts, that, overflowing with joy, we may freely share the blessings of your realm and faithfully proclaim the good news of your Son, Jesus Christ, our Savior and Lord. **Amen.**
—*Minister's Prayer Book*

Father Abraham, Mother Sarah: A Litany (Genesis 12)

Father Abraham has many children.
People of every color, every shape, every size, and every language.
We all claim Father Abraham!
Mother Sarah has many children.
People who are poor and people who are rich.
People who are young and people who are retired.
We all claim Mother Sarah!

I have a story, you have a story, and God has a story.
Look for yourself in the beginning of the story
Of Father Abraham.
And Mother Sarah.
And all people of faith!
—adapted from Safiyah Fosua, *Africana Worship Book, Year A*

Prayer for Illumination (Psalm 13)

Lord, open our eyes to see your grace afresh today. Open our ears, to hear your mercy anew today. We've been suffering for a long time, God, and we need to hear a word from you. We've been a long time in our family dysfunction. We've been a long time in our relationship folly. We've been a long time in poverty and economic pain. We have been too long in sin and shame. Lord, give light to our eyes today and encouragement to our souls, so that our hearts can rejoice in your salvation. Elevate our hopes because of the positive expectations we have in you. Speak Lord, we pray, in Jesus's name. **Amen.**
—Joseph W. Daniels, Jr., *Africana Worship Book, Year A*

Thanksgiving

Offertory Prayer

Generous God,
> you gave us life;
> now we give our lives back to you.

We present ourselves:
> our work and play,
> our joys and sorrows,
> our thoughts and deeds,
> our gifts and resources,

to be used by you
> for the sake of all people everywhere,

through Jesus Christ, our Lord. **Amen.**
—adapted from *Ventures in Worship, Volume 1*

Great Thanksgiving
(Joseph Kim)

Source of Life be with you.
And also with you.
Respond with wonder and awe all that God is doing in our lives.
We receive with openness God's goodness and mercy.

After Pentecost

Let us give thanks to God, who continues to call us.
To the One still at work in the world, we give our thanks and praise.

God, since the beginning, You journeyed with Your people. You formed us out of nothing, and You desired relationship with us that You would be our God and we would be Your people. Even when we turned away, You were still there. Even when all felt lost, You promised Your presence with us.

In time, You revealed Your vision for the world—one of hope, peace, joy, and love. You called our foremothers and forefathers to go from all that they knew and towards a place You would show them. You journeyed with them, and You journey with us.
Therefore, with all your people, past and present, we praise you declaring together:

**Holy, Holy, Holy One,
God of yesterday, today, and forever,
Heaven and earth are filled with your presence
Hosanna in the highest!**

Blessed are You, and blessed is your presence among us. You journey with us, providing for us and caring for us when we are in need, reminding us that as You call us in love, we, too, are to love one another.

In our humanity, in our selfishness and greed, we forget that part of the call, turning too quickly towards our own wants and desires. And so in Your love for us, You made Yourself know in the person of Jesus, revealing to us in Word and Deed how we might be the people You call us to be. In life, and in death, Jesus declared Your love for us, for all of us, and offered a different way to live into Your call for us that all might know Your love.

On the night he was betrayed, Jesus gathered with his friends, and he took bread, gave thanks to You, broke the bread, and shared with his disciples, saying, "Take, eat; this is my body which is given for you. Do this as you remember me."

And after they were fed, he took the cup, gave thanks to You, shared it with his disciples, and said, "Drink from this, all of you; this is the promise of my presence for you and for many. Do this as you remember me."

We remember, and we declare the mystery of our faith:
Christ has died; Christ is risen; Christ will come again.

Pour out your Holy Spirit on these gifts that you have provided and on us who have gathered to receive them. May they be for us a renewing of our commitment to respond to You as You remind us again and again Your faithfulness to be with us all through our lives.

By that same Spirit, make us one with You and one with each other, journeying together towards that day when we live into Your preferred future.

With the declaration of hope in the world, we join our hearts and our voices, praying the prayer that Christ taught us, know that Your love is like that both a Mother and Father as we say these words together:

The Lords' Prayer

(prayer after receiving)
Thank you, God, for this gift of presence—for these reminders of Your grace in our lives, for the provision for the journey, and for Your constant call in us and through us that the world might know Your love. Amen.

Anybody Here? An Affirmation of Faith and Commitment (Psalm 116)

Is there anybody here who loves my Jesus?
I love the Lord.
He heard my voice.
He heard my cry.
He heard my plea.
Is there anybody here who loves my Jesus?
I love the Lord
He bent down low to hear me.
He cares for me
And I will trust him as long as I live.
Is there anybody here who loves my Jesus?
I love the Lord.
As long as I live, I will trust him.
As long as I live, I will praise him.
As long as I live, I will serve him.
—Kwasi I. Kena, *Africana Worship Book, Year A*

Prayers of the People: Lord, We Call on You (Psalm 86)

Our Lord and our God, we call on you this day asking you to be present with us and to visit us in this our time of trouble.

Lord, we are poor and needy materially.
For many of us, there is more month at the end of the money,
than money at the end of the month.

Many of us are living from paycheck to paycheck.
Lord, we call upon you right now to help us and guide us.

Lord, we are poor and needy spiritually.
We have cheated you of the time you desire from us.
We have turned away from having a healthy, intimate relationship with you.
Our prayer lives, meditation lives, study lives, giving lives, have given way to the demands made of us by the world, the job, and creature comforts of life.
Lord, we ask you to be with us this day.

Lord, we call upon the power of your Holy Spirit,
to comfort us in our time of trial,
to guard us in our great hour of weakness,
to have mercy on us in our many moments of anguish.
Lord, would you bring us joy today?

Would you lift our souls from sorrow?
There is none like you, O Lord.
And so we beseech you to hear our prayer.
We invite you to come and be present with us.
We look to you for answers.
We trust you in the time of trouble.
We acknowledge your greatness.

We await your mercies and give you thanks even before they come. Amen.
—Joseph W. Daniels, Jr., *Africana Worship Book, Year A*

Lord, Because You Promised: A Prayer of Lament (Genesis 21)

Lord,
because you promised to be near to the brokenhearted,
    be near us today.
Be with us. We need you.
Come, take our grief and sorrow,
    hear our cries, see our tears, feel our pain.
Be near us. We need you.
Come, take our anger and frustration,
    fight with us, defend with us, plead for us.
Be near us. We need you.
Come, take our regret and despair,
    question with us, bleed with us, die with us.
Be near us. We need you.
We are brokenhearted . . . and. you. promised.
Be near us today, Lord.

Sending

Because God Said

Because God said "I will bless you,"
We will go to bless and be a blessing for our neighbors and the world.
Because God said, "I will surely return,"
We will go to laugh and bring joy till hope is renewed in us and through us.
Because God said "I will hear you,"
We will go to weep and cry out for justice.
Because God said "I will be faithful,"
We will go trusting that the worst thing will never be the last thing.
Because God said,
we believe and will go with God.

Go Forth with the Blessing of God

Go forth with the blessing of God
who called Sarah and Abraham
to leave home
for a land they did not know.
Travel with them
believing
in the assurance of God's presence
in unfamiliar places.

Go forth with the blessing of God,
whose liberation of the Hebrews
stirred Miriam to sing and dance.
Celebrate with her
in song and praise
God's liberating power.

Go forth with the blessing of God,
who raised up prophets
to call for justice
and to renew the earth.
Stand firm with them
for what is good and true and right.

Go forth with the blessing of God,
whose word became flesh
and dwelt among us
full of grace and truth.

Embody with Christ the gifts
of healing, feeding, forgiving, renewing.

Go forth with the blessing of God,
who raised Christ from the dead.
Be raised with him
as a sign
that life is stronger than death.

Go forth with the blessing of God,
who empowered the church
with wind and fire.
Be filled with the Spirit
that your life may shine
with the flame of holy love.

Go forth with the blessing of God,
sustained by the vision
of that great day
when all people
with all the elements of the universe
will sing in a multitude of voices:

Praise and glory,
thanksgiving and honor,
power and might
be to our God forever.
—Thomas Troeger, *Borrowed Light: Hymns, Texts, Prayers, and Poems*

God Is: A Sending

GOD IS. So go with God.
GOD IS Creator, our Maker, in whose image we are made.
GOD IS the Word made flesh, Emmanuel—
    our dwelling place, through whom we have life more abundantly.
GOD IS the lamb that was slain and risen—
    our strong Redeemer, who will never leae us nor forsake us.
GOD IS the soon-coming King of Glory—
    our Victorious Conqueror, with whom we shall reign forever and ever and ever!
GOD IS all that.
GOD IS. So go with God.
—Michelle Riley Jones, *Worship and Song: Worship Resources*

Year A Lectionary Texts

Like This, Like That: Children	Genesis 24:34-38, 42-49, 58-67	Psalm 45:10-17 or Psalm 72	Romans 7:15-25a	Matthew 11:16-19, 25-30
Like This, Like That: Planted Seed	Genesis 25:19-34	Psalm 119:105-112 or Psalm 25	Romans 8:1-11	Matthew 13:1-9, 18-23
Like This, Like That: A Sower	Genesis 28:10-19a	Psalm 139:1-12, 23-24	Romans 8:12-25	Matthew 13:24-30, 36-43
Like This, Like That: Treasure Hunter	Genesis 29:15-28	Psalm 105:1-11, 45b	Romans 8:26-39	Matthew 13:31-33, 44-52

Like This, Like That: A Worship Series for after Pentecost

Signs of God's reign are all around us. Can you see it?
Will you participate in it?

Books are sometimes windows, offering views of worlds that may be real or imagined, familiar or strange. These windows are also sliding glass doors, and readers have only to walk through in imagination to become part of whatever world has been created or recreated by the author. When lighting conditions are just right, however, a window can also be a mirror.
—Rudine Sims Bishop

While Dr. Bishop writes specifically about children's literature, the same holds true for the power of story in general. Stories help us see each other and the world in a more variegated light. Stories help us recognize, acknowledge, and even participate in life in all its beauties and complexities. Stories help us to understand better the sources and depth of our pain, and they help us grasp the real possibility of our potential. Stories matter, because it is the only way we can make sense of the world and ourselves within it.

It is no wonder then that Jesus's teaching primarily consists of stories—or parables—rather than generalities and abstractions. Parables (from the Greek *parabole,* meaning "other speaking") compares two unlike for the purposes of disarming and persuading the hearer towards change. They often feature a surprise or twist that is meant to catch the hearer off-guard. Parables can be in forms as simple as a proverb, metaphor, or simile; or they may be more complex such as figurative sayings or stories (narrative, illustrative, or allegorical). Though Jesus certainly did not invent parables, he used them in all their forms to describe the fullness of God's reign among us. He also used them to challenge the ways we have tried to domesticate or otherwise reshape the kingdom of heaven into something more palatable.

Especially in urban settings, it may be helpful to use less agricultural, more relatable imagery:

- Recast the parables in imagery for your context.
- Invite a small group of creatives to assist.
- Don't replace the scripture reading; use as part of the sermon.

The gospel readings for the 6th-9th Sundays after Pentecost are all parable stories. Whereas the first parable from Matthew 11 presents a mirror to our unimaginative expectations of God's reign, the succeeding parables from Matthew 13 provide window views of the kingdom and doorways to enter in. Using images that were both common and relevant to the daily lives of his hearers, Jesus confronts and challenges us to embrace a dynamic faith in a dynamic God who both creates and embraces a dynamic world teeming with possibility. *Can you see it? Will you participate in it?*

While there are many images to pull from each of these parables, most are agricultural and congregations in more urban settings may find these less relatable. Thus, worship planners may do well to spend time recasting the parable in imagery that is more relatable to your context. Or consider inviting a small group of creatives—from within the congregation or the community—to assist in retelling the parable in terms and images that make sense for your context. Recasting or retelling the parable should not replace the scripture reading itself; rather, it serves as part of the sermonic task of explicating the text.

Ultimately, these stories are meant to help us see God not just in someone else's story, but in our own. What is the kingdom of God like? Well, it is too big to be just one thing, one story, one experience. No, it's like this, and it's like that. So, *take my yoke upon you, and learn from me . . . Let anyone with ears listen!* (Matthew 11:29a and 13:9b).

Week One

Matthew 11:16-19, 25-30 | Like Children

> **Key Images**: children, singing, flutes, mourning, dancing, yoke
>
> **Themes**: repentance, kingdom of heaven, rest and renewal, experiencing God, interpreting scripture

At that time Jesus said, "I thank you, Father, Lord of heaven and earth, because you have hidden these things from the wise and the intelligent and have revealed them to infants; yes, Father, for such was your gracious will. (Matthew 11:25-26)

Matthew 11 introduces something of a narrative shift in the gospel, highlighting a two-fold response to Jesus's ministry and the in-breaking of the kingdom of heaven—some welcome and accept it, while others misunderstand and reject it. Thus, there is confusion about what exactly is happening and who exactly is Jesus. And so, John sends his disciples to ask *Are you the one . . . ?* (v.3), prompting Jesus's response *Go and tell John what you hear and see* (v.4). The problem is that hearing and seeing—that is, perceiving the world as it is and as it could become—requires a release of expectations and an openness to interpretation. Those who refuse to do so are deficient in spiritual understanding and are immature, like children.

And so, Jesus compares this generation (a collective mindset, not an age group) to children in the marketplaces, whose expectation is purely transactional, quid pro quo. It illustrates the fickle responses to both His and John the Baptist's ministries. It is an indictment on the ways in which would-be disciples hold tightly to preconceived expectations of the reign of God and consequently attempt to tame or manipulate God toward their expectation. *We played the flute for you, and you did not dance; we wailed, and you did not mourn* (v. 17). The phrases "we played the flute for you" and "we sang a dirge" highlight their contradictory expectations and their futility. The lectionary reading skips v.20-24 in which Jesus calls out Bethsaida/Chorazin and Capernaum—the two epicenters of his ministry thus far—for how they have emulated this fickleness rather than allowing their experience of *good news* to lead them into repentance.

In v. 25, Jesus then praises the Father for revealing truths to "infants" (νήπιοι nēpioi, meaning "not speaking" referring to the untaught, unskilled), emphasizing the openness required to perceive God's reign. The invitation *Come to me, all you that are weary* speaks to the accessibility of God's kingdom to those who have been wearied and burdened by rigid interpretations of the law. In contrast, Jesus provides "rest" (ἀνάπαυσις anapausis, meaning to give pause, refresh) and a "yoke" (ζυγός zygos, a coupling as in servitude) that is easy (χρηστός chrēstós, "useful and pleasant") and light (ἐλαφρός elaphrós, "light in weight, agile").

The way of Jesus is agile, useful, and pleasant. Can you see it?

Will you participate in it?

Week Two

Matthew 13:1-9, 18-23 | Like Planted Seed

> **Key Images**: seed, soil, planting, plants, stones, thorns, birds, pathway
>
> **Themes**: sharing the word, receiving the word, bearing fruit, understanding the kingdom

> And he told them many things in parables, saying: "Listen!
> A sower went out to sow. (Matthew 13:3)

Matthew 13 opens with Jesus teaching the crowd beside the Sea of Galilee, seemingly a favorite teaching spot, in a series of parables. And though Jesus himself titles it "Parable of the Sower," his interpretation in v. 18-23 focuses on the interaction between the seed and the soil, not the sower nor his actions. So, interpreters are left to wonder about the identity of the sower—is it God or us?

However, one settles the question, the act of scattering seed upon unprepared soil would seem foolish to an audience of farmers. Perhaps the sower is so convinced about the potential of the seed to germinate that it scarcely matters where it lands, because it will produce something. Or perhaps the converse is true and the sower's ability to see potential in every landscape drives him to scatter seed so liberally—because it will produce. Whatever the case, the Greek denotes an ongoing, intentional, dynamic action—the sower is going to sow and won't stop sowing because something will be produced, one way or the other.

Likewise, the interaction between the seed and the soil is a dynamic interplay between gift and receiver. Jesus explains that the seed is the *word of the kingdom*. The "word" (λόγος logos) is more than just speech; it carries the idea of divine revelation. "Kingdom" (βασιλείας basileia) refers to God's reign, not just a future place but an active, present reality. Notice the external forces—the evil one, trouble or persecution, cares of this world and the lure of wealth—that seem that *snatches away what is sown* (v.19). This suggests that while the seed was sown, it lay fallow and static. It did not have any real, meaningful engagement with the earthen matter upon which it lay. What makes the soil *good* is the intentional movement beyond mere receiving of the word towards "understanding" (συνίημι syniēmi, meaning "to bring together"). More than intellectual grasp, this is a dynamic nurturing that brings together the *word of the kingdom* with the *soil* of everyday life (γῆν gen, meaning "land, ground, earth"), leading to deep insight and transformation, i.e. fruit.

The insight here is at least threefold:

- God's reign is continuously and liberally sown—will we have eyes to see the harvest?
- Every seed and soil have potential—will we have faith to trust the process?
- Understanding requires intentional engagement with the world—are we willing to participate?

Week Three

Matthew 13:24-30, 36-43 | Like A Sower

> **Key Images**: seed, soil, fields, harvest, planting, wheat, weeds, bundles, fire, barn, angels
>
> **Themes**: kingdom of heaven, eschatology, the problem of evil, Christian responsibility

> But he replied, "'No, for in gathering the weeds you would uproot the wheat along with them. Let both of them grow together until the harvest. . . ." (Matthew 13:29-30a)

Addressing the crowds, Jesus gives another farming parable, again comparing God's reign to a sower who sows seed. Whereas the previous parable focused on the interaction between the seed and the soil, this new parable focuses on the harvest—how can one ensure a good harvest? Whose job is it to ensure a good harvest? What makes for a good harvest?

Jesus's parable introduces a few surprising elements. The sower sows his own field even though he is wealthy enough to own servants. This would have immediately caught Jesus's first hearers off-guard and, combined with the identification of the Son of Man as the sower, highlights the divine action that initiates and propagates God's kingdom. Whatever God's reign might be or become is solely God's initiative and plan.

Another surprise is both the presence of the enemy and the master's seeming foreknowledge of the enemy's actions. To be sure, the "weeds" (ζιζάνια zizania) are probably darnel or false-wheat, a weed that is undistinguishable from wheat until the grains appear. It is a common nuisance to farmers as it only grows in climates and conditions where wheat grows, so the introduction of the enemy (ἐχθρός echthrós, "a hater") adds a complexity to what otherwise might have been considered a natural occurrence. And the subsequent identification of the enemy as the devil (διάβολος diábolos, "false accuser), implies that there are spiritual forces at work within the world that may easily be missed or mistakenly ascribed to God without divine wisdom.

And perhaps most surprising of all, the master insists on a do-nothing weed control policy. For sure, this goes against usual practice of removing the offending plants as soon as possible to prevent reseeding of the unwanted species and to ensure a cleaner, undefiled harvest. Instead, the master leaves the false-wheat in place because removing them would *uproot* the true wheat, likely because their root systems are too intertwined. Removing one will invariably weaken the other. *Let them grow together*, the master declares, implying that though they may not have been a part of the master's original plan, now they are part of the cultivation and care his slaves will no doubt provide to the wheat in the field.

While some may not readily find comfort in Jesus's eschatological interpretation, the implication is clear: judgment about the seed or the harvest it produces belongs only to the master, not to the slaves nor the reapers. The master alone determines what belongs in the field and what to do with it all in the end. The slaves' job is to care for and steward it all equally, trusting the master to sort it out at harvest time. In a world that so readily categorizes and deals with others in absolutist terms, Jesus's parable speaks of God's reign offering a different way of being with each other—one that wholeheartedly trusts the master's care for all.

The lyrics to the 1976 song "Harvest for the World" by the Isley Brothers offer a great interpolation of this parable:

> Gather everyone, gather all together,
> Overlooking none, hoping life gets better for the world.

When will there be a harvest for the world?

God only knows. Can we live faithfully—celebrating life, overlooking none—in the meantime?

Week Four

Matthew 13:31-33, 44-52 | Like a Treasure Hunter

> **Key Images**: mustard seed, tree, birds, yeast, dough, treasure, field, pearl, net, fish, jars
>
> **Themes**: kingdom of heaven, patience, commitment, wisdom, transformation, discipleship

> "Have you understood all this?" They answered, "Yes." And he said to them, "Therefore every scribe who has become a disciple in the kingdom of heaven is like the master of a household who brings out of his treasure what is new and what is old." (Matthew 13:51-52)

This final reading contains six short parables, the first two of which are addressed to the crowds and the later to the disciples. This collection of parables (mustard seed, yeast, hidden treasure, pearl, net, wise master) reveals the kingdom's unexpected growth, hidden power, and supreme worth. God's reign is surprising and transformative.

Jesus first compares God's reign to a tiny seed that grows disproportionately large, representing the unexpected power of God's reign. Similarly, God's reign is like yeast—a symbol of power and influence—that seems imperceptible but over time and with intention transforms its environment. Both parables highlight the deliberateness with which someone invests the little they have resulting in great impact.

God's reign is also like treasure that has been both found and hidden (presumably in the same field in which it was found). The finder's purchase of the entire field suggests that the treasure's value has now extended to everything it touches. Similarly, in finding such a priceless pearl, the merchant sells everything (perhaps even his livelihood) to purchase this one thing. As Eugene Peterson suggests, the connecting theme between these parables is the word "all." Discovering God's reign hidden in the stuff of daily life elicits joy and requires an "all in" commitment.

In the end, God's reign is like a net—wide in its breadth, magnanimous in its reach, and just in its care. Like the earlier parable about the weeds among the wheat, the catch in this net is to be sorted out in the end. God's reign is both the net and the judgment.

Finally, Jesus focuses on his would-be disciples. "Understanding" (συνίημι syniēmi, meaning "to bring together") is key to both this summation of teaching about the kingdom and the kingdom itself. Jesus affirms that those who do *understand*, who are well-trained in the kingdom, are scribes or teachers of the law who are nimble in their interpretation and application of the law. By bringing together *the word of the kingdom* with their experiences of God's reign in the world, they can deftly practice traditioned innovation, holding the past and future in tension together, not in opposition.

Words for Worship, After Pentecost

Gathering

Call to Worship for the 7th Sunday after Pentecost
(Celia Halfacre)

Your Word, O Lord, is a lamp for our feet.
Give us light, Holy God.
Accept our offerings of praise,
And teach us your ways.

Call to Worship (Matthew 11:25-30)
(Charity Goodwin)

We praise you Lord of heaven and earth.
We show up as babes to learn from you.
Reveal yourself to us, we pray.
We show up struggling and carrying heavy loads.
Receive us and teach us, we pray.
Humble and gentle one, we show up here for You.
Lift our burdens and give us rest.
Show up and reveal yourself to us anew Father, Son, and Holy Spirit, we pray.

Call to Worship
(Celia Halfacre)

Surely the Lord is this place!
Thanks to God.
This is none other than the house of God
And the gate of heaven!
Let us worship the Lord!

Call to Worship /Greeting
(Celia Halfacre)

O give thanks to the Lord
We call upon God's name.
Let the hearts of those who seek the Lord rejoice.
God's covenant and love are forever.

Call to Worship (Matthew 13:44-52)
(Charity Goodwin)

What a view of heaven!
Treasure hidden, covered.
We search and find it.
And joy flows.
What a view of heaven!
Treasure of pearls, precious and valuable
We search and find it.
And joy flows.
What a view of heaven!
Treasure of old and new in a chest
Picked out and displayed
And joy flows.

What a view of heaven!
Treasure and jewels.
We seek, we find,
And joy flows.

Opening Prayer for the Sixth Sunday After Pentecost
(Celia Halfacre)

God of mercy and unending compassion,
we gather to worship you.
Hear us.
Receive our worship with the joy we intend.
We want to offer more, to praise you more,
To give our whole lives, but we do not do the good we want.
Release us from law-captivity and the sin that dwells within us.
We ask in Jesus's name. Amen.

Opening Prayer
(Celia Halfacre)

God, what kind of soil are we? And what could we be, if we committed ourselves to your tending and care? As we gather to worship you, form us; take the dirt of our lives and make fertile soil, where your Word can grow and be fruitful for the sake of others. We pray in Jesus's name. Amen.

Opening Prayer
(Celia Halfacre)

Holy God, you know us better than we know ourselves. You set our path and know our ways and our words. We come into your presence with intention, with purpose, and with joy. You call us here. Your creation calls us here, for we are your children. We worship you with our deep breath, and join the great groaning of creation. Make us worthy of the hope we hold. In Jesus's name. Amen.

Opening Prayer
(Celia Halfacre)

God your word is a seed that grows out of our control. It is a treasure in a field we cannot possess. It is a pearl of great value. Open us to see your glory in the word we hear today. Cleanse us through your Word today; make us like full nets, drawn ashore into your presence, we pray in Jesus's name. Amen.

Prayer of Confession and Assurance of Pardon
(Celia Halfacre)

God of Love, it seems like we're never happy with what we have or who we are. We feel unworthy of salvation, and so we reject it, bit by bit. We feel unfulfilled, and so we buy more. We feel restless, and so we over-burden ourselves with busyness. We are weary, dear Lord. Place your easy yoke on us and free us from needless anxiety. We pray in the name of the One whose burden is easy, Jesus our Christ. Amen.

Beloved of God, hear this call from our Savior:
Come to me all you who are weary
and carrying heavy burdens and I will give you rest.
In Jesus we have our rest.
Thanks be to God.

Prayer of Confession and Assurance of Pardon
(Celia Halfacre)

God of mercy: Sometimes our faith is new and growing, and you fill us with life to build your kingdom within us and through us. Sometimes, the scorching heat dries us up and we're tired. We sense your Word fading within us. Rain your Holy Spirit on us.

The seed of your Word grows like a weed, everywhere it's not supposed to. We exhaust ourselves in toil and sweat to contain it. Release us from that responsibility. Give us assurance that you would share your Word everywhere it will grow, to trust that our roots are deep enough, and our stems strong enough to endure in every situation.

Hear and believe the good news: There is no condemnation for those who are in Christ Jesus. In Christ, you are dead to sin and raised to new life. Alive and made new, you are free to grow, just as you are.
Thanks be to God.

Prayer of Confession and Assurance of Pardon
(Celia Halfacre)

When we're honest with ourselves, God of hope and harvest, we are both good and bad seeds, wanting to do better, and missing the mark. Sometimes we follow your path, yielding fruitful growth, abundant fruit. At other times, we sprout up and pop off like undisciplined weeds. Be patient with us, Loving God. Give us patience with ourselves as we grow more and more into your likeness, into your image. We pray in Jesus's name. Amen.

Beloved, hear and believe the good news: the God who knows us and loves, grows us on the path that leads to everlasting life. God, who began a good work in you, will complete that work in Christ Jesus.
Thanks be to God.

Prayer of Confession (Romans 7:15-25)
(Charity Goodwin)

Lord have mercy on me . . . on my mind and my body
I confess a tug of war pushes and pulls me from good to sin and back again.
My mind desires to honor, love, and live for you.
I desire to do good but I fail time and time again.
God what haunts me is the wrong I do of which I'm not aware.
Bring back to my mind and heart where I have sinned;
Where I missed the mark of showing grace, compassion, empathy,
and an opportunity to do justice.
In this time of silence reveal my sins to me . . .
(Silence)

God says I created you good.
Jesus says I loved you while you were sinners.
The Holy Spirit says I empower you to live under the [Law of] Love.
Your are forgiven in the name of the Creator, Forgiver, and Sustainer. Hallelujah, Amen.

Psalm 72 (Pardon)
(Charity Goodwin)

Let there be awareness of your sin.
Let grace rain on your dry places.
Let empathy be given in abundance.
Let compassion thrive with ease.
Let courage live in you and your generations.
Let justice liberate you as oppressed and oppressor.
Let your mind be Christ's.
Let God's forgiveness shower over you.
Let self-forgiveness be in your words and body.
Let it be in the name of the Father, Son, and Holy Spirit. Amen.

Litany of Assurance (Matthew 13:24-30, 36-43)
(Charity Goodwin)

The Kingdom of heaven is like someone who planted good seed in his field
The Sower keeps sowing seeds.
An enemy planted weeds.
The Sower keeps sowing seeds.
Leave them be to grow together.
The Sower keeps sowing seeds.
Gather the weeds apart from the wheat.
The Sower's angels gather wheat for safekeeping
No weeds shall defeat the sower.
The Sower keeps sowing seeds.

Proclaiming

Prayer for Illumination
(Celia Halfacre)

Lord, we are weak, and we do not know how to pray or to live or to study as we ought. Spirit, intercede for us, in us, with sighs deeper than words. Search our hearts, so they open to hear and believe your Word today. Amen.

Response/Reflection (Lectio Divina)
(Charity Goodwin)

Romans 8:10-11
Based on the traditional version of Lectio Divina this response follows a sermon as an in-worship corporate practice of a spiritual discipline. Invite people to answer the questions after each reading in their heart, writing, or capturing on their phone. Depending on your context you can have people respond aloud for 30 seconds to one minute.

Invite people after worship through your newsletter or a special edition newsletter to share their experience of Lectio Divina. Be sure to share with responses with congregations even those who felt challenged by it. This is a great way to encourage disciple practices into the worship experience.

Read Romans 8:10-11
Ask: What word stands out to you?
Read Romans 8:10-11
Ask: What phrase resonates with you?
Read Romans 8:10-11
Ask: What is God calling you to do or be?

A Reading of Psalm 139 From the Perspective of God
(Charity Goodwin)

Beloved, I know you.
Where you sit and where you stand.
I see you resting and going your way.
I know you, I know your ways.
You speak and I know what you will say.
I'm with you on your front, back, and side.
My hand rests on your shoulder.
Knowing this is overwhelming, I know.
My spirit is forever with you.
You cannot escape my presence, beloved. I'm here!
Come with me to heaven, I'm there.
Be buried in a grave, I, too, am there.
If you could fly over oceans at dawn, I am there to hold you up.
But if darkness surrounded you I will be light for you.
No darkness can keep me away from you.
I see your heart! I feel your anxieties.
I know you even look to idols.
Beloved, I am here to lead you on the path with me, eternally.

Reflect & Respond
(Charity Goodwin)

Lead a time of reflection followed by a simple prayer.

I invite you to consider the kingdom of heaven (or reign of God). For the next 3 minutes reflect on "Where have you seen the Kingdom of God (or reign of God)?"

After 3 minutes have passed, invite people to share in pairs for one minute each, their answer.

Let us come back together for this time of prayer:
May we continue to see glimpses of heaven on earth.
Attune our ears to hear heaven in our daily lives.
Take our hands to craft heaven among our most important relationships.
May we taste and see that you are God and you are good. Here on earth.
In Jesus's name we pray. Amen.

Thanksgiving

Prayers of the People (Matthew 13:1-9)
(Charity Goodwin)

We pray for the earth and us who tend it.
For farmers who labor and toil.
For the earth that struggles to survive.
For our decisions that harm the earth we were entrusted with, we pray . . .
For those who are planting seeds of hope in the earth, their life, work,
and community we pray. . . .
For those blooming and fragrant with joy, blessing, and love we celebrate . . .
For those who know the thorns of life that pierce and prick, we pray . . .

Prayer
(Charity Goodwin)

Loving God we know you are with us in the world
Despite the tragedy and trauma
We still see you at work in us and the world.
At times we feel heavy and weary yet we hold on to hope.
Hope that is You.
Every promise you've made we hold. We remember.
We make it daily because of promises fulfilled and those to come.
Amid the hell that the world can be
Grant us glimpses of your reign.
Grant us to courage to participate in it.
In the name of the one who reigns, Jesus Christ. Amen.

The Great Thanksgiving
(Celia Halfacre)

The Lord be with you.
And also with you.
Lift up your hearts.
We lift them up to the Lord.
Let us give thanks to the Lord our God.
It is right to give our thanks and praise.

It is right and a good and joyful thing, always and everywhere, to give thanks to you, almighty God, and father of Abraham and Sarah, Isaac and Rebecca, Jacob and Leah, Rachel, Zilpah, and Bilhah. You formed us in your image and breathed into us the breath of life. When we turned away, and our love failed, your love remained steadfast. You delivered us from captivity, made covenant to be our sovereign God, and spoke to us through the prophets.

And so, with your people on earth and all the company of heaven
we praise your name and join their unending hymn:

Holy, holy, holy Lord, God of power and might,
heaven and earth are full of your glory.
Hosanna in the highest.
Blessed is he who comes in the name of the Lord.
Hosanna in the highest.

Holy are you, and blessed is your Son, Jesus Christ, who came, as one of us, eating, drinking, enjoying the company of friends, and we called him a drunkard and a glutton. He offered us freedom from the bondage of expectations and burdens of heavy religion. He bid us come, we who are weary and carrying heavy burdens, so that we may receive rest.

By the baptism of his suffering, death, and resurrection you gave birth to your Church, delivered us from slavery to sin and death, and made with us a new covenant by water and the Spirit.

On the night in which he gave himself up for us,
he took bread, gave thanks to you, broke the bread,
gave it to his disciples, and said:
"Take, eat; this is my body which is given for you.
Do this in remembrance of me."
When the supper was over, he took the cup,
gave thanks to you, gave it to his disciples, and said:
"Drink from this, all of you;
this is my blood of the new covenant,
poured out for you and for many
for the forgiveness of sins.
Do this, as often as you drink it,
in remembrance of me."

And so,
in remembrance of these your mighty acts in Jesus Christ, we offer ourselves in praise and thanksgiving as a holy and living sacrifice, in union with Christ's offering for us, as we proclaim the mystery of faith.
Christ has died; Christ is risen; Christ will come again.
Pour out your Holy Spirit on us gathered here, and on these gifts of bread and wine. Make them be for us the body and blood of Christ, that we may be for the world the body of Christ, redeemed by his blood.

By your Spirit make us one with Christ, one with each other,
and one in ministry to all the world, until Christ comes in final victory

and we feast at his heavenly banquet.
Through your Son Jesus Christ, with the Holy Spirit in your holy Church,
all honor and glory is yours, almighty Father, now and forever. **Amen.**

Sending

Benediction (Matthew 13:1-9)
(Charity Goodwin)

May the words that I've heard be sealed in my heart.
May the words that I've heard be sealed in my heart.
May they take root and bear fruit.
May they take root and bear fruit.
In the name of the One who plants, waters, and shines on us now and forever. Amen.
AMEN

Year A Lectionary Texts

Don't Let Go	**Genesis 32:22-31**	Psalm 17:1-7, 15	Romans 9:1-5	Matthew 14:13-21
Don't Let Go	**Genesis 37:1-4, 12-28**	Psalm 105: 1-6, 16-22, 45b	Romans 10:5-15	Matthew 14:22-33
Don't Let Go	**Genesis 45:1-15**	Psalm 133	Romans 11:1-2a, 29-32	Matthew 15: (10-20), 21-28

Don't Let Go: A Worship Series for after Pentecost

Relationships—how we treat one another—are everything. We are called to hold and uphold each other with love, grace, and forgiveness.

. . . Wrestling, I will not let thee go,
Till I thy name, thy nature know.
—Charles Wesley, "Wrestling Jacob"

The first chapter of Genesis offers a beautifully poetic litany of God harmonizing darkness and light, sky and earth, water and dry ground, animals and people. More than organizational unity, God arranges the elements of creation into relationships with each other, and it is this relationship—the way these things relate to each other—that God pronounces "good" [Hebrew, *tov*—meaning having the intrinsic quality of goodness, beauty, and uprightness]. This goodness is then corrupted when sin enters the world—putting God's good relationships out of joint. And this is embodied throughout Genesis through fractured and unresolved family relationships: Cain and Abel, Noah and Ham, Sarah and Hagar, Ishmael and Isaac, Jacob and Esau, Jacob and Dinah, Joseph and his brothers.

And as Wesley's hymn highlights, Jacob's pre-dawn wrestling match with an unknown assailant becomes the prototype by which relationships are made whole—the defining factor being, *never letting go*. As Jacob's story gives way to Joseph's, it is clear that this intentional engagement or wrestling is the model by which reconciliation becomes possible, forgiveness is shared, and love is revealed.

Teach the congregation peacemaking and reconciliation:

- Orient each Sunday around acts of confession, repentance, and reconciliation.

- Use various liturgies to practice using relational language.

- For the final Sunday, invite deeper vulnerability with a sign-act.

- Use *I Need You to Survive* for acts of confession and reconciliation.

In 2006, the Christian/alternative rock band, The Fray, released one of the most popular songs of the era, "How to Save a Life." It was written by band members, Isaac Slade and Joseph King, as a reflection on their work at a rehabilitation center for troubled teenagers. Isaac recalls spending time with one young man who had lost hope. And so, as he writes in the chorus, Isaac walked away from that experience wondering

> Where did I go wrong? I lost a friend somewhere along in the bitterness and I would have stayed up with you all night had I known how to save a life.

After the song's release, "How to Save a Life" became an anthem for those who endeavored to love others who have lost hope. The band received numerous testimonies of how people have been inspired to love someone to life by "staying up all night" with them. The band also received thousands of confessions from individuals who felt lost, waiting for someone to reach out to them with the kind of love that won't let go.

We fulfill God's will and purpose for us when we love each other in this way. This love is not dependent upon familial relationships but is instead dependent upon our ability to see each other as persons of sacred worth who are in need and deserving to be loved and cared for by all God's people. When we cast our lot with each other in covenant community, submitting ourselves to the kind of love that won't let go, then we are able to move beyond merely surviving into thriving through the abundance that God provides.

Worship leaders should consider orienting each Sunday around acts of confession, repentance and reconciliation, with emphasis toward the healing of relationships and the practice of not letting go of each other. Here various liturgies could be used to give or otherwise teach the congregation the words to say for making peace and starting again in relationships. And while each Sunday may certainly include a passing of the peace, the final Sunday in the series could invite more vulnerability through a sign-act, like writing the name of a relationship that needs mending on stone or pottery shard or even paper that is then placed into a mosaic. Or consider using the song "I Need You to Survive" as the call to confession and sign of reconciliation. After some time of confession at kneelers or otherwise, invite the congregation, when they are ready and able, to look each other in the eye and sing or say the words of the second stanza to each other as reconciliation:

> I won't harm you with words from my mouth.
> I love you. I need you to survive.

Over these three weeks, we will move from wrestling to reconciliation. From Jacob's nighttime struggle to Joseph's pit, to his embrace of the very ones who betrayed him. The question each week remains the same: *Will you hold on?* To faith, even in struggle. To love, even when it hurts. To grace, even when it's undeserved. Because with God, relationships are everything.

Week One

Genesis 32:22-31 | Don't Let Go: Hold On Through the Struggle

> **Key Images**: desert/wilderness, river, night, wrestling, daybreak
>
> **Themes**: guilt and shame, self-reflection, change through conflict, humility

> Then he said, "Let me go, for the day is breaking." But Jacob said, "I will not let you go, unless you bless me." (Genesis 32:26)

Up to this point, cunning and deception are the only tools Jacob has known how to use in life. In fact, a survey of his life suggests that this is both his nature (Genesis 25:26) and a product of his nurturing (Genesis 27:5-17). Whichever the case, Jacob has well lived into his name as a "supplanter" and "deceiver," leaving a trail of unresolved, broken relationships—chief of which is his brother, Esau. Their last encounter resulted in Jacob secretly betraying his brother and Esau openly plotting murderous revenge.

Now, afraid to face his brother and the consequences of his actions after these many years, Jacob is alone at night by the Jabbok River. It is seemingly in this stillness that Jacob *wrestles*. This is the only occurrence of this verb in the Hebrew Bible. It is related to the word *abaq* (אָבָק), meaning "dust" or "to be covered in dust." The image is intimate and visceral—Jacob is not just struggling; he is grappling physically and emotionally in the dust of the earth. And this struggle is deeply relational, reflecting Jacob's lifelong wrangling—with Esau, Laban, and now God.

The fact that he wrestles is commendable enough, but the real pivot that enables transformation is in Jacob's refusal to *let go* (שָׁלַח *shalach*, meaning to send away or release), even after being wounded in the struggle. Unlike before, Jacob is determined to hold on to this relationship, which is defined by struggle, until it becomes a blessing (בָּרַךְ *barakh*, favor that implies a bestowal of strength and identity). Jacob, the deceiver, is seeking a relationship that will redefine him.

This is not a story about winning the match but about *not letting go*. And so, Jacob becomes Israel (יִשְׂרָאֵל *Yisra'el*, "one who struggles with God" or "God prevails"), resulting now in a new ability to see the "face of God" in others (Genesis 33:10). Cunning and deception have been supplanted by humility and love. Relationships require us to stay in the struggle long enough to be changed by it.

| Are we willing to be redefined by relationships that force us to struggle?

Week Two

Genesis 37:1-4, 12-28 | Don't Let Go: Hold On Through Betrayal

Key Images: shepherds, goats, Joseph in the pit, torn robe

Themes: sibling rivalry, betrayal, grief

> But when his brothers saw that their father loved him more than all his brothers, they hated him and could not speak peaceably to him. (Genesis 37:4)

One may be forgiven in assuming that Jacob might have been more sensitive to the perils of sibling rivalry. Yet, just as his parents played favorites, so now Jacob stokes the tensions between his sons (perhaps, too, his daughters who are scarcely mentioned save Dinah, the unintentional subject of conflict between father and sons in Genesis 34). Though scripture does not specify Jacob's reaction to Joseph's slanderous report about his brothers, the assumption is that Jacob's justice towards his children is prejudiced and not without bias. And so, Jacob's singular love towards Joseph adds insult to injury and sparks hatred (שָׂנֵא *sane'*, implying estrangement and active opposition).

Curiously, the brothers do not hate their father, who ostensibly is the real source of the issue. Rather, they hate Joseph whose obliviousness to his privilege is infuriatingly insulting. Joseph is a problem, and they want him out of the family. The Hebrew says *they could not speak peaceably to him*—literally, *they could not say shalom*.

And so, they stripped him (פָּשַׁט *pashat*, meaning to strip off violently, like flaying an animal), as an act of dehumanization, and they threw him into the pit (שָׁלַח *shalach*, meaning to cast out or throw away). The brothers are severing ties, choosing division over reconciliation. Instead of holding on, they let go in the most violent way possible, resulting in further estrangement from their father (v. 35).

Though it may not always lead to violent ends, this is what happens when we fail to deal with our wounds. In families, in churches, in communities—resentment brews, silence grows, and before we know it, we have let go and thrown someone into a pit. Letting go is easy because it centers my experience above or at the expense of yours. Holding on, however, forces me to contend with your experience alongside my own—enabling both to inform and enrich the other.

> Who have we let go of too easily?
>
> What pit have we helped create—with our silence, resentment, or fear?
>
> What might it mean to begin the work of repair?

Week Three

Genesis 45:1-15 | Don't Let Go: Hold On Through Forgiveness

> **Key Images**: weeping, Joseph embracing his brothers
>
> **Themes**: reconciliation, forgiveness,

> Then Joseph said to his brothers, "Come closer to me." And they came closer. He said, "I am your brother, Joseph, whom you sold into Egypt. And now do not be distressed or angry with yourselves because you sold me here, for God sent me before you to preserve life. (Genesis 45:4-5)

Here the conflict between the sons of Jacob finally reaches resolution. Whereas before it was the powerful older sibling (Esau) showing mercy towards the weaker younger brother (Jacob), now in a great reversal Joseph the powerful younger sibling chooses to make peace with his weaker, older brothers.

Having heard of his father's reaction to the potential loss of Benjamin (Genesis 44:18-34), Joseph *could no longer control himself* (הִתְאַפֵּק *hit'appeq*, meaning "to restrain" or "to hold back"). Perhaps Joseph is overcome with emotion because of the distress of Jacob or even that of Judah should he not return home with Benjamin. Or perhaps Joseph recognizes the dysfunctional family dynamic that continues to perpetuate perilous sibling rivalry and fosters resentment. Whichever the case, Joseph's first words to his brothers—*I am Joseph. Is my father still alive?*—may reflect less of a concern for his father's health and more of an acknowledgment of his father's continued negative influence over their lives. It is hard to escape the systems in which we have been nurtured.

Nevertheless, Joseph invites his brothers to *come closer* and offers a word of grace—*do not be distressed* (יְרָא *tira,* meaning fear, distress, or guilt)—even while acknowledging the real harm that was perpetrated. Grace always includes accountability. His leaning into the possibility of reconciliation enables him to recast the story of their betrayal as a story of God's faithfulness. Though his brothers cast him (שָׁלַח *shalach*) into a pit in Genesis 37, now in Joseph's retelling God sent him (שָׁלַח *shalach*) ahead of his brothers in order to preserve life.

This is not forgiveness that ignores pain and dysfunction. It is forgiveness that transforms it. Joseph chooses not to let go of his brothers—not to remain in bitterness, but to offer reconciliation. Life with God and God's people is about forgiveness not as forgetting, but as choosing to love again and again.

We are called to hold and uphold each other with love, grace, and forgiveness.

> What hurts must you acknowledge before recasting your story as a testimony of God's faithfulness?
>
> Who do you need to hold again—with mercy and grace?

Words for Worship, After Pentecost

Gathering

Call to Worship (Psalm 105:1-6, 45b)
(Rachel Cornwell)

Come, everyone, young and old, come to worship our loving God!
Let us give thanks to God, call on God's name,
and share the stories of God's goodness with all.
Sing songs of joy,
tell of all the amazing things God has done.
Let's celebrate God's holy name
and be glad in God's presence!
Remember the wonderful things God has done,
and let's praise the Lord together!
Praise be to God, now and always!

Call to Worship (Romans 10:5-15)
(Rachel Cornwell)

Come, seek the presence of God,
and find strength in love that never fades.
For all who trust in the Holy
will find dignity and hope; never disgrace.
We are all one in the spirit of God's love and unity.
Our God is for all,
offering mercy and grace to all who reach out.
All who call with open hearts will find salvation and renewal.
How beautiful are those who bring messages
of hope, peace, and justice to the world!

Prayer of Confession (Genesis 32:22-31)
(Rachel Cornwell)

O God of many names,
We often think that we are wrestling against you when we are really struggling with ourselves. We hold on tight to our habits, attitudes, our biases, and judgments. We cling to our own understanding and perspectives.

Release us, O God, from all that binds us, and bless us with new and abundant life. Open our minds and hearts to your truth and help us to see ourselves inside and out; to be honest about our shortcomings and blind spots, our transgressions and weaknesses. Free us from the grasp of our addictions and our unhealthy egos, so that we might more fully embrace you and the new life you offer us in Jesus Christ. Amen.

Proclaiming

Prayer for Illumination (Matthew 15:(1-10), 21-28)
(Rachel Cornwell)

Spirit of Wisdom, we are listening and trying to understand.
But what you are revealing to us is not always clear.
Open our hearts and minds.
Remove from us our preconceived ideas
and arrogant assumptions.
Surprise us!
We wait with anxious anticipation.
Amen.

Thanksgiving

Offertory Prayer (Genesis 45:1-15 and Psalm 133)
(Rachel Cornwell)

Generous God,
In times of scarcity, you provide for us all that we need.
We are your faithful remnant,
the ones who live to sing your praises.
So we offer to you the thanksgiving of our hearts,
and a willing sacrifice of our hands.
Multiply our gifts so that they may be used to bless others.
In your holy name.
Amen.

Prayers of the People (Genesis 37:1-4, 12-28 and Matthew 14:22-33)
(Rachel Cornwell)

Family of faith,
When we gather together in community,
we bring our whole selves with us.
We carry into worship today our deepest hurts and longings,
Our brightest joys and celebrations.
We long to offer all these things to God,
And to share them with each other.
So let us pray . . .

God of us all, like children we come,
Holding nothing back from you.
We confess that sometimes it can feel like a competition,
seeing which one of us you love the most,
seeking your blessings and favor.
But we know deep down
there is more than enough of your love, grace, and mercy
for each and every one of us.

Sometimes we are afraid.
We feel battered by the storms of life,
But in the early light of this new day
We see you, reaching out to us,
inviting us to step out in faith once more
And to put our trust in you.

So we offer you this day the prayers of our hearts,
For each other and those we love.

For our community, church, and the world.
For places where there is violence and strife,
For those who hunger and long for liberation,
For anyone who is sick or in grief.

God, be with them.
Extend your hand to lift them up
And save them from the rising tide of despair.

Gracious God,
We give you thanks for all that is good, and true,
The love of those we call family,
The dreams of a better future
and work for a more just world now.
The hope we have in each other when we risk it all to follow you.
We celebrate life and love
and all the blessings that you have offered us.

Thank you for lifting us up
from the pits and pitfalls of life;
For saving us when we felt we were sinking,
offering us another chance to try again.
Help us to be bold in our discipleship
and generous in our love for one another.
In the name of the one we know as your beloved Son,
Jesus the Christ we pray. Amen.

Great Thanksgiving (Matthew 14:13-21)
(Rachel Cornwell)

Lift up your hearts
We give thanks to God.

Blessed are you, O God, who with your Word and Holy Spirit
created all things and called them good.
From the edge of the River Jabbock to the shore of the Sea of Galilee,
and beyond, to every place and time,
You meet us face to face.
You feed our hungers, you quench our thirst,
You heal our brokenness and give us new life by water and the Spirit.

In Jesus Christ, your Word became flesh and dwelt among us.
He fed those without food; he healed the sick and ate with outcasts.
He took bread and fish and with a blessing,
Turned fears of scarcity into a meal of abundance.

In the cross of Christ, you took upon yourself our sin and death,
And destroyed their power forever.
You raised from the dead this same Jesus,
who now reigns with you in glory,
and poured upon us your Holy Spirit,
making us the people of your new covenant.

On the night before meeting with death
Jesus took bread, gave thanks to you, broke the bread,
gave it to the disciples, and said:
"Take, eat; this is my body which is given for you.
Do this in remembrance of me."

When the supper was over Jesus took the cup,
gave thanks to you, gave it to the disciples, and said:
"Drink from this, all of you;
this is my blood of the new covenant,
poured out for you and for all for the forgiveness of sins.
Do this, as often as you drink it, in remembrance of me."

And so, in remembrance of these your mighty acts in Jesus Christ,
we offer all that we are and all that we have
as a holy and living sacrifice,
in union with Christ's offering for us.

Pour out your Holy Spirit on us gathered here and on these gifts,
that in the breaking of this bread and the drinking from this cup
we may be filled by the presence of the living Christ
and be renewed as the body of Christ for the world.

May we be sent out into the world
To share this feast with others,
until Christ comes again and we feast at your table forever.
Through Christ, with Christ, in Christ, in the unity of the Holy Spirit,
all honor and glory is yours, almighty God, now and forever.
Amen.
—selections from "A Brief Great Thanksgiving for General Use," *The United Methodist Hymnal*

Sending

Communal Covenant Renewal Liturgy
(Britney Winn Lee)

It is through our sacred covenants—made with one another, in front of God, and by way of grace—that we are held to our healing.
In making these promises, we commit ourselves to ever growing in the understanding of their mystery and their power.
Since the beginning and throughout time, God—in divine humility and hope—voiced vows with God's creation, exemplifying for us, always, that the words we offer matter.

Here, today, we have remembered Word's power.

Out of the power of the Word, the story of the universe was set into motion. In the declaration of the Word, Image Bearers were named good.
Through the mercy of the Word, God's people were held through exile and homecoming. With the truth of the Word, the prophets called us to love once more.
For the promise of the Word, God joined in our humanity. At the table, with his words, Jesus made family of strangers, friends of enemies, and room for the suffering and the sinner.

When the Word-made-flesh was killed, but not forever, he rose again and sent the Spirit, that the Church would be born.

It is for this church and with our own words that we have committed ourselves, expanded ourselves, and now renewed ourselves, again.
What a gift it is to know grace in this way! What an honor it is to serve with these people, in this place, at this exact moment in history!
Give us joy for our promises; grant us peace in upholding them! Root us in the truth of our mission; and fill us with the liberation that you wish for all your people!

Knowing they matter, as they have always mattered, we say these words together today: Now more than ever, we are humbly and wholly committed to the witness of Christ in this world.

In the name of God the Creator, Jesus the Christ, and the Holy Spirit. Amen.

Benediction (Matthew 15: [10-20], 21-28)
(Rachel Cornwell)

Go now into the world to share the good news
with everyone you meet along the way.
Do not withhold God's blessing from anyone,

But see each person as God's beloved.
Extend the table of grace so that none feel they need to beg.
But allow God's abundance to overflow through you.
In the name of Christ, the Shepherd of all.
Amen.

Year A Lectionary Texts

Because Mercy	Exodus 1:8-2:10	Psalm 124	**Romans 12:1-8**	Matthew 16:13-20
Because Mercy	Exodus 3:1-15	Psalm 105:1-6, 23-26, 45b	**Romans 12:9-21**	Matthew 16:21-28
Because Mercy	Exodus 12:1-14	Psalm 149	**Romans 13:8-14**	Matthew 18:15-20
Because Mercy	Exodus 14:19-31	Exodus 15:1b-11, 20-21	**Romans 14:1-12**	Matthew 18:21-35

Because Mercy: **A Series for Worship After Pentecost**

> God's mercy is the lens by which we should both view our
> lives and live with each other, so that by grace our lives
> might become entirely merciful and grace filled.

And so the Christian is called upon not to be like a thermometer conforming to the temperature of his society, but he must be like a thermostat serving to transform the temperature of his society.
—Martin Luther King, Jr., "Transformed Nonconformist"

King would often return to this theme in his sermons as a rallying cry for the church of his day to live more fully into the claims of the gospel—namely that how the Christian lives matters just as much as the fact that the Christian lives. And this *how* is lived out in the minutia of daily life in the here and now, infusing into each thought, word, and action a new meaning and purpose—i.e., an ethic of holiness. This ethic is neither legalistic nor lackadaisical; rather, it is a way of living that is animated by the Holy Spirit and defined by God's mercies.

Like King, Paul writes to an ethnically diverse, socially marginalized, and theologically unsettled community wrestling with the question of how to live with each other. The answer—mercy. God's mercies, revealed through the indwelling of the Spirit, become the ground and the guide for how Christians not only discover hope but give hope to a groaning creation (Romans 8:22). Because of mercy, the Spirit-filled people of God live differently, act differently—especially in the face of hostility, in the face of violence, in the face of distrust, in the face of conflict.

Because of mercy, Spirit-filled people don't write others off. Because of mercy, Spirit-filled people don't stir up mess. Because of mercy, Spirit-filled people don't look for fights. Because of mercy, Spirit-filled people know their lives are not their own, and so they continually and totally submit themselves to the God as holy and living sacrifices, trusting that as the Holy Spirit brings new life into their bodies then their now Spirit-filled lives will bring life into the world.

Consider offering the congregation tangible expressions of mercy:

- Create a covenant banner or wall.
- Ivite people to write their experiences or ideas about mercy on cards, ribbons, etc.
- Place expressions on a banner or wall.

Alternatively, facilitate more direct actions for people to take as part of the church and community.

Worship planners should consider pairing this series with tangible expressions of mercy. Congregations could create a covenant banner or wall, where each week congregants can write their act of mercy or insight on a ribbon, card, or tile and add it to a wall/banner. Or you may choose to do something more direct, such as:

- **Week 1**—Invite congregants to sign up for one new act of service in the church or community that reflects their gifts (e.g., hospitality, music, visiting the sick, mentoring youth). Provide a card or form that says: "Because mercy, I offer, . . ." with blanks for them to name their gift and a way they will offer it this week. [note: be sure to develop a way to acknowledge and respond to each card]

- **Week 2**—Encourage each person to reach out to someone they've been distant from or even hurt by—a simple note, call, or prayer to rebuild or bless without expecting return. Provide sample prayers or phrases for those unsure how to begin.

- **Week 3**—Hold a clothing drive for a local shelter or ministry [note: be sure to ask them first]. Ask participants to not only give clothes but to include a handwritten note of blessing or encouragement with each item.

- **Week 4**—Host a "Because Mercy" community dinner and dialogue, intentionally inviting community members of differing perspectives or faiths. Provide a "Mercy Conversation Card" with reflective questions like:
    - What gives you hope right now?
    - How has someone shown you mercy recently?
    - How might we multiply mercy in our community?

In his *Letter from a Birmingham Jail,* King describes the early church's witness in the world as being very powerful, saying *They were too God-intoxicated to be "astronomically intimidated."* Perhaps this is what makes Christianity so dangerous and offensive and alluring—mercy becomes too intoxicating to ignore, too infectious to control, and too invigorating to ever remain the same.

Week One

Romans 12:1-8 | Because Mercy Re-creates Us

Key Images: living sacrifice, worship, members of the body

Themes: transformed heart and life, spiritual gifts, unity

> "I appeal to you therefore, brothers and sisters, by
> the mercies of God . . ." (Romans 12:1)

Paul's urgent appeal is rooted in the phrase *by the mercies of God*—where the plural *oiktirmoi* (meaning "compassions, manifestations of pity") emphasizes not a singular act but the multitude of God's compassionate acts. The word is deeply emotive, stemming from a root associated with visceral compassion (cf. Hebrew *rachamim* from *rechem*, "womb"). As Paul has explicated in the preceding chapters, these mercies are an essential attribute of God's character and the ground of Christian living.

Thus, a realized Christian ethic is literally a full-bodied reflexive response to God's mercies—present your bodies as a living sacrifice (v.1). Unlike temple offerings, this is a holistic, daily self-offering, literally "logical worship"—the reasonable response to mercy.

The point is to be re-created by mercy. This mercy, revealed in Christ, is not to remain theoretical or internal—it becomes the lens through which we see ourselves, others, and the world. And so, our differences are no longer divisions but become gifts of grace (χαρίσματα, charismata) for the common good.

What must we do now because of mercy?

Who must we become now because of mercy?

Week Two

Romans 12:9-21 | Because Mercy Unmasks Us

> **Key Images:** loving relationships, acts of kindness and hospitality
>
> **Themes:** unhypocritical love, peace as protest, co-suffering solidarity, response to evil

Let love be genuine. Hate what is evil; hold fast to what is good. (Romans 12:9)

"Let love be genuine." The Greek adjective *anypokritos* (ἀνυπόκριτος) literally means "without hypocrisy"—i.e., love that is unmasked, sincere. This aligns with the Hebrew prophetic call to integrity in action (cf. Amos 5:21–24). It conveys a sense of boundlessness in consistency, so that love and all the other virtues that follow are neither biased nor prejudiced in application.

Having been transformed *by the mercies of God* (v.1), this unmasked way of being becomes the dominant theme of Christian community. And so, the call to overcome evil with good encapsulates the essence of mercy in action. Rather than seeking revenge, believers are to respond to enemies with kindness, thereby embodying the mercy they have received.

Ultimately, the invitation is to choose to live *unmasked*. We choose through daily virtuous living that humbly receives and gives God's mercies. We choose by refusing to see or treat those around us as anything other than beloved children of God and fellow partakers in the promises of God.

There's a line in the spiritual *I Got a Robe* that says, *everybody talking 'bout heaven ain't going there*. The idea is that somebody is lying to themselves. Many of us become fluent in the language of mercy while never practicing mercy. We live masked when we sing "Let there be peace on earth and let it begin with me" but we allow rage and vengeance to dominate our approach towards others and the world. We live masked when we quote "Love your neighbor as yourself" but we treat strangers with suspicion and stifle generosity in ourselves or from others.

Mercy unmasks us. What masks do you need to take off?

Week Three

Romans 13:8-14 | Because Mercy Distinguishes Us

> **Key Images**: light vs. darkness, debt ledger, clothing, armor
>
> **Themes**: communal love vs. legalism, accountability and restoration, identity in Christ, salvation

> Instead, put on the Lord Jesus Christ, and make no provision for the flesh, to gratify its desires. (Romans 13:14)

The verb ὀφείλετε (*opheilete*, "owe") comes from a root meaning debt or obligation. The only continuing debt, Paul says, is ἀγαπᾶν (*agapan*), the verb form of agape. This agapē is a mercy-rooted, self-giving love that moves beyond fairness to radical grace. Mercy compels justice and love within the body. In a world of retribution and fractured relationships, Christian community is marked by active, restorative love—a debt we owe perpetually.

This has eschatological urgency—*For salvation is nearer to us now than when we became believers* (v.11). This is not passive waiting but active realization of salvation. Here mercy is not a mood, but an identity. Using baptismal imagery, we are to be clothed in Christ (ἐνδύσασθε *endysasthe*, meaning "to put on, be clothed with). Referring to taking on a new identity, like changing uniforms, this verb calls us to a visible, external expression of mercy that stems from internal transformation.

Clothing is a theme repeated throughout the Pauline epistles (e.g. Galatians 3:27, Ephesians 4:24, Colossians 3:12), reflecting a new identity in Christ—family resemblance. How Christians live, how they treat each other, how they demonstrate self-control, how they are content, how they cultivate joy and make peace and fight for justice—these are all markers of family resemblance.

| How is mercy changing not just what I do, but who I am?

Week Four

Romans 14:1-12 | Because Mercy Unifies Us

> **Key Images**: scales or judgment seat, food, sacrifices, holiday festivals
>
> **Themes**: welcome and hospitality, forgiveness, generosity of spirit

> Why do you pass judgment on your brother or sister? Or you, why do you despise your brother or sister? (Romans 14:10)

Addressing intra-community tensions over standards of holiness, Paul begins with a call to "welcome" (προσλαμβάνεσθε, *proslambanesthe*) the one who is "weak in faith." This is not passive tolerance but an active drawing in—a term often used in ancient hospitality or in receiving someone into one's home. Paul furthers the point in v. 4, using the imagery of a household servant and their master: *Who are you to pass judgment on the servant of another?* Just as one servant has no right to judge another in someone else's household, so believers have no jurisdiction to judge fellow servants of Christ. Thus, mercy is not just something we receive; it's something we *extend*, especially across lines of disagreement and diversity—because all belong to the Lord.

The word "judge" (κρινεῖς *krineis*) appears frequently in this passage, not in forbidding discernment but condemning a kind of judgment rooted in pride or contempt and assumes divine prerogative. The parallel verb "despise" (ἐξουθενεῖς *exoutheneis*) conveys disregard or disdain for another's worth.

Paul addresses a church likely divided along lines of dietary law, holy days, and conscience. But instead of trying to *resolve* the differences, he redirects the focus: Who is Lord? Not us, but Christ. Mercy respects this divine lordship.

Mercy here becomes **spaciousness**—the grace to allow others to belong fully even when they believe or practice differently. This is true unity. As Matthew Skinner puts it, *Love's secure bonds reflect what unity is about, even as its generosity creates the space for unity to occur.* To put it in another context, this is not organizational unity which demands that kind of assimilation that requires you to become like me, think like me, act like me. Organizational unity requires centralized power and the dominance of a particular brand or identity with the suppression of all others. Organizational unity is necessarily based on rigid policies with rigid interpretation.

Paul calls for mutual humility, grounded in the awareness that each of us will give account to God, and none of us is beyond the need for grace. This is a radical redefinition of community. The church isn't a club of the like-minded—it is a communion of the mercied.

Words for Worship, After Pentecost

Gathering

Call to Worship (Exodus 1:8-2:10)
(Tori Butler)

God of Joseph, you have preserved us and sustained us during times of famine.
For that we call you Jehovah Jireh, Our Provider.
God of Shiphrah and Puah, you give us courage to do what is right even when those in powerful positions try to influence us to do otherwise.

For that we call you El Shaddai, God Almighty.
God of Moses, you have saved us from death and destruction so that we might lead others into a deeper and more intimate relationship with you.
For that we call you Deliverer and Savior.
God of us All, we will forever worship and remember your name. Amen.

Call to Worship (Romans 12:1-8; Exodus 2:1-10; Psalm 124)
(Deborah Ann Wong)

We have come here to worship the living God,
to offer ourselves as a living sacrifice, holy and pleasing to God.
Yet it is only by God's mercy that we are able to draw near,
and only by God's grace that we are made holy and pleasing to God.
If it had not been the Lord who was on our side—
If it had not been the Lord who was on our side—
then the flood would have swept us away.
But the Lord drew us out of the water,
so that we might know his great mercy and love.
Let us bless the Lord, who desires that none should perish, but that all should be saved and be called children of God, one body united in Christ.

Call to Worship (Exodus 3:1-15)
(Deborah Ann Wong)

God has called us to this place.
Here we are.
As God told Moses to remove the sandals from his feet, God invites us to remove whatever is keeping us from drawing close to our holy God.
As Moses turned aside to see the burning bush, we turn from the distractions and temptations of our lives and fix our gaze on God.
God is here with us. We are standing on holy ground.
Here we are, God, ready to receive all you want to show us today.

Proclaiming

Prayer for Illumination (Romans 12:9-21)
(Tori Butler)

God you are love. You invite us to love one another deeply, fully, and genuinely. You implore us to bless those who persecute us and to rejoice with those who are rejoicing. You encourage us not to repay evil for evil but to do what is right. Therefore, may your loving Spirit permeate the reading of the scripture, the singing of the songs, and the proclamation of the word. In the name of Jesus, the one who overcame evil simply by being good. Amen.

Prayer for Illumination (Romans 12:1-8)
(Deborah Ann Wong)

God of all truth, we have come to hear your voice, to learn your ways. Give us ears to hear, that we might be transformed as your Word renews our minds and strengthened by your grace to be doers of your Word, using the gifts you have given us to do the work you have called us to, through Jesus Christ our Lord. Amen.

Thanksgiving

Offering Prayer (Romans 12:1-8)
(Tori Butler)

Giver of every good and perfect thing,
We give You thanks for offering Your very body on the cross, showing us the true meaning of sacrifice. God, empower us to give of our tithes and offerings not begrudgingly, but with joy and gratitude. Help us to see our generosity not as an obligation, but as an act of worship—one that reflects Your own love and faithfulness. May our gifts be used to build Your kingdom, bless others, and bring glory to Your name. Let our worship, in giving and in all things, be pleasing and acceptable in Your sight. In Jesus's name, Amen.

A Prayer for Unity (Romans 12:1-8)
(Deborah Ann Wong)

O Lord, you have given us each different gifts, according to the grace given to us. Keep us from using those gifts for self-exaltation and self-indulgence. Deliver us from the fear that causes us to see others as enemies and competition and keep us from seeing others' success as a cause of our lacks. By the work of your Spirit, transform our sight and renew our minds that we might recognize that we are members of one body in Christ, and might offer our gifts in love and service to one another, for the flourishing of your Church, to the glory of your name. Amen.

Prayers of the People (Exodus 1:8-2:10)
(Deborah Ann Wong)

God of love, you have heard the cry of your people. Bind up the wounds of all those who have suffered at the hands of those who do evil. Send your Spirit to comfort us in our pain and let us know your presence in Jesus who weeps with us. When we are tempted to harden our hearts against those who hurt us, soften our hearts with your love. Drive away all fear and keep our desire for justice from turning into a desire to seek revenge. Fill us with a deep trust in your mercy and justice, knowing that you will make all things right in your perfect timing.

God of grace, you have told us to hate what is evil and cling to what is good. Yet you call us also to love those who do evil, those who oppress your people, as Pharaoh did. Give us grace to view everyone, even our enemies, through the lens of your mercy, even as we exercise the power you have given us to resist the evil and injustice that they enact. By your Spirit, pour out your boundless love afresh in our hearts, that your love might transform our sight, and we might see those we have been taught to hate or fear as threats as fellow bearers of your image, in need of your love and mercy.

God of mercy, we confess that we have also been doers of evil, by what we have done, and by what we have left undone. Forgive us for the times when we have failed to take pity on those who cried out in help. Forgive us for the times when we have turned away from those in need out of fear that helping them might result in our own neediness or harm. Like Pharaoh's daughter, may we not blindly follow the evil ways of those in power, but see and act with mercy, as you have shown us mercy. Fill us with your love that casts out all fear, and grant us the courage to do what is right in your eyes, no matter the cost; to love justice, show mercy, and walk humbly with you, our God, in whose footsteps we follow. We offer ourselves as living sacrifices, as clay in the Potter's hand. Shape us and mold us to be more like Jesus, our Savior, in whose name pray and ask these things. Amen.

Sending

Sending (Exodus 3:1-15; Isaiah 61:1-2)
(Deborah Ann Wong)

As you go forth into the world, may you go with the confidence that the great I AM has sent you, and that you are marked by God's presence. Go in the strength of God's Spirit, to bring good news to the oppressed, to bind up the broken-hearted, to proclaim liberty to the captives and release to the prisoners, and to demonstrate the goodness of our God.

Year A Lectionary Texts

Go With Us	**Exodus 16:2-15**	Psalm 105:1-6, 37-45	Philippians 1:21-30	Matthew 20:1-16
Go With Us	**Exodus 17:1-7**	Psalm 78:1-4, 12-16	Philippians 2:1-13	Matthew 21:23-32
Go With Us	Exodus 20:1-4, 7-9, 12-20	**Psalm 19**	Philippians 3:4b-14	Matthew 21:33-46
Go With Us	**Exodus 32:1-14**	Psalm 106:1-6, 19-23	Philippians 4:1-9	Matthew 22:1-14
Go With Us	**Exodus 33:12-23**	Psalm 99	1 Thessalonians 1:1-10	Matthew 22:15-22
Go With Us	Deuteronomy 34:1-12	**Psalm 90:1-6, 13-17**	1 Thessalonians 2:1-8	Matthew 22:34-46

Go With Us: A Worship Series for after Pentecost

> Circumstances can have us looking for God in all the wrong places or doubting God's presence at all. We need God to go with us.

It's a question often asked by children when they are unsure of what lies ahead or of their capacity to do the task before them—*Will you go with me?* Of course, we never quite grow out of the question or the need for wise counsel and guidance and help, because life is filled with uncertainty.

Uncertainty can feel like staring blankly into the distance completely unsure of what to do, where to go, who to call, or who to trust. It can feel like you are waiting for something—or maybe nothing—completely unsure of what comes next or even afraid of what comes next. Whether it is worries about home or finances, relationships or employment, health or estrangement from God, uncertainty can really mess with your mind and your sense of wellbeing, leaving you displaced and utterly exhausted.

Yet, the strength of the child's question is in the confidence that their guardian will answer and be present. In times of wilderness—when clarity is lost, when frustration rises, when delays provoke doubt—we are tempted to question the presence of God. This series traces Israel's wilderness journey through key passages in Exodus and Psalms, and their collective movement from *Is the Lord among us or not?* (Exodus 17:7) to *If your presence will not go with us, do not bring us up from here* (Exo-

33:15). **This is a series for those who have left what was but have not yet arrived where they hope to be.** Rather than asking, "Where is God?" the people of God now declare: "We will not move without you." The journey ahead—whether into unknown futures, new seasons, or hard decisions—only holds meaning if God goes with us.

Though this suggested worship series primarily focuses on the Exodus story, twice it diverts to the complementary psalm for the day. The first instance may fall on what many congregations will celebrate as World Communion Sunday, and the second may fall on what some may celebrate as Reformation Sunday. In both instances, the psalm text offers an elaboration of the series theme that is consonant with the corresponding Exodus text even if not specifically present therein. As such the psalm may offer more creative ground in approaching the respective ecumenical celebrations.

Give thought to defining "us" for your congregation's context. Celebrate with the church universal:

- World Communion Sunday
- Laity Sunday
- Children's Sabbath
- Reformation Sunday

Use other resources to connect within your denomination.

Help your congregants write their own liturgies to express God's presence in your community

Notwithstanding, worship designers should give thought to defining "us" for your context. This series will span dates for many ecumenical celebrations, including World Communion Sunday, Laity Sunday, Children's Sabbath, and Reformation Sunday. Each of these may provide opportunities to help expand the congregation's sense of "us" and its connection with the church universal. Denominational resources will be helpful here. Beyond this, congregations could write their own liturgies using focus statements as liturgical prompts (e.g. for Exodus 16—*Who are the hungry? Where is God for the hungry? What bread is God supplying now?*).

Whichever the case be intentional about curating conversation and imagination around the power and promise of God *with* us—not some of us, but all of us.

> How does God's presence shift us from crisis and complaint—"Is God even here?"—to confidence and assurance—"We will not go if You do not go with us?"

Week One

Exodus 16:2-15 | Go With Us: Provision

> **Key Images**: desert, hunger, bread, quail, cauldron (fleshpots), morning/evening, cloud
>
> **Themes**: divine presence and provision, fear and worry, trusting in God

Draw near to the LORD, for he has heard your complaining. (Exodus 16:9)

It is tempting to see this story as a bad case of being hangry, that is irritable because of hunger. Yet, the Hebrew word for *complain* used in the wilderness stories (lûn, meaning "to murmur") reflects discontent rooted in fear.

In the early days of wilderness life, hunger brings out the worst fears of the people: "Have we been brought out here to die?" (v. 3) The longing for meat seems a bit curious as they left Egypt with flocks and herds (Exodus 12:38) which could have been slaughtered for meat. While their fear may understandably be rooted in the uncertainty of survival resources in the desert for either their flocks or themselves, perhaps it may also be a fear that freedom may cost too much personally—more than they are willing to give or more than they think they can afford.

Whichever the case, the uncertainty inherent in freedom makes them long for the predictability of slavery. Yet amid their desperation and exasperation, God provides daily reminders to the people that though each day holds its own level of uncertainty, one thing remains the same: God will provide. And so, God tests (נָסָה nasah, meaning "to prove or refine") the Israelite's trust in God's ability, willingness, and faithfulness to provide.

The only instruction given to the people is to *Draw near to the LORD, for he has heard your complaining.* (Exodus 16:9). The preposition here (לִפְנֵי panim, meaning "before the face of") implies presence, notably to approach the presence of God in the cloud that has been and remains with them. God's presence is undeterred by their need, their fear, nor their complaint.

Through a daily rhythm of trust, a structure for obedience, and a mysterious provision, God is not only feeding them bread but weaning them off anxiety and into presence-led dependence.

> What does the wilderness reveal about our expectations of God?
>
> What do I do when God's provision looks unfamiliar?
>
> Where might God be feeding me in ways I haven't recognized?

Week Two

Exodus 17:1-7 | Go With Us: Refreshing

> **Key Images**: water gushing from rock, dry wilderness terrain, staff
>
> **Themes**: trust in the midst of suffering, divine presence and provision

> He called the place Massah and Meribah, because the Israelites quarreled and tested the Lord, saying, "Is the Lord among us or not?" (Exodus 17:7)

Significant here is that this is now the second instance of the people's complaint about water (see Exodus 15:22-26). Whereas the first instance ends with a command to *listen carefully to the voice of the Lord your God . . . who heals you* (Exodus 15:26), this passage begins with them journeying *as the Lord commanded* (literally, "by the voice of the Lord") to Rephidim (from a verb meaning "refresh" or "support") where *there was no water for the people to drink* (v.1). And so, immediately the reader is meant to catch the tension of the story and the impending lawsuit (רִיב rîb, "quarrel" or "legal dispute") the people now lodge against God to test (נָסָה nasah, meaning "to prove or refine") God's faithfulness.

The question—*Is the Lord among us or not?* (v.7)—is the central theological issue. Does the same God who promised healing also lead us *into* suffering? Is God with us in our suffering? Such questions underscore the tension between understanding God's presence as utilitarian performance rather than abiding support.

God seemingly answers the question positively by using something old to do something new. The instruction to Moses to *take in your hand the staff with which you struck the Nile* (v.5) is a visual reminder to the people of what God has already done when they were suffering the most. Now it is used to bring water—refreshment—from a hard place. If God did it before, God can and will do it again. *What does trust in God really look like when following God leads to a hard place?*

| What does it mean to intercede for a community that is afraid?

Week Three

Psalm 19 | Go With Us: Guidance

> **Key Images**: nature (sky, sun, earth), honey, honeycomb, gold, rock
>
> **Themes**: God's guidance, wisdom and discernment, God's presence with creation

> But who can detect one's own errors? Clear me from hidden faults. . . .
> Let the words of my mouth and the meditation of my heart be acceptable
> to you, O Lord, my rock and my redeemer. (Psalm 19:12, 14)

The lectionary pairs the giving of the Ten Commandments in Exodus 20 with Psalm 19, both marking a distinctive turning point: an invitation to listen. Whereas God's speaking in Exodus 20 results in fear—*You speak to us, and we will listen, but do not let God speak to us, lest we die.* (v.19)—the counterpoint in Psalm 19 results in resounding praise. The juxtaposition of these passages underscores how God's presence is mediated through both nature and torah (law) itself—if we listen.

The psalmist notes in v.1 that the heavens "declare" (סָפַר *saphar*, meaning to narrate or recount as a storyteller) God's glory. In other words, creation is not silent, it testifies through its very existence that God is in relationship with creation. Just as listening to the voice of creation gives one knowledge (דַּעַת *da'at*, discernment, perception, wisdom), so too listening to God's torah *enlightens the eyes* (v.8) and keeps one from *hidden faults* (שְׁגִיאוֹת *segia*, "unintentional errors or mistakes").

Ultimately the invocation to be found "acceptable" (רָצוֹן *ratson*, meaning delight or pleasure) denotes that which is pleasing to God—a word of relational intimacy. Thus, intimacy with God—through active listening for and to God's ongoing revelation—enables flourishing.

> Am I listening to the multiple ways God speaks—through creation, Scripture, and conscience?
>
> Is God's word shaping not only my actions but my thoughts and desires?
>
> What does it mean for my life to be "acceptable" in God's sight?

Week Four

Exodus 32:1-14 | Go With Us: Orientation

> **Key Images**: golden calf, revelry, broken tablets
>
> **Themes**: patience, idolatry, control, repentance and forgiveness

> And the Lord changed his mind about the disaster that he
> planned to bring on his people. (Exodus 32:14)

Moses has been gone too long, and the people below are restless. *We do not know what has become of him* (v.1)—a confession laced with fear, disorientation, and the deep human need for visible leadership. They're in-between: delivered from Egypt, but not yet at home. And it's in the in-between that orientation slips.

The phrase *go before us* (יֵלְכוּ לְפָנֵינוּ yelechu lefanenu) echoes God's earlier promises to "go before" them (Exodus 13:21)—but now, the people seek that leadership from something they control. They cry out not just for a god, but for direction—it's a longing for leadership, clarity, movement. In the wake of uncertainty and doubt, they melt gold, shape it with their hands, and point to the work of their own making and say, "This is what brought us here." When we lose sight of God, we often reach for substitutes—but what we really need is a re-orientation of our hearts toward God's presence.

It may be too easy to read God's response in v.10 merely as divine temper. The word for "let me alone" (יָנַח yanah, literally: "leave me so that . . .") shows God creating space for Moses—inviting intercession, opening the door for re-orientation. Perhaps this is a re-orientation for Moses—a kind of test to see if he, too, will distance himself from the people to secure divine favor for himself. Or perhaps it is God's re-orientation: Is God as temperamental as the Canaanite gods or can God's wrath be otherwise tempered?

Moses' intercession hinges on two points: God's reputation and God's promises. Here on the same mountain Moses was first introduced to God and the covenant promises, God is now reminded by Moses of the very same. And just as that first introduction sends Moses back to his people, so now Moses' intercession sends God back to God's people—*And the* LORD *changed his mind about the disaster he planned* . . . (v. 14). The Hebrew word *nacham* (נָחַם) means to repent with great sorrow and compassion. God was re-oriented back toward mercy, not because God had wandered, but because this is what love always chooses.

Both the people and God, in different ways, are turning. One turns toward a false image. One turns back toward mercy. The entire story pulses with questions:

> Where are we facing?
>
> And who is leading us?
>
> Are we oriented toward the presence of God—or simply toward movement?

Week Five

Exodus 33:12-23 | Go With Us: Companioning

> **Key Images**: rocks with significant fissures, tent of meeting
>
> **Themes**: power of presence, intimacy with God, the character of God, intercession

> And he said to him, "If your presence will not go, do not bring us up from here. (Exodus 33:15)

In the aftermath of betrayal, the people are still alive but something vital has fractured—not just trust, but the very relationship between God and the people. Earlier in Exodus 33, while God assures Moses and the people that the promises will be fulfilled and they will enter the land flowing with milk and honey, God will not go them. Instead, God will send a messenger—a distant guide. A functional blessing, but no fellowship.

And while it may accomplish the goal of getting to the Promised Land, for Moses the idea is unbearable. In verse 12, Moses pleads: *You have said, 'I know you by name, and you have found favor with me.' If that's true, then show me your ways . . .* He's not asking for a map—he's asking for companionship. The word "ways" (דֶּרֶךְ *derekh*) can mean path or journey, but it also implies shared life. Moses wants to know not just *where* to go, but *who* is going with him.

If your presence does not go with us, do not bring us up from here. (Exodus 33:15). Moses' request is not about efficiency or victory—it's about relationship. Here again is the Hebrew word for presence or face (פָּנִים *panim*). It conveys not just proximity but intimacy, attention, and mutual regard. Moses isn't asking for a distant oversight. He's asking for God to walk with, dwell among, remain beside.

This is companioning in its deepest form: shared experience, mutual presence, walking the same path together. The journey only matters if God shares it. Without God, the land is just geography. Without God, the journey is just wandering. Without God, freedom is hollow.

Ultimately, Moses doesn't want a promised future without the Promiser in the present. Moses isn't afraid of journeying into Canaan. He is afraid of journeying without God. This is a fundamental pivot for all spiritual life:

> Do we want what God offers, or do we want God Himself?

Week Six

Psalm 90:1-6, 13-17 | Go With Us: Viewpoint

> **Key Images:** mountaintop, a home or dwelling, dust being swept away, hands lifted in work
>
> **Themes:** faithfulness, God's steadfast love, perspective and wisdom

LORD, you have been our dwelling place in all generations. (Psalm 90:1)

The final words of the Pentateuch given in Deuteronomy 34 describe Moses' final moments on Mount Pisgah/Nebo. Here Moses has come to end of his journey, and after surveying the Promised Land, he dies and is buried. This is not failure but perspective. From this vantage point, Moses sees what he could not see in the valley: that God has been faithful, that the journey mattered.

Psalm 90, traditionally attributed to Moses, sounds like it may have been written from this very moment—a prayer not from the middle of the journey, but from its end. It is the prayer of someone who has walked with God, seen the brevity of life, and still believes that God is home. In the opening verse, "dwelling place" (מָעוֹן) *ma'on*) is perhaps better understood as not just a shelter, but a home base. The idea being: "You are where we return, where we rest, where we are known." It carries the sense of refuge, stability, enduring presence. In contrast to the wilderness tents, God is the permanent habitation across all generations, all time.

The psalm zooms out: from dust to dawn, from a thousand years to a breath. It is the viewpoint of eternity, spoken by someone who's learned that the point was never just to arrive—it was to walk with God. And though life may be fragile and uncertain—*You turn us back to dust . . . you sweep them away like a dream. (v.3-5)*—the psalmist is confident that God will "satisfy" (*śāba'*), implying fullness, a sense of being sated by *hesed* (חָסֶד steadfast, covenantal love). The psalmist does not ask for long life, or conquest, or completion. He asks to be filled—with love, with purpose, with the beauty of God upon us (v.17).

From this perspective, even unfinished stories are complete. Even when the journey ends on the mountain, the work of our hands is established because it has been companioned by God. The journey wasn't merely about reaching the land. It was about walking with God. In the end, God is the Promised Land.

Words for Worship, After Pentecost

Gathering

Call to Worship for Exodus 2: 1-15
(Trenton Teegarden)

In the wilderness, we often feel hungry and weary, asking ourselves whether God is truly with us.
Like the Israelites, we sometimes look for help in the wrong places, doubting God's presence.
Rest assured, God hears us, reminding us that we are not alone.
We gather today, longing for certainty and asking God to walk beside us.
Let us open our hearts to the God who sustains and guides us through the wilderness.
All: We come to worship, trusting that God goes with us today and always.

Call to Worship (Psalm 90: 1-6, 13-17)
(Trenton Teegarden)

Lord God, you have been our dwelling place in all generations.
In times of trouble, we seek your refuge.
Let us rejoice and be glad all our days!
When we feel discouraged and alone, we find hope in your eternal presence.
Let us rejoice and be glad all our days!
As we gather today, your steadfast love reassures us,
and we find hope in your eternal presence.
Let us rejoice and be glad all our days!
God with us, Lord, all our days, and give us strength
so we may share your love with the world.
Let us rejoice and be glad all our days!

Call to Worship (Exodus 16:2-15)
(Christie Hale)

O God, you are always faithful to your promise in all the places you've led us;
Gather us. Focus us. Enlighten us.
You hear our complaints in the desert when we are hungry.
Turn our hearts and minds to your presence and promise.
You send manna in the morning; you provide meat in the evening.
Go with us God, always.

Call to Worship (Exodus 17:1-7)
(Christie Hale)

O God, you are always faithful to your promise in all the places you've led us;
Gather us. Focus us. Enlighten us.
We hear the noise of our quarreling; how we tested you in the desert.
Turn our hearts and minds to your presence and promise.
You sent Moses with the elders to the rock; You made waters gush for your people.
Go with us God, always.

Call to Worship (Psalm 19)
(Christie Hale)

O God, you are always faithful to your promise in all the places you've led us;.
Gather us. Focus us. Enlighten us.
You instruct our lives and revive our very being.
Turn our hearts and minds to your presence and promise.
Pardon our unknown sin; save us from willful misdeeds.
Go with us God, always.

World Communion Sunday Call to Worship
(Britney Winn Lee)

The blood of Christ is translucent green, deep red, well-water clear, and black with three sugars.
It is offered this day from golden chalices, plastic pop-tops, hollowed calabashes, and borrowed mugs.
With the world that God loves, we share in its gift.
The body of Christ is paper-thin, Hawaiian sweet, sun-toasted cassava, and scraps under overpasses.
It is offered this day from ceramic saucers, goldfish baggies, tribal cloth, and paper towels.
With the world that God saves, we share in its gift.
The earth over, many hands will hold Christ today; many tongues will proclaim, "Remember."
With them all, we join our bodies and voices in worship and in sacrament. Amen.

Call to Worship (Exodus 32:1-14)
(Christie Hale)

O God, you are always faithful to your promise in all the places you've led us;.
Gather us. Focus us. Enlighten us.
You called your servant Moses up to Sinai; we felt afraid and abandoned.
Turn our hearts and minds to your presence and promise.
Moses reminded you of your mercy. You returned him to us with the covenant.
Go with us God, always.

Call to Worship (Exodus 33:13-23)
(Christie Hale)

O God, you are always faithful to your promise in all the places you've led us;
Gather us. Focus us. Enlighten us.
Moses begged for help to lead your people and you did exactly as he asked.
Turn our hearts and minds to your presence and promise.
You are determined to be compassionate, and bring us near to you.
Go with us God, always.

Call to Worship (Psalm 90)
(Christie Hale)

O God, you are always faithful to your promise in all the places you've led us;.
Gather us. Focus us. Enlighten us.
You have been our help, generation after generation.

Turn our hearts and minds to your presence and promise.
Let your servants see your mighty acts and our children see your glorious deeds.
Go with us God, always.

Confession & Pardon
(Christie Hale)

Let us join together, confessing our sins before God and each other.
Patient God, we argue, quarrel, complain and ignore you, day in and day out. You give us perfect instructions to revive our being—and we forget. You give us faithful laws to make us wise—and we ignore them. You give us right regulations to gladden our hearts—and we turn away. We are lost and return to our old ways when we don't see you. We doubt your promise and presence even though we know you to be faithful. You go with us, and provide extravagantly for us. Break open our hard hearts to your presence. Soften our hardheadedness to respond to your graceful ways. We seek your forgiveness for our sins, individually and collectively. We humbly ask to be brought into right relationship with you.
(Silence may be kept)
Hear the good news. Though we have broken our relationship with God, creation, each other, and ourselves: God is gracious and loving. In the name of Jesus Christ, you are forgiven.
In the name of Jesus Christ, you are forgiven. Thanks be to God. Amen.

Proclaiming

Prayer for Illumination
(Christie Hale)

Glorious God, **open our eyes to see your presence and our ears to hear your word. Open our minds to practice your teachings growing our faith and action. For in the strength of the Spirit we ask this. Amen.**

Thanksgiving

Offertory Prayer (Matthew 21:33-46)
(Trenton Teegarden)

Gracious God, as we offer our gifts today, we thank you for your unfaltering love and the global community of Christians across cultures and denominations. May our gifts reflect our gratitude and commitment to your work and bless them to bear fruit in your Kingdom. Bringing hope and unity to all those in need. Go with us as we share your love and grace with all. We pray in the name of Jesus Christ, who unites the world. Amen.

Prayers of the People
(Christie Hale)

Let us gather our prayers together lift our petitions collectively to God.

We pray for the whole of the earth: **grant restoration to creation.**
We ask for wisdom among the leaders of the world: **endow them with discernment to govern justly.**
May all nations have unity of purpose: **to care for all people.**
To our churches **may we serve you with gladness and singleness of heart;**
For all who are suffering **grant your peace;**
For all who are lonely **grant your comfort;**
For the needs of our congregation **grant your guidance;**
We bring these petitions and those in our hearts into the prayer that Jesus taught to us saying, **Our Father . . . (The Lord's Prayer) . . . Amen.**

Sending

Benediction
(Christie Hale)

As we go forth today receive this benediction
May God the Creator fill us with faithful love:
let us rejoice and celebrate our whole life long!
May God the Redeemer strengthen our faith:
let our trust in your presence and promise be restored.
May God the Sustainer nurture us throughout our lives:
let us love in all we say and do!
May the grace of the Holy and Blessed Trinity God, the Creator, the Redeemer and the Sustainer, be upon you this day and always. **Amen.**

Year A Lectionary Texts

The Kingdom Is Yours	Revelation 7:9-17	Psalm 34:1-10, 22	1 John 3:1-3	**Matthew 5:1-12**
The Kingdom Is Yours	Joshua 24:1-3a, 14-25	Psalm 78:1-7	1 Thessalonians 4:13-18	**Matthew 25:1-13**
The Kingdom Is Yours	Judges 4:1-7	Psalm 123 or Psalm 76	1 Thessalonians 5:1-11	**Matthew 25:14-30**
The Kingdom Is Yours	Ezekiel 34:11-16, 20-24	Psalm 100	Ephesians 1:15-23	**Matthew 25:31-46**
The Kingdom Is Yours	Deuteronomy 8:7-18	Psalm 65	2 Corinthians 9:6-15	**Luke 17:11-19**

The Kingdom Is Yours: A Worship Series for After Pentecost

The joyous message of the gospel is realized through faithfulness to the reign of Christ.

Rev. Will D. Campbell was an ordained Baptist minister who became known as a renegade preacher. He joined the civil rights struggle in the 1950s, quit organized religion and fought injustice with nonviolent protests. Once, when asked if he could boil the Christian faith down to ten words or less, he famously quipped: "We're all bastards, but God loves us anyway." However, when his friend Jonathan was killed by a member of the KKK while working on voter registration in black communities in Alabama, Campbell found himself wrestling with feelings of anger and vengeance. Eventually, someone asked him whether he thought both his friend Jonathan and the Klansman who killed him were bastards—and if so, did God love them both equally. In recounting this story, Campbell said that this question "made a Christian out of me."

As Campbell was forced to acknowledge, deep faithfulness to the claims of the gospel strains the boundaries of ordered religion—stretching even well-conceived notions of just who can participate in God's kingdom and how. Throughout Matthew's gospel Jesus speaks of the kingdom of heaven—that is, the reign of God in the present and future—in expansive terms, challenging the exclusionary impulse of his would-be followers. Just who are the "poor in spirit"? Who really are "the ready" and "trustworthy"? Who will be "blessed" and who will be "made whole"? In a world where excommunication and cancellation are normative, "To whom does the kingdom belong?" becomes the fundamental question, and to those who are willing to take seriously the demands of the kingdom Jesus emphatically answers: "yours."

In this season of endings—and new beginnings just on the horizon—the Gospel texts of late Ordinary Time speak with increasing clarity and urgency. Jesus calls us to see the Kingdom of God not as a distant hope but as a present reality breaking into the world through mercy, readiness, faithfulness, and compassion. Worship leaders should consider using this as a moment to invite critical reflection on the past year, celebrating all the ways the congregation has seen and participated in the in-breaking of the kingdom. The bookends of the series—All Saints and Thanksgiving Day—form an excellent frame for this. Think of ways to solicit from the congregation kingdom stories that could be shared either digitally (e.g., weekly email stories or social media posts) or physically within your space (e.g., an artistic display or bulletin boards). Select stories could be incorporated within the liturgy as a testimony or as a gathering meditation or used as part of the sermon.

Each Sunday invites us to lean more deeply into the character of the Kingdom: a place where the lowly are blessed, where faithful readiness and bold stewardship are honored, where judgment is rooted in compassion, and where gratitude reveals the fullness of salvation. This is no distant kingdom. It is as near as the hands that serve, the oil that burns, the talents entrusted, and the stranger welcomed. To those who are willing, *the kingdom is yours.*

Week One

Matthew 5:1-12 | To the Lowly, the Kingdom Is Yours

> **Key Images**: mountain, kingdom of heaven, blessing, images of comfort
>
> **Themes**: blessing, the reign of God, humility

> . . . for theirs is the kingdom of heaven. (Matthew 5:3)

Addressed to a primarily Jewish audience with more quotes from the Hebrew scriptures than any of the other gospels, Matthew paints Jesus as a new Moses. From the perilous escape from infanticide at the hands of a ruthless king to the mountain top farewell, Matthew envisions Jesus as the fulfillment of Deuteronomy 18:15—*The LORD your God will raise up for you a prophet like me from among your own people; you shall heed such a prophet.*

And so, in v.1 Jesus ascends the mountain and sits, assuming the posture of teaching associated with Moses. And just as Sinai established a new community in Exodus, so Jesus establishes a new community of the faithful. No longer is God's community to be distinguished merely by well-ordered bloodlines and legalistic fervor, but by humble fidelity to God. Blessedness (μακάριοι *makarioi*, denotes a state of being in divine favor, suggesting joy, approval, and flourishing) becomes defined not by tribe, prestige, or prosperity but by one's need for and practices of humility, mercy, and justice—the poor, the mourners, the meek, the hungry, the merciful, the pure in heart, the peacemakers, the persecuted, the slandered. The kingdom of heaven is entrusted to those who both participate in and need God's reign now.

Jesus speaks blessing over the very people the world forgets. And this is not an aspiration, because the community Jesus describes already exists. God's kingdom isn't given to the powerful or the pious, but to those who know their need. All those who have trusted, mourned, hungered, served, and endured—these are the ones Jesus calls "blessed."

> What is your role in a kingdom that belongs to the lowly?
>
> Who else needs to know that the kingdom is theirs?

Week Two

Matthew 25:1-13 | To the Ready, the Kingdom Is Yours

Key Images: lamps flickering in the night, a door that shuts

Themes: eschatology, faithfulness in uncertainty

And while they went to buy it, the bridegroom came, and those who were ready went with him into the wedding banquet, and the door was shut. (Matthew 25:10)

Prompted by the disciples' question concerning *when* and *what* (Matthew 24:3), Jesus culminates his teachings in the gospel with a series of parables, each intensifying both the call and demands of the kingdom of heaven. Jesus and his disciples have been in the temple in Jerusalem every day (the center of religious, cultural, economic and political life), teaching about the practices and systems of faith that were prevalent but not always relevant for God's saving purposes. Now, while feeling the mounting tension between the now and not yet, his disciples want to know about the end. They want Jesus to fix their uncertainty with certainty.

Yet Jesus won't let us off with easy settlements. Instead, while questions about the uncertainty of our world and what the end holds for us are prevalent, Jesus insists that the more relevant question is not about when or what the end will be but rather what God is doing.

And so, the kingdom of heaven belongs to those who are ready or wise (φρόνιμος *phronimos*), who bring more oil "just in case because you never know what might happen." These are those who amid uncertainty remain alert with faithful, spiritual discernment to see and anticipate the in-breaking of God's reign at any moment. By contrast, the foolish (μωραί mōrai, connotes moral irresponsibility) are so dependent on certainty that they altogether miss the possibility for participation in what God is doing.

Faithfulness is not just a moment of decision but a lifestyle of alertness. We are called not simply to wait, but to watch—to live today in light of the coming kingdom.

> What keeps you spiritually awake and alert?
>
> How might you cultivate watchfulness without anxiety?

Week Three

Matthew 25:14-30 | To the Faithful, the Kingdom Is Yours

> **Key Images:** money bags, enormous sums of treasure or gifts, shovel, buried treasure
>
> **Themes:** spiritual gifts, mission of the church, eschatology

> His master said to him, "Well done, good and trustworthy slave; you have been trustworthy in a few things; I will put you in charge of many things; enter into the joy of your master." (Matthew 25:21)

Continuing the theme of faithfulness to the claims of the kingdom, Jesus gives another parable about responsible stewardship. The implication is that the reign of God demands active participation right now.

Key to this is Jesus's use of the term *slaves* (δοῦλος doulos), denoting willful service as if in worship (cf. Matthew 6:24). The good slave can be entrusted with incredible resources (τάλαντον *talanton*, a massive sum), because they understand the time is always now—that every moment is the opportunity for joyful obedience and uncertainty must not lead to fear.

It is this fear that consumes the last slave, immobilizing his work and becoming his judgment. The harshness of the master is a direct result of the slave's own fear—a stark contrast to the joy anticipated and experienced by the other slaves. So, the judgment is that God has work for us to do right now and you reap what you sow.

Jesus makes clear that the kingdom of heaven belongs to the faithful who have courage to act, not in some prescribed heroism but *according to his ability*. God's gifts are never meant to be buried but to grow, so that all might experience *the joy of your master*.

> What does courageous stewardship look like in this season of your life?

Week Four

Matthew 25:31-46 | To the Compassionate, the Kingdom Is Yours

> **Key Images:** Christ the King, sheep and goats, throne, images of vulnerability
>
> **Themes:** compassionate care for the vulnerable, faithfulness, mission, eschatology

Then the king will say to those at his right hand, 'Come, you who are blessed by my Father, inherit the kingdom prepared for you from the foundation of the world, for I was hungry and you gave me food . . . (Matthew 25:34-35)

Whereas the previous parables describe a sudden return of the bridegroom/master triggering unexpected judgement, the scene now takes an apocalyptic shift to the final judgment that echoes the vision of Daniel 7. The Son of Man sitting in judgment of all the nations is an immediate indictment of the arrogance of human empire because God judges all. Again, the emphasis here is on the present/future character of God's kingdom and its elusiveness—some will see it, some won't.

The six categories of judgement—hungry, thirsty, stranger, naked, sick, imprisoned—highlight the immediacy of the kingdom and the real-world implications for participation in the kingdom. The God's reign, personified by the Son of Man, is to be found among *the least* (ἐλάχιστος *elachistos*, denotes extreme humility or insignificance). And faithfulness by would-be disciples is characterized by service amongst these. The phrase *Inasmuch as you did it . . .* (eph' hoson epoiēsate) implies an intimate link between actions and Christ himself.

The question is simple: *Did you see me?* In the hungry, the stranger, the prisoner—did you see me? Here, mercy is the measure. This isn't charity, but shared humanity—not obligation, but solidarity. The Kingdom belongs to those who practice compassion as the rule, never the exception.

It's worth noting that both the righteous and the unrighteous are surprised by the impact of their respective actions. Perhaps they may have been surprised by each other's actions as well.

> How would you describe your actions?
>
> Would anyone be surprised?

Week Five

Luke 17:11-19 || To the Grateful, the Kingdom Is Yours

> **Key Images**: borders and thresholds, 10 lepers
>
> **Themes**: gratitude and thanksgiving, faithfulness, reign of God, humility, worship

> Then Jesus asked, "Were not ten made clean? So where are the other nine? Did none of them return to give glory to God except this foreigner?" Then he said to him, "Get up and go on your way; your faith has made you well. (Luke 17:17-18)

Aside from its uniqueness in Luke's gospel, the story of the ten lepers stands out for how it portrays faithfulness to the already-not yet rule and reign of God. Sandwiched between the disciples' request to *Increase our faith[fulness]* (v.5) and the Pharisees questioning *when the kingdom of God was coming* (v.20), the lepers' healing provides an answer to both questions, ultimately revealing the one leper as both the model for faithfulness and a sign of the inbreaking of the kingdom.

Of particular note is the emphasis on *sight* (ἰδὼν *idōn*, "to see, perceive, recognize"), a recurring motif throughout the gospel that signifies revelation, recognition and faith. Jesus's sight enables physical healing for all, and the Samaritan's sight (v. 15) activates deeper spiritual healing through gratitude. The supposed foreigner seems to understand more clearly the connection between loving neighbor and loving God—one neessitates the other.

To be sure, the story is not an indictment of the nine who needed and received healing; rather, it is an encouragement to any would-be disciple to move beyond a consumeristic faith. The nine seem content with what they have received, but the tenth leper *recognized* his healing as a catalyst for worship—*He prostrated himself at Jesus's feet and thanked him* (εὐχαριστῶ *eucharistō*, "to give thanks"). In so doing, the second blessing—*Your faith has made you well* (implying a completed, enduring wholeness) —is greater than the first.

The inbreaking of the kingdom belongs, not just to those who are healed or saved, but to those who through faith are able to recognize Jesus as the source of their healing through worshipful gratitude. Knowledge of the kingdom is in direct correlation with one's ability and willingness to say "Thank you, Jesus."

> What are you "seeing" but not recognizing as a gift from God?
>
> How does your spiritual perception shape your response to God's grace?

Words for Worship, After Pentecost

Gathering

Call to Worship
(Lisa Hancock)

Beloved Saints, we gather to join the multitude of saints across the generations from every tribe, every people, and every language, to proclaim:
Salvation belongs to our God, who is seated on the throne, and to the Lamb!

We gather to remember, to grieve, and to celebrate the saints who came before us, yet whose lives and witness continue to shape us as we all proclaim:
Salvation belongs to our God, who is seated on the throne, and to the Lamb!

We gather as the family of Christ, siblings and saints, diverse yet united by grace to declare with our voices, our hearts and our lives:
Salvation belongs to our God, who is seated on the throne, and to the Lamb!

As we gather, may the Lamb who is our Shepherd guide us, comfort us, and tend us as a community of saints—past, present, and future.
May we join in the work of the Shepherd to build a world with no more hunger, no more thirst, no more suffering, and no more pain that all the saints of all times, tribes, peoples, and languages may share in God's abundant life. Amen.

Call to Worship
(Lisa M. Straus)

With those seeking your blessing,
we come looking for the Kingdom of God!
With those who need oil for their lamps,
we come looking for the Kingdom of God!
With those who squandered their gifts,
we come looking for the Kingdom of God!
With those who missed the chance to serve,
we come looking for the Kingdom of God!
With those who were healed,
we come looking for the Kingdom of God!

Call to Worship (Psalm 34)
(Lisa M. Straus)

Come! Let us bless the Lord;
let us speak God's praise always.
May our souls rest in the Lord;
let us listen and be glad.
Let us magnify the Lord,
and let us exalt God's name together!

Call to Worship
(Lisa M. Straus)

Holy God, we come to you eager to sing your praises!
God help us keep our lamps trimmed and burning!
Loving God, we come to you filled with wonder and awe!
God inspire us keep our lamps trimmed and burning!
Gracious God, send the power of your Holy Spirit among us!
God empower us keep our lamps trimmed and burning!

Call to Worship (Psalm 123)
(Lisa M. Straus)

Lift your eyes to God in heaven!
We lift your eyes to God with joy and expectation
Pray to be filled with the love of Jesus!
We will share Christ's love with our neighbors near and far.
Receive the peace of the Holy Spirit!
We will worship God filled with peace!

Call to Worship (Psalm 100)
(Lisa M. Straus)

Make a joyful noise to the Lord, all the earth.
Let us worship the Lord with gladness
and enter God's presence with singing.
Know that the Lord is God.
It is God who made us,
and we are God's people.
Enter God's gates with praise and thanksgiving.
We will give thanks to God and bless God's holy name.
For the Lord is good;
God's steadfast love endures forever.

Call to Worship for Thanksgiving Day (Deuteronomy 8:7-18)
(Lisa M. Straus)

The Lord your God is bringing you into a good land, a land with flowing streams.
We give thanks and praise to God!
The Lord your God has provided you with ordinances and commandments.
We give thanks and praise to God!
The Lord your God will keep the covenant established with your ancestors.
We give thanks and praise to God!

Opening Prayer
(Lisa M. Straus)

Holy God,
We come before you with praise and thanksgiving!
May our songs and prayers bring you glory and honor.
May our worship draw us closer to you.
May we leave this place ready to share your Kingdom with the world. Amen!

Opening Prayer
(Lisa M. Straus)

Grace-filled God,
We come into your presence today with gratitude for all the blessings you have already given us. May the work we do in worship through our prayers, our words, and our songs bring honor and glory to you. Amen!

Opening Prayer
(Lisa M. Straus)

Faithful God,
This is the day that you have made! We hope to be glad and rejoice in it! We come to you today hoping that all that our worship will light a fire in us so that we can share your light in the world. Amen!

Opening Prayer
(Lisa Hancock)

God of Justice and Mercy,
You call us by your grace and draw us together as the Body of Christ. Teach us today to be builders of the kingdom of heaven. Help us invest in the flourishing of all and divest from unjust systems. Give us wisdom to know the difference between accountability and exploitation. Show us how to lead with love and resist the love of power. Empower us and form us to live as citizens of your kingdom here and now. Amen.

Opening Prayer
(Lisa M. Straus)

Loving God, we rejoice in your creation and we come today prepared to worship and praise you! As we sing, and pray, and listen this morning, may our hearts be filled with your peace and may our faith in you grow stronger. Amen.

Opening Prayer for Reign of Christ
(Lisa M. Straus)

Most Loving God, may we worship you today in a way that honors all of your children. May all that we pray, sing, and speak shine your light on those who need your love. Amen.

Opening Prayer for Thanksgiving Day
(Lisa M. Straus)

Loving God,
We come to you today ready to receive healing for our bodies, minds, and spirits. May we offer you praise and thanksgiving for all the ways you transform us through worship! Amen!

Prayer of Confession/Pardon and Assurance
(Lisa M. Straus)

God of grace,
We come before you this morning aware that we have ignored the needs of your kingdom.
We have not taken care of your creation.
We have not listened to your people in need.
God, forgive us.
Guide us back to the work you would have us do to bring your kingdom closer. Amen.

Prayer of Confession
(Lisa Hancock)

Merciful God, we live in a world where the power and wealth of a few take precedence over the survival and flourishing of us all. We know what the scriptures say, we tell the stories of Jesus and sing songs about God's good news that sets us free. Yet, in our actions and in action, we allow the narrative that we are powerless to resist the forces of this world to drown out the gospel.
God, forgive us for our complacency and complicity.

Merciful God, we live in neighborhoods where prejudice and discrimination happen every day in large and small ways. In our actions and inaction, we heap the burdens of marginalization, isolation, despair, and poverty on our neighbors who the world calls abnormal, incapable, and undeserving. Yet we know that all of us—including the most vulnerable in our midst—are your children who you call beloved, known, and worthy.
God, forgive us for our complacency and complicity.

Merciful God, we live in a community where leaders refuse to listen to the voices of those who speak out with truth and wisdom. In our actions and our inaction, we silence and ignore the everyday prophets among us who show us how to live into the kin-dom of God instead of the kingdom of this world.
God, forgive us for our complacency and complicity.

Merciful God, in our inmost being we know the big and small ways we have been complacent and complicit in living as your kin-dom bearers in the world. We confess these to you now in the silence of our hearts.

Silent prayers of confession.

Beloved, receive this good news:
The Bridegroom comes to us again and again,
redeeming and inviting us to join in the kin-dom of God
on earth as it is in heaven.
In the name of Jesus Christ, you are forgiven.
In the name of Jesus Christ, you are forgiven.
Glory to God! Amen.

Proclaiming

Prayer for Illumination
(Lisa M. Straus)

God of Wisdom,
Fill our hearts and minds with your Word. May all that we hear open us to the Kingdom work you need us to do. Amen!

Thanksgiving

Offertory Prayer
(Lisa M. Straus)

Loving God,
We are grateful for all the blessings you have given us and as we return to you a portion of what you have shared with us, help us know how best to use these gifts to show others the blessings you give to all your children. Amen!

Offertory Prayer
(Lisa M. Straus)

Loving God,
As we try to be people who are good stewards of all that you have already given us, help us know how best to return to you all that you would have us give. Help us know how best to use all our gifts in a way that brings honor and glory to you. Amen!

Offertory Prayer
(Lisa M. Straus)

Omniscient God, as we return to you some of what we have so faithfully received from you, we pray that we can be faithful in all that we do to share what we receive with others. Amen!

Offertory Prayer
(Lisa M. Straus)

Faithful God, may our gifts today be shared with all who need them: the hungry, the thirsty, the naked, those who are sick or in prison. May they fill the needs of those who have them and may they fill the hearts of those who receive them with your love. Amen.

Offertory Prayer
(Lisa M. Straus)

Faithful God, as we return to you what you have already shared with us, may we learn to use it to transform those around us who are in need of your love and mercy. Amen!

Litany of Remembrance
(Lisa Hancock)

Living God, our Guide and Guardian,
Who sits on the throne and delivers us into eternal life,
we give you thanks for the saints of every time, tribe, and tongue
who now rest in the shelter of your embrace.
We set aside this moment to remember
those saints who are dear and precious to us
who have died and entered into glory
during the last twelve months.

As each name is called, ring a bell and/or light a candle in honor of each person. Where possible, have family members or close friends of the person named come forward to light a candle or rise where they are sitting.

We thank you for the life and love of these dear saints,
and rejoice that they have entered
into the fullness of life with you.

We remember those saints we hold in our hearts
who have not been in our present for some time,
yet whose life, love, and witness
continue to form and shape us as your disciples.
We honor them now by lifting their names aloud or in our hearts.

Allow space for people to speak names aloud from where they are seated.

On this All Saints Sunday, we remember
that we too are living saints,
members of the family of God
with all the saints of the past, the present, and the future.

And so, we remember:
We are God's children.
What we shall be has not yet been revealed;
but we know that when Christ appears, we shall be like him,
for we shall behold him as he is.

So today and every day,
may we put on Christ and live as saints
who tend the poor,
comfort the mourners,
learn from the meek,
affirm those who seek righteousness,
offer mercy alongside the merciful,
and work for peace with the peacemakers
until Christ comes in final victory
and we feast as the family of God
at the heavenly banquet. Amen.

Sending

Jesus, Now Lead On

From where we are
to where you need us,
Jesus, now lead on.
From the security of what we know
to the adventure of what you will reveal,

Jesus, now lead on.
To refashion the fabric of this world
until it resembles the shape of your kingdom,
Jesus, now lead on.
Because good things have been prepared
for those who love God,
Jesus, now lead on.
—Wild Goose Worship Group, Iona Community, *Worship and Song, Worship Resources*

A Sending Forth

Go! Never stop going out from church,
out from the peace and stillness,
out into the noise and discomfort,
out to tears and laughter.
Carry with you the living bread that you were given here,
as a treasure between your hands and in your heart,
and share it again and again.
It will suffice forever, as long as you continue to break it.

Come! Never stop coming back to this place.
Never come with empty hands.
Bring with you the cry that is pressing behind your lips.
Let it sound here.
Bring with you the hunger that is never filled,
the fight that is not yet won.
Bring with you one who has always been at your side,
without you knowing it.
Here is the meeting place, in the light of the face of God.
—"Go! Never Stop Going out from Church," *Worship and Song, Worship Resource*

Special Times of Worship

Always With You: A Different Liturgy for Mother's/Father's Day
(Britney Winn Lee)

Supplies: A candle and lighter, something to represent bread and wine for communion (a cracker and juice, toast and milk, etc), and a little cup of dirt (plus a seed, if available). If reading with people, one voice will read all unbolded sections while the **group joins in for the bolded sections.**

"If ever there is a tomorrow when we're not together, there is something you must always remember. You are braver than you believe, stronger than you seem, and smarter than you think. But the most important thing is, even if we are apart, I will always be with you."
—Christopher Robin to Pooh, *Pooh's Grand Adventure*

Right now, we push aside all the feelings we "should" have and people we "should" be, and we open wide our doors to what *is*
Welcome, old grief;
Welcome, new reality;
Welcome, fear;
Welcome, worry;
Welcome, exactly who we are right now

As we light this candle, we declare this space for remembering and honoring the children and parents we miss during Mother's (and/or Father's) Day(s)
Be with us, saints;
Be with us, Spirit

Song: "Let It Be" by The Beatles

For children who had to say goodbye to parents when they should have had so much more time
We hold you now: *(name any names aloud)*
For children who have watched the minds and bodies of parents deteriorate, no longer able to recognize or remember
We hold you now:
For children whose parents were unable to offer their presence or resources, children who ached to know a different kind of paternal or maternal love
We hold you now:
For children who have lost parents to suicide, disease, estrangement
We hold you now:
For children who wrestle with the complexities of their birth parents, adoptive parents, and foster parents
We hold you now:
For children who are navigating the milestones of life without their mothers or fathers there to call for recipes and family histories and old stories that have faded with years
We hold you now:
For LGBTQIA+ children who do not have homes to which they can return
We hold you now:
For children who were abused in a multitude of ways:
We hold you now:
For children who dread the holidays because of their voids
We hold you now:

Scripture: Matthew 5:1-12

For parents who birthed babies straight into the arms of God
We hold you now:
For parents who have lost young children to disasters that make this life seem too unfair for the human heart
We hold you now:
For parents who have raised their grandchildren or other relatives because of a lost life or reality
We hold you now:
For parents who have lost children to suicide, disease, estrangement
We hold you now:
For parents whose children were unable to offer their presence or connection, parents who ached to know a different kind of familial love
We hold you now:
For parents who have received a gutting diagnosis

We hold you now:
For parents who are raising children, and working jobs, and running households by themselves
We hold you now:
For birth parents who wrestle with the complexities of hard decisions and limited resources
We hold you now:
For adoptive and foster parents who wrestle with the complexities of hard questions, identity narratives, and ethics
We hold you now:
For migrant and refugee parents who are risking everything (even separation) for a better life for their children
We hold you now:

> "If I had lost a leg—I would tell them—instead of a boy, no one would ever ask me if I was 'over' it. They would ask me how I was doing learning to walk without my leg. I was learning to walk and to breathe and to live without Wade. And what I was learning is that it was never going to be the life I had before."
> —Elizabeth Edwards, *Resilience: The New Afterword*

To those who are not biological parents, but who step in to mother and father so many around them
We honor you now:
To those who chose not to be parents in a culture that so often pressures otherwise
We honor you now:
To those who would choose to be parents, or parents again, but who grieve the loss of a dream
We honor you now:
To those who have redefined family to go past lines of biology, nationality, and economics
We honor you now:
To those who did the best they could with what they had when they had it
We honor you now:
To those versions of ourselves that we never turned into, and the versions of ourselves that we did
We honor you now:
To the voices we wish we could hear say "Happy Mother's and Father's Day"
We honor you now:
To the ears to which we wish we could say "Happy Mother's and Father's Day"
We honor you now:

Scripture: John 1:5

"Sorry, but you don't really get a choice—you keep waking up and you keep breathing and your heart keeps on beating. . . . It's like your heart knows that if it keeps going, so will you. And your heart hasn't forgotten how good it is to be in the world, so it pushes on, propelling you along to the fridge, the shower, a family dinner, coffee with a friend. . . . If you too are mired in the early days of unimaginable loss, the only thing to do is follow your heart. Then listen to your body. And keep . . . going."
—Jamie Wright

Song: "Great Is Thy Faithfulness"

Hear our words to those we miss
Meet us in our celebration and in our grief

Communion
The body of Mary's son, broken for us
The blood of God's son, poured out for the world
Thank you Jesus for the bigger picture of resurrection

God's family table is open to all who wish to partake, in your homes, on these screens, though separated we are one.
(Participants hold cup of soil—and a seed if possible—in their hands.)

Remind us, God, that our faith makes room for death, that our faith can hold endings, though they are excruciating and devastating.
(Participants push seeds into dirt.)

Remind us that in a backwards kingdom, end is beginning, last is first, and burial is birth . . . eventually.
Thank you for love that was, is, and is to come. Amen.
Go now in the peace that passes our understanding.

(Note: Words for Worship on World Communion Sunday are included in the Go With Us *series in the season After Pentecost, page 230.)*

A Call to Worship for Reformation Sunday
(Eleanor Colvin)

For everything there is a season, and a time for every matter under heaven.
In all seasons, at all times—we praise God!
For everything there is a season; this is the season for reformation—a time to remember who God created us to be.
In all seasons, at all times—we glorify God!
Glorifying God calls for very clear vision! God calls us to write the vision and make it plain.

In all seasons, at all times—we seek God!
For everything there is a season, and a time for every matter under heaven.
All: This is the time to worship the One in whose image we were formed. On this Reformation Sunday, we take time to seek, glorify and praise our God. Amen!

(Note: Words for Worship on Thanksgiving Day are included in the series The Kingdom Is Yours, *week five, in the season After Pentecost, page 241–42.)*

Opening Prayer for Christ the King
(Eleanor Colvin)

Good Shepherd,
Lay me on your shoulder Lord.
I am tired.
I am weak.
I am worn.
Anoint my torn flesh.
Bind my breaking heart.
Bless my consciousness.
Only You can heal.
Only You can cleanse.
Only You can restore.
Anoint me. Lay me on your shoulder. Carry me home.
Amen.

A Kyrie for the Earth and an Alleluia for God
(John Thornburg)

Worship leaders are encouraged to choose a musical setting of the Kyrie Eleison, and a setting of the word 'Alleluia' to be sung at the places indicated

Eternal God, you not only made the air and the wind,
    you also taught our bodies how to breathe.
        Twenty-five thousand times a day, you give us the power to breathe.
            We thank you more than we can say.
But we've decided that exhaust and toxic fumes are your problem.
    We figure you'll clean up after us.
        If the beauty of the mountains is obscured by our pollution,
            you'll just bring some wind and blow it away for us.
                Forgive us.

KYRIE ELEISON.

Eternal God, you've made four oceans and twenty-seven seas.
You've made so many lakes and rivers that not even Google
knows how many there are.
> Our bodies are sixty-six percent water.
> But we've decided to use rivers as industrial toilets,
> and we've decided that a few million barrels of oil in the ocean
> won't hurt anything.
>> We figure you'll purify everything. You'll clean it up for us.
>> Forgive us.

KYRIE ELEISON

Eternal God, you made everything.
> Everything that walks. Everything that crawls.
>> Everything that flies. Everything that swims.
Everything that burrows, dives, swoops, and runs.
You made day and night, you made sea and land, you made sun and moon.
> You made the eagles' wings catch the wind.
>> You made whales sing to each other.
>>> There is nothing you cannot make.
And you made everything fit together and work together.
> We praise you for that.
> We sing Alleluia to you.

ALLELUIA

Make us into people who care about the earth.
> Remind us that being earth keepers is hard work and great work.
>> Remind us again and again that the earth is yours, not ours.
>>> Make us stewards, not abusers.
>>> There is nothing you cannot make.
>>>> And you made everything fit together and work together.
>>>> We praise you for that.
>>>>> We sing Alleluia to you.

Contributors

R. DeAndre Johnson is an ordained deacon, author, musician, and preacher serving in the Texas Annual Conference of the United Methodist Church. He has served as music director, worship leader, and consultant for churches and conferences, including the General Conference of the United Methodist Church, and the World Methodist Conference. He has served as chorus master for the Houston Ebony Opera Guild and as a member of the editorial team for Worship Arts magazine. He is the author of *Yes and Amen: A Prayer Collection* and is a contributor to *The Methodist Book of Daily Prayer*.

For this volume, DeAndre conceived and developed the sermon and worship series, authored the accompanying commentaries, curated liturgies and prayers from a wide variety of sources, and composed original liturgical pieces. Liturgies appearing in this book without attribution are DeAndre's work.

Contributing Writers

Laura Jaquith Bartlett serves as a minister of music and deacon in the Oregon-Idaho Annual Conference of The United Methodist Church.

Scot C. Bontrager serves as a local church pastor in the Horizon Texas Annual Conference of The United Methodist Church and is a member of the Order of Saint Luke.

Diana Sanchez-Bushong serves as executive director of Worship Ministries for Discipleship Ministries, The United Methodist Church.

Tori Butler serves as a local church pastor in the Baltimore-Washington Conference of The United Methodist Church.

Jo Ann Cooper serves as a local church pastor in the Louisiana Conference of The United Methodist Church, and as a spiritual director and mentor with Backstory Preaching.

Rachel A Cornwell serves as a local church pastor in the Baltimore-Washington Conference of The United Methodist Church.

Charity Goodwin serves as pastor of spiritual formation and groups in the Missouri Annual Conference of The United Methodist Church and as a speaker and teacher on topics related to emotional intelligence.

Kallie Green serves as a local church pastor in the Rio Texas annual conference of The United Methodist Church.

Ginny Griggs serves as a local church pastor in the Texas Annual Conference of The United Methodist Church.

Christie Hale serves as a local church pastor in the Texas Annual Conference of The United Methodist Church.

Celia Halfacre serves as a local church pastor in the Rio Texas Annual Conference of The United Methodist Church and is a member of the Order of Saint Luke.

Lisa Hancock serves as director of Worship Arts Ministries for Discipleship Ministries, The United Methodist Church.

Jackson Henry serves as pastor of worship and music in the Tennessee-Western Kentucky Conference of The United Methodist Church.

Heather Josselyn-Cranson serves as a hymn writer and scholar of liturgical music at Regis College, in Weston, Massachusetts, and is a member of the Order of Saint Luke.

Joe Kim serves as a local church pastor and district superintendent in the Pacific Northwest Annual Conference of The United Methodist Church.

C. Scott Maderer serves as a stewardship coach and certified lay speaker in the Rio Texas Annual Conference of The United Methodist Church.

Bromleigh J. McCleneghan serves as a local church pastor in Hinsdale, Illinois, and is an author and writer on topics of religion, children, and family.

Michelle Mejia serves as a local church pastor in the Baltimore-Washington annual conference of The United Methodist Church.

Felicia Patton serves as a director of music in the Northern Illinois Conference of the United Methodist Church.

Katie McKay Simpson serves as a local church pastor in the Louisiana Conference of the United Methodist Church.

Lisa M. Straus serves as a local church pastor in the Rio Texas Annual Conference of The United Methodist Church.

Trenton Teegarden serves as minister of modern music and director of men's ministries in the Arkansas Annual Conference of The United Methodist Church.

John Thornburg serves as a United Methodist pastor, hymn writer, poet, and worship planner based in Texas, whose hymn and liturgical texts have appeared in more than 40 publications.

Jennifer Veres-Schrecengost serves as a local church pastor in the Texas Annual Conference of the United Methodist Church.

Deborah Ann Wong serves as a worship leader for theologians and a theologian for worship leaders, and is a scholar at Duke Divinity School in Durham, North Carolina.

Joseph Yoo serves as a church planter and Episcopal priest in Texas.

Sources

Gathering

Page 5: Call to Worship
    R. DeAndre Johnson, adapted from "Old Stories Become New Songs" by Walter Brueggemann as found in Walter Brueggemann *Prayers for a Privileged People* (Abingdon Press, 2008).

Page 7: Prayer of Confession
    R. DeAndre Johnson and Jorge Lockward with words adapted from "On Controlling Our Borders" in Walter Brueggemann *Prayers for a Privileged People* (Abingdon Press, 2008).

Page 9: Invitation to Passing of the Peace
    Valerie Bridgman Davis, in *The Africana Worship Book, Year A,* ed. Valerie Bridgman Davis and Safiyah Fosua (Discipleship Resources, 2006).

Proclaiming

Page 11: Introductory Material
    Fred B. Craddock, *Preaching* (Abingdon Press, 1985).

Page 12: In the Name of
    R. DeAndre Johnson, *Yes and Amen: A Prayer Collection* (Upper Room, 2023).

Thanksgiving

Page 15: A Prayer of the People
    Susan A. Bock, *Liturgy for the Whole Church: Resources for Multigenerational Worship* (Church Publishing Incorporated, 2008), 99.

Sources

Page 16: A Prayer of the People
Mary Freedlund, *Women's Prayer Services*, ed. Iben Gjerding and Katherine Kinnamon (Twenty-Third Publications, 1983), 46.

Page 17: A Payer for the Church
R. DeAndre Johnson, *Yes and Amen*.

Page 18: Praise for Today
R. DeAndre Johnson, *Yes and Amen*.

Page 18: A Prayer for Exodus
R. DeAndre Johnson, *Yes and Amen*.

Page 19: A Prayer of Lament and Fear
John D. Witvliet, *Reformed Worship*, Issue 56, p. 36. "Don't Be Afraid" is by John L. Bell. Glasgow: Wild Goose Resource Group, Iona Community, 1995.

Page 23: A Prayer for a Couple About to Marry
Wesley's Daily Prayers: Prayers for Every Day in the Year, ed. Donald E. Demaray (Bristol House, 1998), 424–25.

Page 23: A Prayer for Married Couples
Wesley's Daily Prayers, 424–25.

Page 24: In Times of Disaster: A Prayer of Praise and Intercession
Discipleship Ministries: https://www.umcdiscipleship.org/resources/prayers-for-those-facing-disasters.

Page 24: A Litany of Social Penance
Walter Russell Bowie, in *The Wideness of God's Mercy: Litanies to Enlarge Our Prayer*, ed. Jeffrey Rowthorn (Church Publishing, 2007).

Page 26: Invitation 3
Lillian C. Smith, in *The Africana Worship Book, Year A*.

Page 27: Invitation 4
Valerie Bridgeman Davis, in *The Africana Worship Book, Year A*.

Page 26: Offertory Prayer
Hélder Pessoa Câmara, OFS., *The Hodder Book of Christian Prayers*, ed. Tony Castle (Hodder and Stoughton, 1986).

Page 28: Baptism
"The Services of the Baptismal Covenant of The United Methodist Church as Revised to Align with the 2008 Book of Discipline and Book of Resolutions" (United Methodist Publishing, 2009).

Page 28: Thanksgiving over the Water
Susan A. Bock, *Liturgy for the Whole Church,* 84–85.

Page 31: Invitation 1
Barbara Hamm, *Worship and Song* (Abingdon, 2011), #3168.

Page 31: Invitation 2
Tim Warner, in *The Africana Worship Book, Year A.*

Page 31: An Alternate Great Thanksgiving
Jackson Henry, with words adapted from *The United Methodist Book of Worship* and *The United Methodist Hymnal* (United Methodist Publishing, 1989).

Page 32: An Abbreviated Communion Liturgy
Words of Institution adapted from *The United Methodist Book of Worship*, Matthew 26:26-28 (NRSVue), 1 Corinthians 11:23-25 (NRSVue). Initial statement adapted from "A Statement of Faith of the United Church of Canada," *The United Methodist Hymnal,* #883.

Sending

Page 38: A Closing Prayer
Valerie Bridgeman Davis, in *The Africana Worship Book, Year C,* ed. Valerie Bridgeman Davis and Safiya Fosua (Discipleship Resources, 2008), 164.

Page 39: Dismissal 3
Lillian C. Smith, in *The Africana Worship Book, Year A.*

Advent

Page 44: Introduction to Worship Series for Advent
Gordon, Mack, and Harry Warren, "At Last" (EMI Robbins, 1941).

Page 49: Call to Worship
Emily Dickinson, "'Hope' is the Thing with Feathers," from *The Complete Poems of Emily Dickinson*, ed. Thomas H. Johnson (Belknap Press, 1983).

Christmas and Christmastide

Page 60: Introduction to Worship Series for Christmas and Christmastide
Jaroslav J. Vajda, "Now the Silence," UMH #619.

Page 62: Introduction to Worship Series for Christmas
Esau McCaulley, "Christmas Is Weird," *The New York Times* (Dec 23, 2021).

Page 62: Introduction to Worship Series for Christmas
Howard Thurman, *Meditations of the Heart* (Beacon, 2023), 29.

Page 70: A Watchnight Prayer for Wisdom and Courage
Adapted from "A Year of Prayer Guide Book: Co-Laboring with the Living Lord, Ignatian Companions on Mission" by the Maryland Province Society of Jesus, 2005. The African American Lectionary, http://www.theafricanamericanlectionary.org/PopupWorshipAid.asp?LRID=304, The African American Pulpit, 2011.

Page 71: Opening Call to Worship and Prayer: Seeking Light
From the website of Grace Church in Ealing, London. http://www.freshworship.org/. Reposted: https://re-worship.blogspot.com/2018/11/opening-prayer-seeking-light.html.

Page 73: Call to Worship for Baptism of the Lord
Martha Brunell, *The Abingdon Women's Preaching Annual, Series 2, Year A* (Abingdon Press, 2001), 58.

Page 73: Litany: "Lord, I Want to Be a Christian?"
Kwasi I. Kena, in *The Africana Worship Book, Year A*, 103.

Page 73: Gathering Words for Epiphany / Baptism of the Lord
Cole Arthur Riley, *Black Liturgies: Prayers, Poems, and Meditations for Staying Human* (Convergent, 2024).

Page 74: I Believe: An Affirmation of Faith
Bruce Prewer, http://www.bruceprewer.com/. Reposted at https://re-worship.blogspot.com/2012/06/affirmation-of-faith-john-1.html.

Page 78: Benediction for Christmas Eve
Heidi Neumark, *The Abingdon Women's Preaching Annual, Series 2, Year A*, ed. Leonora Tubbs Tisdale (Abingdon Press, 2001), 38.

Page 78: A Sending Forth for the Christmas Season
Adapted from a prayer by Christine Sine on Godspace. http://godspace-msa.com/. Posted on the website of the Irricana United Church. Reposted at https://re-worship.blogspot.com/2014/01/litany-light-of-god-has-come.html.

Page 79: A Watchnight Benediction
Nancy C. Townley, "Watchnight (New Year's Eve)," Ministry Matters, Dec 7, 2012.

Page 79: Benediction
Martha Brunell, *The Abingdon Women's Preaching Annual, Series 2, Year A* (Abingdon Press, 2001), 59.

Page 100
J. J. Heller, "Coming Home" (2019).

Page 104
Karl Rahner *Encounters with Silence*

Holy Week and Easter Sunday

Page 141: A Week Where Transformation Will Meet You
B. Kevin Smalls, in *The Africana Worship Book, Year B* (Discipleship Resources, 2007).

Page 141: Maundy Thursday: Low Enough to Wash Dirty Feet
Kwasi I. Kena, in *The Africana Worship Book, Year B.*

Page 142: A Sending
Adapted from *United Methodist Book of Worship.*

Eastertide

Page 144: Introduction to Worship Series for Easter
Bob Marley, "Redemption Song" (Island, 1980).

Page 147: Introduction to Worship Series for Easter
Taylor Swift, Joy Williams, John Paul White, and T Bone Burnett, "Safe and Sound" (Big Machine, 2011).

Page 149: Introduction to Worship Series for Easter
Andra Day and Jennifer Decilveo, "Rise Up" (Warner, 2015).
"Higher Love"

Page 150: Introduction to Worship Series for Easter
John Legend, Lonnie Lynn, and Che Smith, "Glory" (ARTium, Def Jam, GOOD, and Columbia, 2014).

Page 155: Ritual of Healing for Isolation
Adapted by Dr. Lisa Hancock, Discipleship Ministries, October 2022; from "A Service of Healing I" © Copyright 1992 UMPH. Thanksgiving and Communion © 1972 The Methodist Publishing House; © 1980, 1985, 1989, 1992 UMPH. Dismissal with Blessing, alt., from *The Book of Offices and Services After the Usage of The Order of Saint Luke*, ed. Timothy J. Crouch (OSL Publications, 1988).

Pentecost and Trinity Sunday

Page 169: Who Will Go
  Tony Peterson, in *The Africana Worship Book, Year B.*

After Pentecost

Page 179: A Prayer of Confession (Genesis 18:1-15)
  Joseph W. Daniels, Jr., in *The Africana Worship Book, Year A.*

Page 180: A Prayer of Confession (Genesis 18:1-15)
  Joseph W. Daniels, Jr., in *The Africana Worship Book, Year A.*

Page 181: O Gracious Power: A Confession (Genesis 12)
  Thomas Troeger. *Borrowed Light: Hymns, Texts, Prayers, and Poems* (Oxford University Press, 1994).

Page 181: Prayer for Illumination (for the second Sunday after Pentecost)
  Nelson Cowan, in *Worship Any Time or Place,* ed. Nelson Cowan (Abingdon Press, 2023).

Page181: Father Abraham, Mother Sarah: A Litany (Genesis 12)
  Adapted from Safiyah Fosua, *Africana Worship Book, Year A.*

Page 182: Prayer for Illumination (Psalm 13)
  Joseph W. Daniels, Jr., *Africana Worship Book, Year A.*

Page 182: Offertory Prayer
  Adapted from *Ventures in Worship, Volume 1,* ed. David J. Randolph (Abingdon Press, 1969).

Page 184: Anybody Here? An Affirmation of Faith and Commitment (Psalm 116)
  Kwasi I. Kena, in *The Africana Worship Book, Year A.*

Page 184: Prayers of the People: Lord, We Call on You (Psalm 86)
  Joseph W. Daniels, Jr., in *The Africana Worship Book, Year A.*

Page 186: Go Forth with the Blessing of God
  Thomas Troeger. *Borrowed Light: Hymns, Texts, Prayers, and Poems.*

Page 187: God Is: A Sending
  Michelle Riley Jones, *Worship and Song: Worship Resources* (Abingdon Press, 2011), #170.

Sources

Page 193: Introduction to Worship Series for After Pentecost
Ernie Isley, Marvin Isley, Chris Jasper, Rudolph Isley, O'Kelly Isley, and Ronald Isley, "Harvest for the World" (T-Neck Records, 1976).

Page 204: Introduction to Worship Series for After Pentecost
Isaac Slade and Joe King, "How to Save a Life" (Epic, 2005).

Page 205: Introduction to Worship Series for After Pentecost
David G. Frazier, "I Need You to Survive" (Mezzo Agency, 202).

Page 210: Great Thanksgiving (Matthew 14:13-21)
Quotations from "A Brief Great Thanksgiving for General Use" Copyright © 1972 The Methodist Publishing House; Copyright © 1980, 1985, 1987, 1989, 1992 UMPH.

Page 214: Introduction to Worship Series for After Pentecost
Martin Luther King, Jr., "Transformed Nonconformist" (1954).

Page 247: Jesus, Now Lead On
© 1999 Wild Goose Resource Group, admin. by GIA Publications, Inc. *Worship and Song: Worship Resources* #163.

Page 247: A Sending Forth
English translation by Ninna Edgardh, 2008, in *Worship and Song: Worship Resources* #167.

Special Times of Worship

Page 249:
Pooh's Grand Adventure: The Search for Christopher Robin. Directed by Karl Geurs (Walt Disney Home Video, 1997).

Page 251
Elizabeth Edwards, *Resilience: The New Afterword* (Crown Archetype, 2010).

Page 252
Jamie Wright, "I used to think that if I ever lost a child," Instagram, May 11, 2019, https://www.instagram.com/p/BxVRopRJwg9/.

Be prepared at a moment's notice.

WORSHIP ANY TIME or PLACE

The Compact Book of Methodist Liturgies, Prayers, and Other Acts of Blessing

From pulpits to pews, from altar tables to dinner tables, from sanctuaries to streets, *Worship Any Time or Place* is a compact guide that equips the Methodist pastor, worship leader, or layperson to create meaningful worship moments for any group of people, any time, any place.

It includes liturgies and prayers suitable for traditional settings such as worship services, funeral services, and administration of the sacraments, plus words to use during hospital visits, retreats, church meetings, other conventional settings, and more.

Nurture Children (and Adults and Families) as Disciples through Worship

Discover a new approach to ministry with children and families, one that goes beyond simply increasing attendance numbers. In *Let the Children Lead: Models for Worship with All Generations*, you'll dive into five innovative congregational models that faithfully and intentionally engage children in worship. Gain insight from real-life success stories and learn how to contextualize and scale the models, implementing them with the laity and leaders in your congregation.

The book offers theological perspectives on the importance of worship in children's faith formation. And it provides practical help as your congregation learns to support and serve children, not as a means for church growth, but as an act of faithfulness.

www.ingramcontent.com/pod-product-compliance
Lightning Source LLC
LaVergne TN
LVHW020523060925
820214LV00005B/15